GILLIAMESQUE

~~A PRE-POSTHUMOUS MEMOIR~~

~~TG's Bio (degradable.) Autography~~

~~A singular person's first~~
~~first person singular~~
Palin-dromic biograph

My Me, Me, Me Memoir

Terry Gilliam
and Ben Thompson

CANONGATE

Edinburgh – London

First published in Great Britain in 2015 by Canongate Books Ltd,
14 High Street, Edinburgh EH1 1TE

www.canongate.tv

1

p. 8, Terry Gilliam and Johnny Depp, *The Man Who Killed Don Quixote* © 2000 Francois Duhamel;
p. 10, Ernie Kovacs © Fred Hermansky/NBCUniversal/Getty Images; Sid Caesar © NBC/MBCU Photo
Bank via Getty Images; p. 25, *MAD* magazine covers © DC Comics; p. 60, Algonquin Hotel lobby
© Barry Winiker via Getty Images; p. 72, sketchbook report © Robert Crumb; p. 102, El Cordobes ©
Hulton Archive via Getty Images; p. 173, *Nude on a Sofa* by Francois Boucher, photo © bpk/Bayerische
Staatsgemaldesämmlungen; p. 184, *Time Bandits* © Criterion Collection; p. 196, Terry Gilliam as Little
Bo Peep in *The Meaning of Life* © 1983 Universal Studios. All Rights Reserved. Courtesy of Universal
Studios; p. 218, John Neville and Sarah Polley, *The Adventures of Baron Munchausen* © 1989 Columbia
Pictures Industries, Inc. All Rights Reserved. Courtesy of Columbia Pictures; p. 223, three *The
Adventures of Baron Munchausen* images © Sergio Strizzi, courtesy of Contrasto Agency; p. 228, *The
Adventures of Baron Munchausen* cast © 1989 Columbia Pictures Industries, Inc. All Rights Reserved.
Courtesy of Columbia Pictures; p. 248, Terry Gilliam and Johnny Depp, *Fear and Loathing in Las Vegas*
© Peter Mountain; p. 248, Benicio Del Toro © Peter Mountain; p. 251, Johnny Depp, *The Man Who
Killed Don Quixote* © 2000 Francois Duhamel; pp. 257–9, six *The Man Who Killed Don Quixote* images
© 2000 Francois Duhamel; pp. 260–1, Terry Gilliam, *The Man Who Killed Don Quixote* © 2005 HanWay
Films/Photos by Francois Duhamel; pp. 265–7, five *The Brothers Grimm* images © 2005 Dimension
Films/Photos by Francois Duhamel; pp. 268–9, three *Tideland* images © 2005 HanWay Films/Photos
by Francois Duhamel; p. 272, two *Faust* images © Tristram Kenton; p. 273, two *Cellini* images © ENO/
Richard Hubert Smith; p. 273, *Cellini* poster © ENO, illustration by James Straffon; p. 274, Terry Gilliam,
The Brothers Grimm © 2005 Dimension Films/Photos by Francois Duhamel; p. 276, Christopher
Plummer and Lily Cole, *The Imaginarium of Dr Parnassus* © 2008 Liam Daniels; p. 277, Terry Gilliam and
Amy Gilliam © Dave Hogan via Getty Images; pp. 280–1, three *Zero Theorem* images courtesy of Voltage
Pictures; p. 282, Monty Python Live (Mostly) entrance © Ralph Larmann; p. 283, Monty Python Live
(Mostly) 'Spanish Inquisition' © Dave J. Hogan via Getty Images; p. 284, Monty Python stamp © Royal
Mail Group Ltd, 2015; p. 288, Gilliam family © David M. Bennett via Getty Images.

Except where explicitly stated, all images of the members of Monty Python are courtesy of Python
(Monty) Pictures Ltd.

British Library Cataloguing-in-Publication Data
A catalogue record for this book is available on
request from the British Library

ISBN 978 1 78211 106 1

Curation & Project Management: HDG Projects Ltd
Design: gray318
Art direction: Rafaela Romaya

Printed and bound in China

Mel Brooks made me want to be a JEW!

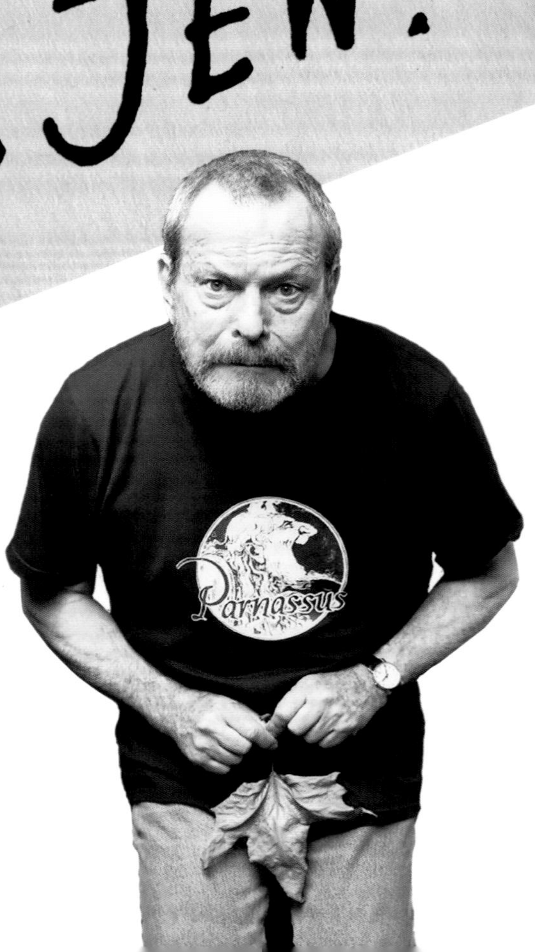

A WARNING!

This is not the book that my daughter, Holly, and I intended. The plan was to produce a large, expensive, high-class coffee-table book of my artwork for the Cognoscenti of Fine Art. It would include a choice selection of historical tidbits for those who could read. Unfortunately, once the tape recorder started rolling I couldn't stop babbling, and we have ended up with something closer to a Grand Theft Auto-biography: a high-speed car chase through my life with lots of skids and crashes, many of the best moments whizzing by in a blur. As a result, I have had to insert handwritten or typed notes to adjust the story, apologise for the egocentric nature of the reminiscences, name the ignored, fill in the glaring gaps, or just try to get control of my story-telling self. The Cognoscenti will have to buy something else for their coffee tables.

Unlike my good friend Michael Palin – who knew where the real pot of gold was buried from the very beginning – I have never bothered to keep a diary and, as my wife Maggie never tires of reminding me, such memory as I do have left is dangerously – if not actionably – selective. On top of this, as the years have passed, more and more of those I've relied upon to be custodians of our shared but forgotten experiences – wonderful warm slabs of my life – have been sadly laid out on cold slabs of their own.

It's in looking back on the lavish gifts of love and creative collaboration which other people – in harness with providence – have continued to recklessly foist on me that I come as close as I am ever likely to get to true humility. And since I haven't tested the accuracy or otherwise of my alleged memories by cross-checking them with any of my small – and ever-dwindling – number of living friends and relatives, you'll just have to take my word for it that the account that follows is 100% undisputed objective fact.

ANOTHER WARNING! If you are the type of reader who is looking for cuddly tales of domestic and family bliss, be prepared for disappointment. Those are mine to keep.

T.G.X

CONTENTS

TERRY GILLIAM

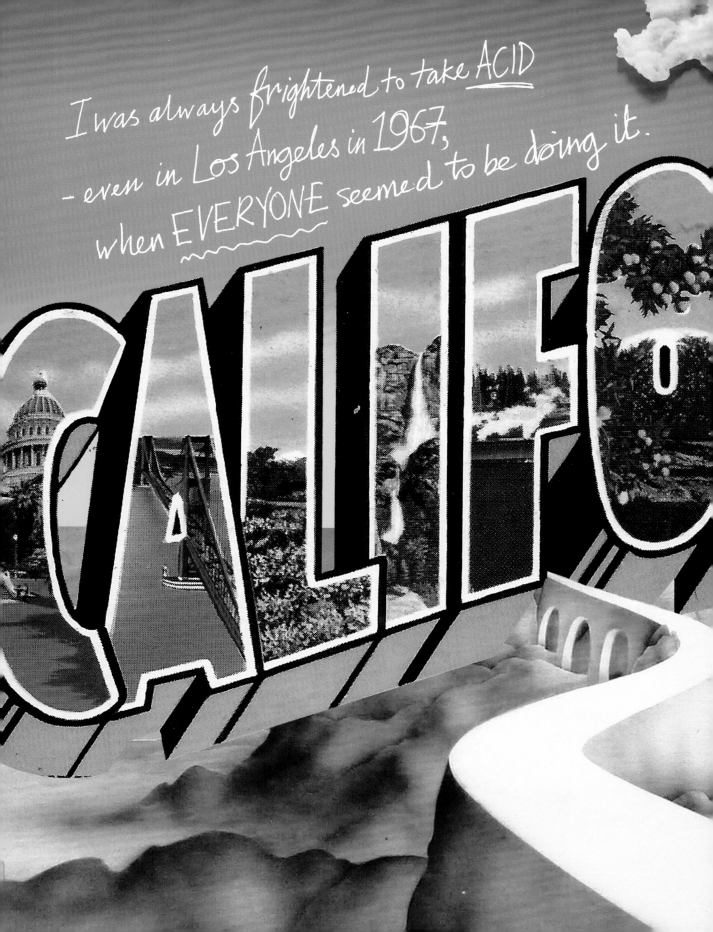

I was always frightened to take <u>ACID</u>
– even in Los Angeles in 1967,
when EVERYONE seemed to be doing it.

Chapter

1

Going to California

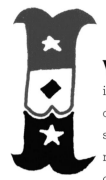

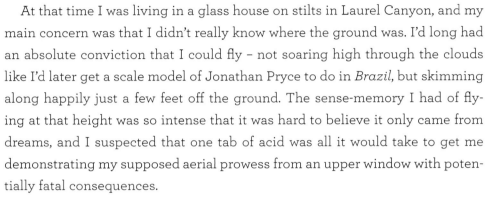

I was always frightened to take acid – even in Los Angeles in 1966–7, when everyone seemed to be doing it. You could see the way it was fucking people's minds up right from the start, and being lucky enough to have occasionally accessed the realm of the imagination LSD was meant to take you to without chemical assistance, I wanted to make sure the itinerary for those visits stayed strictly under my own control.

At that time I was living in a glass house on stilts in Laurel Canyon, and my main concern was that I didn't really know where the ground was. I'd long had an absolute conviction that I could fly – not soaring high through the clouds like I'd later get a scale model of Jonathan Pryce to do in *Brazil*, but skimming along happily just a few feet off the ground. The sense-memory I had of flying at that height was so intense that it was hard to believe it only came from dreams, and I suspected that one tab of acid was all it would take to get me demonstrating my supposed aerial prowess from an upper window with potentially fatal consequences.

People have sometimes accused me of not being able to distinguish dreams from reality, and it's true that when it came to my recurring night-flights of fancy I had been mercifully spared the process of (literally!) disillusionment where you wake up thinking 'That really happened,' but then the vision gradually leaves you. I suppose if the mind really is more powerful than the body, then my brain could have convinced all those little muscles that this momentous event had earned its place in their individual memories – which is pretty much how it works for phantom limbs, but in that case you're dealing with a nervous system trained over a long period of time to assume that certain things are going on down below.

Maybe all dreams of flying are just your subconscious response to the fact that your dad threw you up in the air a lot as a little kid. I know Freud would offer another, earthier interpretation, but I was never a big fan of his, being more of a Jungian myself. A Neil Jungian, that is. I've always really loved Neil's music – Buffalo Springfield, Crazy Horse, all of it – as well as identifying strongly with his no-bullshit approach to the human psyche. So fuck you, Sigmund, I'm sticking with the 'dad throwing you up in the air a lot' theorem.

The first chance my dad got to throw me up in the air was in November 1940. I was born a month after John Lennon and half a year before my fellow

Minnesotan Bob Dylan (who took a while to realise that was what his name should be). In American terms I was a pre-war baby, because the land of my birth decided to sit out the first few dances of the Second World War, until the Japs marked our card at Pearl Harbor.

My dad, James ('Gill') Gilliam – who'd been in the last operational cavalry unit of the US army for a while before the war – tried to re-enlist, but they told him he was too old and his horse-riding skills would be no use against the Nazi *blitzkrieg*. In any case, his primary duty was to throw me up in the air a lot, so I'd have an excuse for all those flying dreams in later life. As a consequence of this enlightened intervention on the part of the US military (which would not be the last benevolent decision it would make on behalf of the male Gilliams, but more of that later), the war had no impact on my early life at all.

There was none of that formative trauma which is normally so vital to the evolution of the artistic mind (although that absence would in itself become traumatic in later life, proving a serious obstacle to any attempt to pass my-self off as a Renaissance man). I arrived two years before my sister Sherry and eight-and-a-bit before my brother Scott, so I'd made sure my feet were firmly under the table before any competition arrived. I was smart, happy and in good health – in short all the things you'd want in a child. I'd later joke (and if a man can't use material he's been road-testing all his life in his own memoir, when can he?) that my father was a carpenter and my mother was a virgin, so what other choice did I have than to be the chosen one?

I love the out-of-focus-ness of this kid. I was moving too fast for the cameras even then. My mum's hair is the subject of the piece - look at those precise curls, and that's a really good parting - but the object of her attention is, well, what exactly? My parents appreciated what they had, and they always admired the creature, but they could never quite grasp the true nature of its identity . . . There's an element of vanity about Mrs Beatrice Gilliam that I find very interesting in retrospect. The meticulousness of her parting once almost got her lured off the straight and narrow. In the mid-1930s, when she was working in a Minneapolis restaurant called Hasty Tasty, a smartly dressed woman kept admiring her hair and asking if she would come and do her and her friends' the same way, and my mum found out afterwards that this potential client was the wife of the notorious Minneapolis gangster 'Kid' Cann who used to procure local women for him and his good friend Al Capone.

There are a few family pictures of us outside rented houses in Minneapolis, but the first home I actually have memories of is the one at Medicine Lake, out of the city, which my parents bought and moved us to when I was four. The house was basically a summer cottage – not made for 40-degrees-below-zero winters, and not really meant to be lived in at all in the cold season, but it was all they could afford at the time, so we made the best of it. I remember my dad insulating the whole place and digging out the basement.

We lived there for several years with an outside toilet, which we called a 'biffy'. It was a two-holer – presumably to delineate us from the poor people, who only had one hole. You'd think we might've complained about having to troop out there in Arctic conditions, but it was normal to us. That's the great thing about kids – normal is normal, so what are you complaining about? That's just the way the world is.

Years later, once I'd run away to join *Monty Python's Flying Circus*, I used to drive my parents crazy by referring to myself as 'poor white trash'. They hated me doing that, because they weren't poor white trash – they worked very hard. We didn't have much money, but we never felt ourselves to be poor.

My dad did lots of different jobs to keep the grizzlies from the door. At one point he worked on the Alaskan highway – driving earth-movers – at another as a coffee salesman. Either way, he was away a lot, and the template of a hearth maintained by the mother, and a father who comes back from his travels as a glamorous figure, is one I have tried to build upon as an adult – to the extent that my wife Maggie claims she raised our three children as a one-parent family.

It's intriguing how these patterns repeat themselves without one necessarily being aware of it. I never realised I was away that much when my kids were young, and similarly when I was growing up, I never felt like my dad wasn't around. Even if L Ron Hubbard himself were to audit me, I don't think he could come up with a memory of an absent father. Because Dad was always building stuff and fixing things up, we were constantly aware of his presence. Who could forget the day he finished work on the inside toilet and made a tree-house out of the remains of the old biffy?

The thing I remember most clearly about the winters was when Dad would tie an inner tube to the back of the car and whoosh me around the lake, whip-lashing all over the place, shouting at the top of my voice. That was fantastic.

Those three destructive little words 'health and safety' had yet to reach Minnesota. My dad took me out shooting from a very early age. We had three

Look at the wisdom in this child's eyes. And that's obviously a nice man standing behind him.

My dad died in 1982, and what still intrigues
me about him is that even though he was always
doing things, and his work was normally very
physical, he was incredibly kind and gentle. He
wasn't pushy and aggressive and ambitious, like me,
whereas my mother was the controlling and organising
force. You can see there's real power in her, and she
was definitely the disciplinarian of the house. If I had
to be whipped — which I did sometimes (let's say if
I was defending my tree house with a bow and arrow,
and someone inadvertently got hit in the eye King Harold-
style) — my dad would do it, but it wouldn't be his idea.
I don't ever remember feeling that I'd been punished unfairly;
getting spanked with a belt every now and again was just what happened.
It wasn't just locking you in your room — what would be the point of that?
There had to be something physical. I think there's something a little crazy
about the age we live in now where you're not supposed to smack a kid or even
shout at them. Maybe this is more true of boys than girls, but the need for
physical limitations is very strong when you're growing up, because you're
always pushing at them.

shotguns in the house – a 12-gauge, a 16-gauge and a 22. They were definitely there for hunting rather than protecting us from the evils of the world. You'd go out and get what you needed for the table, and then come back and pluck the pheasant or gut the sunfish you'd caught by driving onto the frozen lake, drilling a hole and plonking your line down.

Of course, the ice brought its own hazards. When you were out sledding and went over a bump, it was so cold that if your tongue touched the metal it would get frozen stuck. You'd have to walk all the way home holding the sled up to your face and hopefully get some hot water to get the thing off. That was some horrible shit, but it was absolutely standard.

Luckily, the dog falling on my head was more of a one-off. In winter, when the snow ploughs would come down the road outside and heap the snow and ice up onto the side, we would tunnel into it to make a cave to play in. One day a dog climbed up on top of it and took a piss, and the piss melted the snow and suddenly the whole thing – dog plus piss – came down on my and my friends' heads. It was all quite elemental, but the great thing about growing up in the country is that you can't avoid learning about the functions

that our bodies have, and the fact that animals have insides, and that we eat them and they die. Frogs' legs were a great local delicacy in Minnesota – you hold him by the back legs, then whack him with a knife or an axe as he tries to jump, and you've got a nutritious snack. Food is immediate. There's a living creature, there's a dead creature, and there's a full creature slightly higher up the food chain. This is knowledge that has served me very well creatively.

Sometimes we'd go to a relative's farm on Sundays, and we'd see chickens get their heads cut off and still be running around afterwards. As a kid there is nothing more entertaining than that, because you are actually seeing life after death. These youthful farmyard experiences don't make you callous, they just give you a respectful understanding of how cruel nature can be. One of my clearest – and most upsetting – childhood memories is of a mother garter snake being run over by a car, and me finding its belly split open and all these baby snakes swarming out across the road to their inevitable doom. Clearly this particular snake was trying to evolve into a mammal as it crossed the road.

I've always wondered how city kids learn these things. Obviously nature's still there underneath all the tin cans and the breeze blocks, but its workings are harder to discern

I like how confident I am in the saddle here – you can see it's not the first pig I've ridden.

when cats and dogs are the only animals you come into regular contact with.

An ambivalence about the relationship between the rural and the urban has been a major underlying theme of the films I've made. On the one hand, I love cities for their architecture and as hothouses of culture and art. On the other, I hate them as man-made excrescences conspiring to obscure our view of the natural world.

I've tried to do my bit over the years to bridge that gap. While we were making *Jabberwocky*, I wanted to find some actual animal tissues for the skin of the monster, so I went to visit an abattoir near Shepperton in West London. When you've watched a big old cow walk in there on four legs, very much alive, there's something really shocking about the moment when it's given the bolt to the head, and this thing with all its muscles and its energy just turns to dead weight. To add to the fun, it was a small family-run abattoir – what Americans call a 'mom-and-pop operation'. So when the carcass was hoisted up in the air and all the intestines were coming out, who was there to clear up but this kid of ten or eleven who was home on his school holidays? Watching him scoop up all the slops and the blood, I did think that anyone who eats meat (as I do) should spend a few hours in a place like that at some point in their lives, just to understand the process you're part of.

It's crazy how isolated the Western world has
become from reality. Apart from anything else, nothing sets your imagination free like a direct connection to the planet you actually live on. When I think back to the landscape I grew up in, I know that across the dirt road passing in front of our house was a big swamp, and further down the road was a terribly frightening wood with a house in it that was sort of ruined and no one was exactly sure who lived there. Straight away, the mind goes flying. The swamp was magical too, because one year they cut down a load of trees and piled them up along the edge of the road, and if you crept down among the trunks you'd find all these wonderful mossy spaces to hide out in.

In 1966, my mum began to assemble a retrospective diary of family illnesses (in later years I have sometimes wondered if my relative freedom from health-related anxiety can be attributed to the fact that Beatrice Gilliam did all my worrying for me). In the entry for 1948, when I was seven years old, she wrote as follows: 'Terry had a number of terrible sieges with the croup. His temperature would be very high and he would see horrible creatures on the ceilings and

At one with nature in a summertime Minnesotan variant of the Garden Of Eden.

And then again, sixty years later, by a Spanish waterfall with Johnny Depp, trying – and ultimately failing – to film DON QUIXOTE.

(This was just before the moment in the documentary <u>Lost in La Mancha</u> where Johnny's got the fish in his trousers and he ad libs the line 'You're a fish – I'm a man.') How did I get from one place to the other? If you look closely at the first photo, you can see I'm actually standing by a tombstone, so maybe it wasn't so very far after all.

walls and think they were after him. I was so frightened that his mind wouldn't come out of these hallucinations . . .'

Some might argue that these fears were not without foundation in the long term, but I have no memory of those particular hallucinations. I think she may have conflated my troublesome outbreaks of coughing with a recurring nightmare I started to have after seeing Alexander Korda and Michael Powell's *The Thief of Bagdad* at around this time. Cineastes will tell you what proportion of my films contain images inspired by that landmark of Arabian adventure, and I suspect more do than don't. The spider in it loomed so large in my dreams that I'd wake up in the night with my bedclothes strangling me like a suffocating web.

Luckily, not all my formative cinematic experiences were so traumatic. I'd go to the cinema and see *Snow White* or the bad boys' world in *Pinocchio* and think, 'This is a world I want to be a part of.' As a kid, once you've had your first taste of Robin Hood or 'cowboys and Indians' on celluloid, that's it, it's done – you just want to be on your horse, outspeeding the Sheriff of Nottingham or hunting down that Redskin (or Native American as you will later more respectfully come to know him).

I also read an enormous amount. My favourite books tended to be by a Scottish author called Albert Payson Terhune, who seems to be more or less unknown in Britain these days, perhaps because while he wrote a lot of excellent stories about loyal dogs, someone else wrote the most famous one – *Greyfriars Bobby*.

We always had dogs in the house – usually setters, along with the odd spaniel – so these books did not require great intellectual leaps of understanding on my part. But the great thing about reading as a spur to the imagination (as opposed to say *Grand Theft Auto* – not that I don't enjoy that too) is that you're doing all the visualisation yourself. However good the author might be at painting a picture with words, the final stage of translating that mental picture from two dimensions into three is up to you.

It's the same with the radio, which was all-powerful in America at that time. There was a children's radio show called *Let's Pretend*, which was one of my very first gateways to the fantastical. It might seem a strange thing for a cartoonist to say – that radio was the medium that first taught him how to conjure up visuals – but it's certainly true in my case. Even later on, when I started to get actively interested in animation, the name of a voiceover artist like Mel Blanc still probably meant more to me than Chuck Jones' did. And once I started making films of my own, I loved doing the voices and sound effects every bit as much as the images.

We didn't have a TV during the time we lived at Medicine Lake,
but I do remember going round to a neighbour's house to watch Sid Caesar's *Your Show of Shows*. Caesar was the one commanding your attention, but I realised when I went back to that show years afterwards that it was the less prominent Carl Reiner who was truly breathtaking.

Another comedian I discovered on that same neighbour's TV, who made a huge impression on me right from the off, was Ernie Kovacs. Even though I saw him ridiculously early in life – I was just ten or eleven years old and pondering

Ernie Kovacs and Sid Caesar (handsomely pictured here) were so anarchic that it was hard to imagine how they got on the telly. But TV was a fairly new medium then and clearly couldn't support the legions of executives that are now available to get in the way of talent. In a way these shows were my first connection with what became Python.

the economic benefits of my first paper round – I think Kovacs was the one who did more than anyone else to bring alive my interest in what I would later learn to think of as surreal comedy. No one else was doing that kind of thing on TV at the time, and he died far too young in a car crash, but not before he had introduced my receptive mind to the entrancing notion of a thing not having to be what it was.

In terms of constructing a home for my youthful imagination, the two sure foundations which Ernie Kovacs and Walt Disney had to build upon were Grimms' fairy tales and stories from the Bible. Decades later, when I eventually came to try to film Grimms (an experience that was a *mittel*-European horror story all of its own, but we'll come to that later), I'd find out that they had been every bit as bowdlerised as the Old and New Testaments have been. But just because a sacred text has been tampered with by a few old men with beards over the years, that doesn't make it any less powerful.

The version of the Bible I read at least

twice all the way through was the King James, which is a pretty good run at the material, all things considered. Once you've got a book like that in your hands, you want to

As well as a tree-house, my father also made me a special table for backyard performances of the secret knowledge imparted by this magic set. It wasn't so much about becoming a master of illusion, as learning how to keep the audience on your side when things almost invariably went wrong . . . useful preparation for my later career as a film-maker.

get to the end just to find out what happens – was it the butler who did it, or the Messiah?

Either way, I was raised to know the whole thing – Genesis, Exodus, Leviticus, Numbers, Deuteronomy, Joshua, the lot – and I do think the generations who've grown up without learning the Bible (and to my own secular regret I include my own children in that) have really missed out. Stories like David and Bathsheba are the building blocks of our culture, but who knows Bathsheba now? Who even knows David?

It's not necessarily a question of having a reverential attitude. What's interesting is sharing a culture that has grown out of those tales, because it's easier to have fun with things when everyone understands what the references are.

Ours was a relaxed religious household. Christianity was a normal part of life, like fresh water and mosquitoes; everyone we knew went to church on Sunday, listened to the sermon and sang vigorous non-conformist hymns like 'Onward Christian Soldiers' (which are much better than the standard Anglican hymn book – that is fucking horrible).

Lawnmowing for candy is one of the essential human transactions.

Credit			Debit		
Amt.	Date	Reason	Amt	Date	Reason
20	6/21	Father gave it to me	.10	6/29	Bible School
.04	6/29	Groc. Change	.65	6/30	Bible School
.02	6/29	Found it	.05	7/1	Bible School
$1.00	6/29	Lawn Mowing	.10	7/4	Fireworks
.50	6/30	Weeding	.61	7/4	Lost it
.04	7/1	Groc. Change	.35	7/4	Show
.35	7/1	Weeding	.60	7/7	Swimming
.03	7/3	Groc. Change	1.00	7/8	Scout Stuff
1.00	7/3	Lawn Mowing	.05	7/8	candy
1.00	7/4	" "	.25	7/11	Swimming
5.00	7/16	Parents gave to me	5.00	7/?	Jamboree
	7/?	Dishes	.77	7/20	"
		Groc. Change	.30	8/1	Show
1.00	8/10	Lawn Mowing	.10	8/10	Scout Dues
30	8/10	Weeding	.50	8/15	Whitsett

Contrary to the propaganda of certain studio executives, tight budgeting has always been really important to me ... whether I was saving $1.30 out of every $2.10 earned as a kid, or trying to get by on $50 a week and still save up for a film camera in New York in the mid-sixties. Obviously the numbers are bigger now, but it's still the same fucking thing. To me it's always been about buying the freedom to do what I want and nothing else ... I don't have to clean those cars or make that advert, because I've got a dollar thirty for a sketch book and some pencils. I owe my forensic record-keeping to my mother, who even kept the hospital bill (totalling $76.60) for the week of my birth – room, drugs, laboratory anaesthetic, Thanksgiving dinner for Gill, circumcision for Terry ($2).

That first brutal edit was standard practice in America – every kid (well, all the boys at least) got circumcised, and I suppose $2 wasn't a bad deal, given the excessive amount they took off. I've suffered with that all my life, but that's another story – let's call it the director's cut.

Going to church was the big social event of the week, and any other large-scale gathering which took place at the weekend – a square dance or a barbecue – was likely to be organised around that same social hub. It gave you a real sense of community. The same way that knowing that if you wanted to buy something, you'd have to save hard to get the money, prepared you for the realities of your working life as an adult.

When I was eleven years old, our family underwent what should in theory have been a great upheaval. Like so many of our fellow Americans before – and after – us, we sold our house and drove out West to try our luck in California. A two-wheeled trailer was hired, all our moveable possessions packed into it – including my grandmother on my mother's side (although eventually we heeded her protests and let her come in the car with the rest of the family) – and we set off into the future.

The whole thing felt like a big adventure to us kids, but must have been pretty stressful for the adult members of the party, given my dad's uncertain employment prospects. He knew there were possibilities with a company called 3M, which had been based in Minneapolis, but it was nothing definite. And by the time we'd moved into a little pink house in one of aluminium giant Henry J. Kaiser's tract developments – serried ranks of more-or-less identical brand-new houses, with much less space around them than we'd been used to back at Medicine Lake – the Gilliams' California dream was losing a little bit of its lustre.

My mum's diary recounts my reactions in the same melodramatic terms she so often (and so mystifyingly) tended to ascribe to me: 'Terry was very disappointed. He said, "I thought we were coming to Paradise."'

It was true that at first everything did seem kind of contained and not natural, but LA hadn't been completely valley-ised by then. From where we lived in Panorama City, you had only to go fifteen minutes down the road to reach open fields. If you were willing to drive a little further, you could get to the mountains or the beach in under an hour. And by the time we'd gone into the mountains a few times at the weekend, and my dad had built fences in the back yard and clad the kitchen units in walnut, the San Fernando Valley soon started to feel like home.

Panorama City was not far from Stoney Point, which was one of the places where stock footage was filmed for Westerns and cowboy-themed TV shows. When you saw the standard shot of the posse running or the cavalry or someone shooting and someone else fall, that would often be where it was.

The phantasmogoric WILD WEST wallpaper of my LA bedroom is a definite step on from Minnesota's more austere domestic environment. Life there wasn't about decoration, it was just about what you needed, whereas once we were in CALIFORNIA, cowboys became an option. This is GILLIAM in his larval stage – a young boy newly arrived in LA in search of the Western experience... I was ready to RIDE.

When you go somewhere for the first time thinking it's going to be something it turns out not to be, that's always disappointing, but the funny thing about Stoney Point was, we kept going there. It still had an allure. You're at this place, and it's not quite what you hoped for because it looked much more dramatic on film, but then you start looking at what is really there and your imagination starts making it interesting again. I suppose that junction – the place where reality and myth or fantasy meet – is where a lot of my films ended up being located.

It wasn't like I particularly needed an escape route. I didn't have any problems adjusting socially to life in California. No one laughed at how we talked – we all spoke American. When you moved into a new community in the 1950s, the neighbours were there to welcome you, and going to the church a few blocks away was how you got to know everyone. We'd been Episcopalians or Lutherans in Minnesota – I can't actually remember which – but the church we joined in LA was Presbyterian. It didn't seem to matter too much.

We were Protestants, that was the main thing. People weren't zealots. They believed in the basic stuff, but nobody spent too much time thinking about how the Trinity actually functions. We didn't buy transubstantiation – we had to draw the line somewhere. I mean, come *on*. The Catholic Church was the competition – they took their orders straight from Rome.

The one thing that was truly different about arriving in California was that this was the first time I knew there were Jews in the world – not just in the Bible. Most of the people who lived near us in Minnesota had been of Scandinavian origin. But our new next-door neighbours were Jewish, and Jews were like magnets to me.

They just seemed smarter and funnier than everybody else I knew. I don't think I necessarily thought of them as more glamorous than my existing family and friends, just a bit more exotic and better read. I always used to complain about our own relatives when my parents suggested we go and see them: 'Why? They're not interesting.' But I'd find any excuse to spend more time at my new Jewish friends' houses. I'd got a whiff of something heady there that I definitely wanted more of. Looking back now, I suspect that 'something' might've been showbiz, as a lot of them seemed to have some connection – and even the vaguest pointer in that direction was a giant green 'walk this way' sign to me – to Hollywood.

Here I am at the piano with my siblings Scott and Sherry. I had to go without Christmas presents for a year or two to help pay for this, but it was worth the wait. I loved (and still do love) the way that to play Scott Joplin you have to get the rhythm going with your left hand while your right hand does something completely different. I now have a Steinway Grand, which I bought from Rocky Horror Picture Show star Tim Curry (and he'd bought before that from Pink Floyd's Roger Waters). You wouldn't guess its illustrious pedigree if you heard me play it, though.

Aside from putting on my magic shows and hammering away at my little blonde wood piano like an Aryan wannabe Fats Waller, I'd found one other reliable outlet for that instinct for showing off, which seemed to be so much stronger in me than my parents' genes might have suggested. And that outlet was drawing.

It started back in Minnesota after a school trip to the zoo. We'd been driven into Minneapolis by special bus, and when we got back to class the teacher told us to draw one of the animals from memory. I cheated and copied a bear from a book sneakily tucked on my lap beneath my desk and got a lot of praise for it. The pattern of my creative life was set.

In the days before video games, comic books were the main corrupting influence on American youth. But they were also more part of the cultural furniture there than they ever were in Britain. You grew up with *Superman* and *Batman*, and a whole section of the newspaper was given over to strips like *Terry and the Pirates*, *Mutt and Jeff*, *Dick Tracy*, *Dagwood and Blondie* (an earlier generation thrived on *The Katzenjammer Kids*, *Gertie the Dinosaur*, *Little Nemo* and *Dreams of the Rarebit Fiend*). Trying to emulate the cartoonists was a large part of the pleasure of reading them from a very early age for me.

You draw something and straight away it either works, or it doesn't. That was (and indeed still is, on the ever rarer occasions when I get around to it) the

I learned everything I know about drawing from this book. Talent borrows, cartoonists copy.

delight of cartooning for me – the instant feedback. It's not like making a film or writing a book, where you've got to work on it for years and then somebody's still got to go to the cinema or buy a copy to see what you've done – it's more like a kind of performance. Quick – do it – then, *Boom!* You get the hit of an audience, even if it's only an audience of one, liking (or hating) it.

I guess there's always been a kind of smart-arse quality about me, where when someone says something I've got to come back with a quip that says, 'I'm here, and I'm pretty clever.' Maggie, my wife, still finds that pretty irritating, and I guess by doing it in the form of a drawing, I shift the whole transaction onto ground that I feel confident on.

These are some of the earliest original cartoons I can't remember doing, and I actually think they're better than some of my much later stuff I did at college. They just seem more confident. I really like the two pupils in one eyeball, and those suction cup things are incredible.

PICASSO had his blue period, but my formative
works were predominantly concerned with Hoover attachments.
I guess that was tech paranoia of the Fifties doing its deadly work.
Once when I had scarlet fever as a kid I hallucinated that my
parents went into the other room and the refrigerator blew up
and killed them.

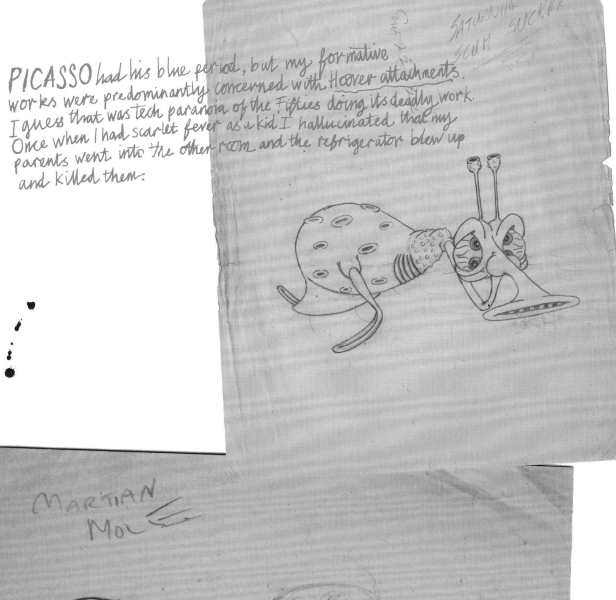

The film THE WAR OF THE WORLDS
might have been another key influence.
That came out in 1953, making me twelve or
thirteen at the time I did this.

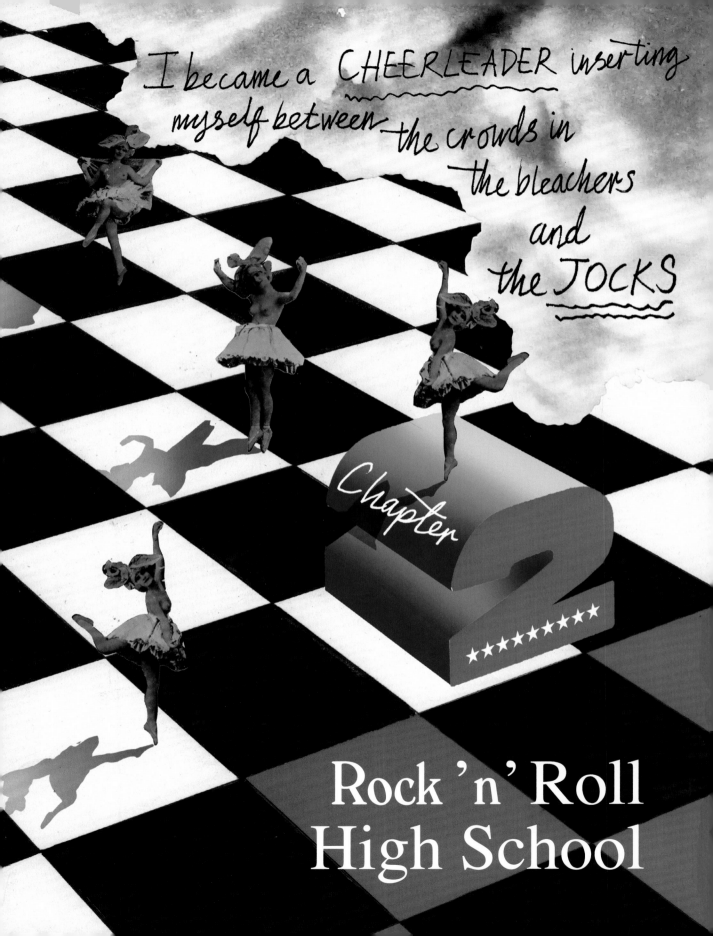

I became a CHEERLEADER inserting myself between the crowds in the bleachers and the JOCKS

Chapter 2

Rock 'n' Roll High School

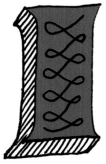**I** never met my grandfather on my mother's side. His and my grandma's marriage had broken up after he got ripped off in a business deal and turned to drink, but I wasn't encouraged to ask about that as a child, because it was perceived as such a disgrace to the family. Years later, when my mum gave me her journal to read, I found out that one of my grandpa's other shameful accomplishments was running a cinema in Bismarck, North Dakota – which she initially tried to pass off as 'a theatre' (as if that made it more respectable!). So the cinematic gene was definitely in there somewhere.

If we're going to get into genetics, although I'm a bit of a neo-Lamarckian when it comes to the inheritance of acquired characteristics, I've spent most of my life trying to counteract my genes (whether by acquiring as many Jewish friends as possible as soon as we moved to LA, or by voluntarily exiling myself to the colonial motherland as an adult). You know that feeling you get as a kid at Christmas when you see your relatives sitting around and think, 'I've got to get out of here . . .' Surely it can't just have been me who felt that way? It wasn't that I'd had a bad time in the bosom of my family, or that they were genetically unsound, I just wanted to see a bit more of the world.

My grandfather on my dad's side was an early stepping-stone into a different kind of landscape. He was a Baptist preacher (albeit one who qualified via mail order rather than theological college), a big, charming guy who lived in the South, in Hot Springs, Arkansas. We'd driven down there from Minnesota a couple of times and my memories of those early trips are a splashy blur of swinging out and jumping into creeks on big tyres on ropes. All that shit was great, except that when you rolled around in the tall grass you'd get covered in ticks and chiggers – a.k.a. nasty little biting fuckers that burrowed under your skin, and when you tried to pull them off their heads broke off inside you, causing days of painful itching.

Another thing that stuck in my mind about the South in the forties and fifties was how civilised it seemed. Everybody was always so polite – black and white, everyone would say 'Good morning' on the street – you couldn't have asked for nicer people. Of course, I'd realise later on that all this politeness was conditional on everyone staying in their place. (Although many years later I did meet a black woman who shared my surname in the foyer of a London film company, so the Gilliams must have done the odd bit of mixing and matching on the quiet.)

The first time I went out to Hot Springs on my own, in the summer of 1955, I experienced a foretaste of later dissenting tendencies, but in this case the seeds of disenchantment were planted – as so often – in the fertile mulch of self-interest.

The same July weekend that I was first trusted to embark on the long train journey East from LA all by myself also turned out to be a historic occasion on a larger scale – the grand opening of the original Disneyland, an hour down the road from Panorama City, in Anaheim, California.

I was tremendously disappointed to be away from LA for what, by my reckoning – then as now – was one of the major cultural events of the twentieth century. Missing out on what turned out to be a famously disastrous opening ceremony (notwithstanding the reassuring presence of Ronald Reagan – a man from whom both California and the world in general would later hear more than they might've expected – as one of the three TV anchors) was about the closest I ever came to real childhood trauma. That's what kills me; I've always wanted the scars, but I just don't have them. In fact, that's probably why I had to go into film-making – to acquire the deep emotional and spiritual wounds which my shockingly happy childhood had so callously denied me.

Once back from Arkansas, I wasted no time in making good my Disneyland deficit, returning to Walt's magical kingdom many times in the years that followed. The thing that made Disneyland a genuinely enchanting place for me was the quality of the craftsmanship. Previously, theme parks had always been pretty tacky, gimcracked places, but so much love and care went into making Disney's dream a reality – there were no shortcuts.

Everything you could ever think of, he put in there . . . it wasn't just about seeing the favourite cartoons of your childhood in 3-D. Disneyland was also where I first learned about architecture – the way the windows would be scaled on Georgian buildings to give them a greater sense of height – and Sleeping Beauty's castle became the template for all my ideas about Europe. OK, it was a fantasy land, and some might say I've been living there ever since, but at least now I know where the dirt is hidden.

It wasn't all about Yurp (as Europe was pronounced in

America). On the African ride, you'd get on the boat from *The African Queen*, and the animals would poke their heads up from the water or suddenly appear roaring from behind a tree – it was everything you could want from travel, but without the bugs. Then there was the World of Tomorrow, featuring the Monsanto House of the Future (which didn't seem as sinister an idea then as a genetically modified future does now). You could drive little cars in the miniature Autopia, even though you weren't yet old enough to have a driving licence. And Main Street was like a dream version of America: idyllic and historical at the same time.

My imagination was always stimulated by enclosed worlds with their own distinct hierarchies and sets of rules – whether that be the virtual reality of Disney's Tomorrowland, or the medieval castles or Roman courts of the 'sword and sandal' movie epics, which I loved just as much. Such well-defined social structures give you something to react against and take the piss out of, and I've always – and I still do this – tended to simplify the world into a series of nice, clear-cut oppositions, which I can mess around at the edges of. It's when things become more abstract and unclear that I start to struggle.

There are few more exotic and compelling examples of
a self-contained community than the travelling show, and some of my most vivid childhood memories were supplied by the annual visits of the Clyde Beatty circus, which used to set up in the car park in Panorama City and put

the word out for local kids to come and help raise the tents. They'd give you a bit of money in return for the work you did, but I found the carnival atmosphere so intoxicating that I'd probably have done it for nothing. They always needed extra pairs of hands and one year, when I was thirteen or fourteen, I ended up helping out in the freak-show tent. The experience of seeing all the exotic circus acts sitting around playing cards – just like everyday people, except they were pin-heads or dwarves – has stayed with me to this day. It wasn't just the

I must have been about fourteen when I helped raise Clyde Beatty's freak-show tent. It was not to be the only circus in my life.

22

revelation that these extraordinary people would behave in such a normal way that fascinated me – in retrospect, that should have been obvious – it was the moment when the show would begin, the barkers would introduce them, 'All the way from darkest Africa . . . ', and they'd have to instantly make that transition to being 'the leopard man' or 'the alligator boy'.

The idea of someone subsuming themselves completely within another identity has always intrigued me, I suppose because that's something I've never felt quite able to do myself. As far as my first forays into public performance as a junior magician were concerned, I was so bad that I'd generally find myself fucking up the tricks themselves and then having to do something ridiculous to get myself out of the resulting mess. It seemed much easier to just act the goat as a way of keeping people at a certain distance – for a while I earned myself the nickname of 'clown' from other kids of my age for my willingness to make a fool of myself in order to distract audiences from my technical shortcomings.

I was always very gregarious and loved making people laugh, but I think ultimately the reason I was never going to become a performer first and foremost – and certainly not an actor – was that at heart I don't have the neediness or incompleteness that will ultimately drive you in that direction. I like showing off, and I don't mind making a fool of myself or playing the grotesque, but I've never been comfortable exposing whatever subtler sensitivities and emotions I may or may not have buried deep-down inside. That's the well a good actor is willing to dip into and reveal to the world. I prefer to hide behind a mask or a cartoon.

The most important single cultural influence

on my teenage years was *Mad* comics. They had a very distinct brand of humour, which kids of my generation had in common (and subsequent ones too, as the magazine went from strength to strength – commercially, if not artistically – in the years after its co-founder and my comic book superhero Harvey Kurtzman moved on in 1956), in much the same way that *Monty Python* or *South Park* would end up uniting people in later years.

NOT WANTED

THE BEAST OF BIRMINGHAM

The Beast is back! Again it is loose on the campus of Birmingham. The Beast returns every semester with its evil handi- | food lying neatly beside trash cans, celery sticks floating in clever little puddles of cherry punch. Only the warped mind of the Monster could possibly con-

Still a little way to go here in terms of background detail, although the trash-can is a start. But I make no apology for the civic-minded undertone – people dropping litter have always made me angry.

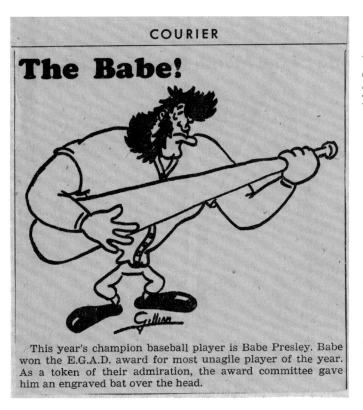

COURIER

The Babe!

This year's champion baseball player is Babe Presley. Babe won the E.G.A.D. award for most unagile player of the year. As a token of their admiration, the award committee gave him an engraved bat over the head.

BABE PRESLEY – that's old Elvis, in an early drawing from my high school magazine. You can see how much care I've taken over the signature. You get the signature right and everything else follows – that's how it worked for Picasso, too.

I've been lucky to be exactly the right age at the right time at several different points in my life, and 1956 was definitely a good year to be sixteen (just as ten years later, being a bit older than most of the first generation of hippies probably helped stop me getting as badly fucked up as some of my friends did). I remember sitting in a parked car outside my high school when 'Heartbreak Hotel' came on the radio and thinking 'Shit! I've never heard anything like that before.' But there was no danger of me trying to follow in Elvis' blue suede footsteps. I played the French horn in the school band and openings were few and far between for people lumbering around wrapped in one of those at Sun Records. I didn't care, though. I loved the way the sound of that instrument came from another space, and I was good at dancing, so the benefits of the rock 'n' roll era were not completely denied to me in an out-of-school context.

Looking back, there were some similarities with Python, in that *Mad* could be very intelligent and unbelievably silly at the same time, and this was obviously a mixture I liked. Its highest purpose was to entertain, but if you could have fun while saying something important at the same time, then so much the better.

The first lesson I learned from *Mad* comics was that one of the most effective ways of making a comedic point is to take a well-known character with certain widely accepted attributes, and then turn them on their head or use them in illicit ways. Whether that meant subverting a pre-existing comic strip or TV show or – because *Mad* mainstay Harvey Kurtzman loved movies so much – using familiar faces or storylines from the cinema as grist to the mill of political satire (Humphrey Bogart's Captain Queeg in *The Caine Mutiny* was a particular favourite), I found the audacity of it breathtaking and hilarious.

The other key thing about *Mad* comics, apart from the boldness of its parodies and appropriations, was that it was beautifully drawn. The penmanship of Jack Davis was so amazing that I just had to try to copy it – that was how I schooled myself as a draftsman, not with Rembrandt but with Jack Davis: looking at the effects he'd achieved and trying to work out how he'd done it by having a go myself. All the main *Mad* artists brought something different to the table – Willy Elder was the gag-master. Harvey would write a basic storyline and

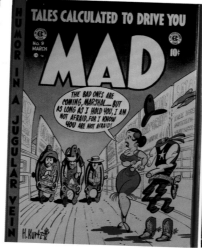

then Willy would add all these little accretions of humorous detail (which he called 'chicken fat'), so you could go back to his work time and time again and keep finding new things in it. Years later, Elder's drawings would end up being maybe the biggest single influence on how I'd make movies – inspiring me to try to fill up each shot with so much detail that it would repay second, third and even fourth viewings.

Last but not least among the building blocks of *Mad* comics' irresistible allure was the unabashed sensuality of Wally Wood's female characters, which were so unbearably sexy that they almost felt like pornography. As a precautionary acknowledgement of the vague sense of impropriety associated with the publication, I used to hide my *Mad* comics in the garage. On one unfortunate occasion they were discovered, and I got a whipping with a belt for my pleasures, but if that was meant to be aversion therapy, it didn't work, probably because the leathery strictures were applied by my dad, who didn't think it was entirely justified and was just doing my mother's dirty work for her.

It wasn't that I didn't take anything seriously

when I was growing up. On the contrary, I was so intensely engaged with all the things that did interest me that it sometimes made me oblivious to salient facts about my broader situation. In some ways, this inner directedness was a good thing – it meant other kids found me quite easy to be around, because I had no issues, and basically inhabited my own private world, which at least made sense to me. But it could also lead to unwelcome surprises, when my naive vision of the world came into conflict with reality.

Harvey Kurtzman's magazines were, in a sense, movies without movement. I learned from Mad and Help! how to do zooms, tracking shots, close-ups – all the grammar of film.

For many people, such a conflict might have manifested itself in the form of unexpected public humiliation at the hands of malevolently inclined school-mates. For me, it was more likely to involve having the mantle of unsought social responsibility thrust upon me. At the tender age of fourteen, just a couple of years after my arrival at Chase Street Elementary School in Panorama City, I found myself giving the school's graduation address on the subject of 'Mexico', a topic about which I knew extraordinarily little. Later on at Birmingham High School – which was one of the largest in LA, with more than 2,000 students in an old army hospital that had been converted into classrooms after the war – one of the most painfully embarrassing moments in my educational career would see me elected king of the senior prom, in preference to my infinitely better-qualified best friend Steve Gellar, who just happened to be Jewish.

Before we can dip a nervous toe into that particular WASP-plagued swimming pool, the particular chronology of my personal odyssey from teenage paragon of civic virtue to subversive cartoonist-in-waiting requires a digression into scouting. Being a boy scout was great fun because it took me out into nature, and you had to work as a group and learn new skills – two activities I still enjoy to this day. The Morse code I don't use so much, but I can still do knot tying, and if I was trapped in a well with a broken arm, I could probably tie a bowline around myself with just the other arm to pull myself out, which is a reassuring ability to have.

Scout meetings were once a week, but every now and then they'd take us on these amazing camping trips up in the mountains. That's what's wonderful about LA – how close the San Bernardino mountains are. We'd go up there for the weekend and sit around the campfire at night, where tales would be told – all these things which are so primal, and which I've never quite grown out of. (Luckily I went into showbiz, so I've never had to.)

Even at one with nature in the wilds as we were, Hollywood's magic Kingdom still cast a long shadow.

Among the stars who came out to dazzle us in the light-pollution-free skies of Irvine Ranch were several — Danny Kaye and Debbie Reynolds among them — who I'd later get to know via friendships with their diversely talented offspring. If you'd broken this big news to the thirteen-year-old me, I would've found it immensely unlikely.

Debbie Reynolds

Danny Kaye

The most spectacular of these outward-bound excursions was the 1953 National Scouts Jamboree at Irvine Ranch in southern California. It's probably all identical tract homes now, but then it was a huge temporary hormonal metropolis of 45,000 teenage boys in shorts.

We stayed there for a whole week — it was our Kumbh Mela — and hopefully these extracts from the beautifully designed official souvenir brochure (design standards were stratospheric in 1950s America, as the pristine layouts of my high school yearbooks will also attest) give you some sense of the mood of this infectiously purposeful corralling of youthful vitality.

HOLLYWOOD MOVED TO THE JAMBOREE

Where there's life, there's Hope.

Doreen O'Dare

Lanny Ross

Debbie Reynolds

Preston Foster

Danny Kaye

Who missed television? Who missed the movies? Not us that week at the Jamboree. The Oscar winners came to the Jamboree, and we're nominating all our Hollywood visitors for special Oscars. We had no less than three big-time shows going on in different areas every afternoon—plus that super "Hollywood Salutes the Jamboree" in the main arena Tuesday night. Bob Hope . . . Dottie Lamour . . . Victor McLaglen . . . Mitzi Gaynor . . . you name 'em—they were there.

The Camp Chief presents Hollywood's George Murphy with a "Scout Oscar" for producing our Jamboree movie.

45,000 SCOUTS AND EXPLORERS CAME TOGETHER

We marched and marched and marched, as if those winding columns, streaming into the arena from a dozen different directions, would never end. We began to understand how many boys 45,000 means. As we sat together in one vast group, how we sang! Folk songs, Scout songs, patriotic songs. While we sang the old melodies, we felt very close to each other, and very glad we were there. As we sang, and listened to inspiring messages, and saw the pageants of our nation's history and of Scouting, we felt how great our country is and how lucky we are to live in it. We were proud of being Scouts and Americans.

As if to suggest that there might be some truth in the old adage that 'politics is show-business for ugly people', another distinguished visitor – vice president Richard Nixon – also dropped by to briefly rejoin his old troop.

'The Veep squatted on his haunches [it says here] and whipped up one of the 44,000 best patrol pancake breakfasts eaten on the Irvine Ranch that morning.' Pity the 1,000 scouts who didn't get breakfasts. Just the previous year he had failed in his attempt to become governor of our fair state – famously telling reporters, 'You won't have Nixon to kick around any more' – but he could still make a mean pancake: truly, there was no stopping that man. Richard Nixon was certainly an interesting character – you couldn't take that away from him. Years later I sat near him on a plane and noticed for the first time how huge his head was. I was in the row right behind him at first, but then his security guys pushed me back – I think they needed more room for his head.

Marching, carrying flags, these are the kinds of things we did in the fifties. The Cold War was very much in everyone's minds, from the 'duck and cover' exercises we had to do at school to ensure that we would be properly prepared for a possible Soviet nuclear attack, to the hysterical witch hunt of the McCarthy hearings. That's why we were healthy, we were strong and we were good – we weren't quite America's Hitler Youth, but there was definitely a militaristic undertow. Our scout troop was a little army in miniature, and if cold-war push ever came to shove, the communists didn't have a chance: tomorrow belonged to us.

Or so I thought, until the time came for me to make the inevitable transition from Life to Eagle Scout, the scouting equivalent of a scientologist going 'clear'. While not necessarily the highest achiever in our troop, I was certainly one of the top two or three, having been awarded approximately fifty-three merit badges in useful disciplines such as cooking, carpentry, safety, firemanship, fishing and animal industry. (What exactly is 'animal industry'? I guess it's battery chickens – how to raise poultry in the smallest space imaginable.) And yet for some reason our scout leader wouldn't accept that I'd earned all my badges in the proper way.

It wasn't so much him refusing to make me an Eagle Scout which really pissed me off – though that was bad enough – as the fact that these bureaucratic fuckers were effectively accusing me of lying. Didn't they know that the lying skills would only come later in life (you can't make films if you can't lie), and you certainly don't get a badge for them?

At that far-off juncture in my life, the Christian ideals of justice and morality I had been taught in Bible school were still holding firm. So when the scouting bigwigs finally confirmed that they had no intention of admitting their mistake, my response was to say – not in so many words, as such foul-mouthed insubordination would come later, but this was definitely the underlying gist of it: 'Well, in that case, I am no longer a scout of any kind. Goodbye, and fuck you.'

It would be stretching a point to describe this moment as the beginning of my life-long struggle against injustice, but I do remember sitting in the scouts' review board – which is sort of like a military court-martial, except you don't get shot at the end – with my hands in front of me on the desk, imagining that I was playing the piano. It was an incredibly vivid sensation; related to later flying dreams, but not wholly overlapping, and less an out-of-body than an extended-body experience, as my hands felt like they were a million miles away and yet still connected to my arms.

A lot of kids my age would probably
have been alarmed by such a strange feeling of bodily alienation, but I found it fascinating. It was probably no coincidence that in later life I would end up marrying a make-up artist, because from an early age I was very intrigued – in a Lon Chaney-esque rather than Liberace-ish way – by the changes in people's appearance that could be effected

It took me twelve hours to get this Phantom look, using the same techniques as Lon Chaney. I'd read up all about Lon and his clever use of collodion – which had previously been used for sealing wounds – and then built the layers up with cotton.

I wore my creation to a Halloween party with a bag over my head like Lon's MAN OF MYSTERY. One girl pulled it off and she just screamed and ran... That's how I seduced women in those days, and to be fair to her (and me), I did look genuinely horrific.

I suppose at seventeen years old it's nice to be confident that you're only getting that reaction because of the make-up. And thanks to Michael Crawford and Andrew Lloyd Webber, the Phantom of the Opera is now recognised as a great romantic lead, so maybe I was just ahead of my time.

This biblical character took even longer to sort out. I can't remember if he was meant to be Moses or John the Baptist. Either way, it was a role Charlton Heston would have relished.

I know what you're thinking: 'How on earth did this fine upstanding young man grow up to be in Monty Python's Life of Brian?'

cosmetically. Not just for the potential for mischief in putting on a disguise, or for the act of transformation itself, but more for the combination of the two. I suppose it was the idea of what you might get away with on the journey to becoming something different that excited me.

The funny thing was that my single-minded dedication to achieving those effects probably – in terms of mischief at least – closed far more doors than it opened. My mum's diary captioned her photographic record of my most phantasmagoric transmogrification as follows: 'This is Terry as the Phantom of the Opera . . . he had all the girls screaming and afraid to get near him.'

It's possible that there was subconscious method in my Lon Chaney madness. As keen as I was to extend my as yet woefully limited (come on, this was the 1950s – and as the great reproductive historian Philip Larkin pointed out, sex wasn't properly invented till 1963) portfolio of erotic experience, my mum's diary also mentioned me reassuring her that I had no intention of becoming 'seriously involved with a woman' for the foreseeable future because I had 'too much left to accomplish'.

With the benefit of hindsight, I can see that looks a little pompous, but as high school drew towards its close, there was definitely a sense that nesting time was at hand. Girls were getting themselves knocked up and guys were getting themselves trapped.

I understand how when you're eighteen years old and wondering what you're going to do on leaving school, getting married and having kids (not necessarily in that order) can look like a short-cut to becoming a grown-up, but I saw a lot of really smart people get stuck up that particular cul-de-sac, and I was always adamant that this sorry fate would not be mine. I wouldn't say that I was actively keeping myself pure, more that girls were helping me to achieve that goal, despite my best efforts.

Looking at the way me and my friends Mel Metcalfe, Richard Lotts and Bob and George McDill, the sons of the minister Rev'd McDill [far right], the man who would eventually help me get a Presbyterian college scholarship, are standing in this photo – in a kind of arrowhead – you might be tempted to think 'Gilliam the leader!'

I probably was the nominal head of the church youth group we all belonged to, but that didn't cut too much ice with Lois Smith, the girl (standing, appropriately enough, in the centre) we all had the hots for. I wasn't a sensualist in those days — I think Mel and Richard had made more progress than I had in that direction. They're both much more tanned than me, and Mel was quite smooth and ended up being a sound mixer in Hollywood. I presume the book we're all holding might be a prayer guide for young people wanting to know how to keep clean and pure — I certainly needed one.

Mel and Richard aside, most of my best friends in high school were Jewish. They tended to live up in the slightly more well-to-do town of Sherman Oaks, and their parents were often involved in the film business, either as editors, or working on the accounting side. But much as the voice in my head was honing its heady mantra of 'Hollywood! Hollywood! Hollywood!', the question of how my own mundane reality could somehow be made to intersect with that impossibly glamorous realm – so physically close, yet so practically distant – was no closer to finding an answer.

My dad still stubbornly refused to find work in the movie industry, inexplicably choosing to spend his working life constructing pre-fab movable office partitions. It never once occurred to me that he might find this occupation as tedious as I did – an oversight on my part which can probably be ascribed in equal parts to my dad's dignified, craftsman-like approach to the need to put food on the family table, and my own adolescent egotism.

The one upside of my dad's job was that he'd come home with these giant 8-foot by 4-foot cardboard boxes that his pre-fab partitions came in, which were great for making stage sets with – you'd have this huge slab of a thing that took paint beautifully. All you had to do was stick a frame on it and it was practically a canvas. I was constantly laying these things out on the patio at the back of our house, rushing against the clock to finish some ludicrously over-ambitious school project or other. My parents would always be there to help me through when I needed more hands to get a job done. Far from resenting me for these demands, they seemed to really enjoy it – marvelling at the fact that there was this kid living in their house who was so excited about having all these ideas and making all these things.

By the time my junior prom came around, I was building this huge castle out of cardboard boxes for the set. Inevitably, the project fell behind schedule – though luckily there were no studio executives on hand to pull the plug – to the extent that by the time my classmates were arriving with all their tuxes and corsages immaculately in place, I was still rushing around the hall covered in paint.

A year later, the famous jazz musician Stan Kenton played at our senior prom, which probably wasn't where his ambitions would have lain at the start of his career.

Teen of the Week

Citizen-News Art by John Waltz
Terry Gilliam . . . ASB prexy at **Birmingham High** . . . B12 class vice president . . . cheerleader . . . pole vaulter on track team . . . CSF . . . Lettermen's Club . . . member of Knights . . . plans to attend Occidental.

This not-remotely-embarrassing appearance in a local newspaper's 'Teen of the Week' spot reassures those who might have worried about me appearing insufficiently clean-cut that my cartooning is only a 'hobby' and I 'do not plan a career in the art world', preferring to focus my energies on higher-minded philanthropic goals of the kind with which my name is now rarely, if ever, associated.

How did I come to be trapped in such a suffocating web of civic virtue? Sporting mediocrity probably had something to do with it. I was reasonably athletic at school and had always remembered myself – perhaps encouraged by the local print media's wildly inaccurate description of me – as a 'pole vaulting star'. Sadly, mediocrity had a firm grasp on my skinny legs and I never rose above the 'B' team. Still, I sported a cool 'Balboa' hairstyle (crew cut top, Fonzie-like back and sides) to distract from my failings.

Obviously sporting achievement has a much higher

social value at school than academic excellence. I think that is one truth that holds good equally on both sides of the Atlantic. And if I wasn't going to be in the forefront of the action on the field of play itself, there was one other option, a strategy to which any red-blooded American adolescent male could not help but feel himself drawn: I became a cheerleader, inserting myself between the crowds in the bleachers and the 'jocks' tens of yards further out on the playing field.

As a pole vaulter, I made a pretty good physical comedian. The worst thing that can happen to you in that athletic discipline is to come down straddling the crossbar. It is as painful as it looks, and I suffered this indignity all too often, invariably (or so it seemed to me) with a large crowd gathered watching in the stands.

On those occasions, I found the secret was to round the humiliation off with a nice little showbiz flourish — 'Ta daah!' That way you could win the public over and turn the whole situation in your favour, much in the same way as (say, for the sake of argument) an incompetent magician might redeem themselves by getting a laugh out of the failure of a trick.

I had always sung in the church choir — following my mother's and grandmother's leads — and how better to adapt and expand that primal impulse to collective music-making than to surround myself with the pom-pom waving cream of Birmingham High School's pulchritudinous crop of senior cheerleaders?

Naturally there was an element of emotional awkwardness involved, in that however much we fancied the girls, they were only ever interested in the jocks who were actually on the football team, but at least we could lurk yearningly in their midst.

Observant readers may well have found their eyes being drawn to the good-sized Bs adorning the alluring frontage of my fellow cheerleaders. In case anyone was wondering, the 'B' stood for 'Braves'. Birmingham High School was one of many US institutions to include Native American imagery as part of the rich stew of iconography upon which mid-century sports fans were invited to dine. Lurking at the left-hand edge of the yearbook (page 33) – as if about to be edged out into the margins of history – you can see the beautiful ceremonial head-dress that was brought out on grand sporting occasions. This was later banished to the back-rooms by a new kind of McCarthyism – one which deemed such powerful and aesthetically meaningful historical images 'derogatory'. The 'Brave' in this case was none other than Larry Bell, who went on to become a famous sculptor in the 1960s and '70s, and interestingly is one of the cut-out figures on the cover of The Beatles' *Sgt. Pepper's Lonely Hearts Club Band*.

Cheerleading in animated form via the school newspaper.

These 'trophies' are pretty basic, but there is some character in them. As you can see, I'm still refining my signature at this point – the big V in the middle was an experiment I soon dropped out of a prudent desire not to emphasise the fact that my middle name was (and is) Vance. Why do you think I blessed my own progeny with the middle names Rainbow, Thunder and Dubois? I'd suffered for my parents' thoughtless disregard for naming convention, so why shouldn't they?

Pondering my collection of high school badges,

it's interesting how large the kind of heraldic imagery I would later explore on film loomed. By the time I was an American film-maker in Britain some years later, people found it strange and anachronistic that an upstart colonial would have such an interest in the knights of the round table. Yet this stuff was actually the common currency of my education – and once you got to college, with all the fraternities vying for your attention with their fancy Greek names, things would get even more classical.

The tiger actually came from college a little later on, but check out the natty blue chariot on a pink and grey background, which was the beermat-like insignia of my senior class, The Phaetons. The original Phaeton, as the classical scholars among you will already know, lost control of the sun chariot in a bid to prove himself the son of a deity – not an example I would be following in any way.

By the time I was in my final year of high school, a complex overlapping network of school, church, sporting and charitable organisations seemed to be forming a kind of protective cocoon from which a grown-up, responsible Terry Gilliam – at once a man of action and a pillock of the community – would inevitably emerge. One day I was approached by several girls, who turned out to be the behind-the-scenes kingmakers, asking if they could put me forward as a candidate for student body president. I had no ambitions along these lines, but I find it hard to say 'No' to lovely ladies, so I agreed, and before I knew what

hit me I was banging a gavel and pretending to be in charge. Again, I had no knowledge of what was required to lead the student body and had to learn as I went along while pretending I knew exactly what the job entailed.

Here I am with the Knights of Birmingham High School – committed to the preservation of high school law and order but secretly itching to work in conjunction with 'Ladies'

My friend Steve Geller is the one holding the left-hand end of the banner.

In my new position of unasked-for authority in my final year at Birmingham High School, I began to feel the tug of some of the dark undercurrents swirling beneath the supposedly still waters of the late 1950s. As student body president, you were inundated with reams of right-wing propaganda from conservative lobbying groups like the John Birch Society, whose logo incorporated the Statue of Liberty with the word 'communism' as a snake entwining it. If we didn't all change our ways, America would be under communist control within the decade, there was no doubt about it. And as for the threat black men posed to decent white women . . . well, it was no wonder all those guys were getting lynched in the South.

I used to get into big arguments about all this ridiculous bullshit. A sense of injustice seemed to be bubbling under everywhere you looked, and when you think of what was going on in the cinema around that time – from *High Noon* to Stanley Kubrick's *Paths of Glory* – it was basically all these lefties and commies showing how much more humane they were than the people who wanted them to stop making films.

If only my high school valedictorian's speech had been recorded for posterity, you wouldn't have to take my word for just how politically revolutionary it was... Not!

OCCIDENTAL

Chapter 3

Camelot

**ith the help** of a Presbyterian church alumni scholarship specifically designed for golden children like myself, I attended a very fine university. Occidental College was as Ivy League as you could get on the West Coast; they used to call it 'the Princeton of the West'. Barack Obama would study there a few (oh, alright then, twenty . . .) years later – which may or not be a recommendation, depending on your point of view. Either way, with only 1,200 students it was a lot smaller than my high school, and the campus in Eagle Rock – just forty-five minutes away from Panorama City, but there was no reason to go home except during the holidays – was a beautiful place to be.

It's a testament to what a great job Occidental did for me that I arrived a ferociously well-motivated, high-achieving eighteen-year-old, on what was technically a missionary scholarship, and left four years later as a directionless ne'er-do-well with an academic record of stunning mediocrity. I'm not being remotely sarcastic when I say that, because the opportunities I was given to broaden my understanding of the world and experiment with different ways of looking at it are still standing me in good stead to this day. It saddens me greatly that so many twenty-first-century students are too hemmed in by career worries and pressures of debt to enjoy the kind of liberating academic experience that my time at college brought me.

There was an amazing sense of freedom involved in escaping from everything I'd known before and throwing myself into a totally new environment. What I'd initially thought I was hoping to get out of Occidental was a career that would give me a legitimate reason to see the world while feeling fairly confident that I was doing something to make it a better place. Becoming a missionary was one possibility, as I'd arrived at Oxy with the full weight of the church behind me, but diplomat would have done me just as well – I wasn't talking to Jesus every day, so it wouldn't be essential for me to work for him directly.

What I ended up leaving with was something much more valuable: the ability to question some – if not all – of the assumptions I'd grown up with, and to carry on questioning them if I didn't like the look of the answers I was getting. If this sounds like a process of disillusionment, that's not quite right. It felt more like an expansion of possibilities, and one that was historically aligned with a broader opening out within American society.

In the more restrictive atmosphere of the 1950s, all the most powerful forces around you – family, science, design, the church – seemed to be ushering you in the same direction as far as the future was concerned. But at some point in the next decade, all the signposts suddenly seemed to be pointing to different destinations, and for me, college was the start of a feeling – not so much of alarm, more of excitement – that I was going down a new road, which my education up to that point hadn't really prepared me for.

This mood of flux initially expressed itself in a series of rapid shifts in my educational focus. I arrived at Occidental as a physics major, maths and science being the kinds of things we studied in America after the war. It was all about building the technology of the future, and patriots had to step up to the plate as escaped Nazis couldn't run our space programme on their own for ever. But within a couple of months I'd realised that college-level physics was a different animal to the one I was used to. It was just too abstract and difficult for a simple creature like me, so I switched horses to fine art in midstream. (I always preferred the practical and physical, yet have never stopped being seduced by ideas and ideals that are utterly abstract; ideas like freedom, democracy, truth, God; ideas that people are willing to do the most physical of activities to defend – namely killing those who disagree with them – so it's lucky I've not been the man of action I once wanted to believe I was.)

It wasn't too long before I was on the move again. I loved the painting, drawing and sculpture classes, and the main professor – Robert Hansen – was a brilliant artist. He'd been to India and was what you might call an enlightened human being – there were certainly, I wouldn't say religious, but definitely spiritual qualities to his work. He always liked what I did, but I could tell he felt I was spending too much time cartooning for quick laughs – 'Showtime . . . *Ta-dah!*' – when I was capable of doing something deeper. The art history teacher on the other hand was boring as shit. And I must've abandoned his course just in time, because now I'm very interested in art history.

In the end – and benefiting from a large measure of tolerance on the part of both scholarship and college authorities – I found myself majoring in political science, which was useful, because there were only four required courses, and you could basically design your own liberal education by choosing elective subjects like drama, oriental philosophy and even Russian (if the commies really were taking over, I'd better at least learn to say '*tovarisch*'). The head of

From the moment I arrived at Occidental, I was constantly designing sets and costumes for theatrical productions, as well as appearing onstage – generally in the kind of ~~that were all the Pythons would ever trust me with later on~~ broad supporting roles. I got huge laughs playing this slightly camp character in a college revue – or 'fraternity sing' as we called them – a triumph undimmed by either the subsequent discovery that what was really amusing the audience was the fact that my flies were undone, or the coining of the popular sobriquet 'Sir Terence of the Open Fly'. I like to try to dignify this memory by suggesting that this photo could be a still from an early German Expressionism-influenced Orson Welles film.

department, Raymond McKelvey, was one of those great educators who are full of ideas and energy but can still appreciate a fool – someone who maybe doesn't have time to study for an exam, but will fake it with panache, even if that means describing 'hegemony' as 'a hedge made out of money', which was leaping years into the future, as nobody even knew about hedge funds yet.

Before I settled on my third and final choice of major, I also had to go through a process of social transformation. One of the reasons media revelations about waterboarding and all those things never caused too much of a ripple in the mainstream of American public opinion is that so many people have been through something quite similar in the course of fraternity 'hazing' rituals. In order to become a member of the 'Sig-Al' family, there was a whole week where you were forced to wear sackcloth underwear and clean the toilets with toothbrushes – among other degradations. Maybe this was where the kind of people who ended up in the CIA got their ideas from.

The fact that, as freshmen, most of you have probably just left home for the first time only adds to everyone's sense of disorientation and vulnerability. The sleep deprivation you had to go through – where older students would come in and turn the lights on, and you'd all have to get up from the hard floor you were allowed to sleep on because one of you was talking – was certainly quite effective at making you want to kill the person they told you was responsible. And they'd do that night after night, so you're going to classes the next day in your scratchy burlap underwear feeling totally destroyed.

At the same time, you do get through it, and I suppose there must be a certain deadening of feeling involved. I know similar things used to go on in the English public schools that my fellow Pythons went to, and I've often heard it said that this process of brutalisation automatically produces brutal people, but I don't think that's necessarily true. To me, it all depends on the way the brutalisation is administered. If it's meted out with a sense of humour, and an awareness that this is just a gauntlet that has to be run as a prelude to some kind of social acceptance, then the cruelty of it can be a vehicle for creativity.

Cardigan sweaters will be tremendous on campus this year. For that rugged man on campus, Dave wears a bulky knit shawl collar sweater by Towne & King. Notice the contrasting trim on sleeve. These handsome all wool sweaters come in olive, charcoal and smog @ **$18.95**

That bulky knit look by Jantzen is the Canadian Cardigan, worn by Dick. This bold stripe sweater of all wool is a winner in red, blue, olive and tan @ **$15.95**

The cardigan jacket shown by Terry is an all wool brushed flannel with contrasting trim. This cardigan is fully lined and can be worn for school or on more dressy occasions. In charcoal, red, tan, brown and blue @ **$13.95**

No doubt many readers will have asked themselves how a fine figure of a man like Terry Gilliam could have avoided modelling professionally at some point in his career. Here are the results of what – astonishingly, I'm sure you will agree – proved to be a one-off outing as a clothes horse. The San Fernando Valley hot spot, the Munroe's Mens & Boys Shop, was based in Panorama City, and my fellow mannequins were old school friends, Dick and Dave. We were just local college boys — innocents caught up in a misfiring campaign to lend credibility to a potentially incendiary combination of man-made fibres.

MUNROE'S MENS & BOYS SHOP
8416 VAN NUYS BLVD.
PANORAMA CITY, CALIF.

OPEN MON., THURS. & FRIDAY TILL 9 P.M.

BULK RATE
U. S. POSTAGE
PAID
Permit No. 123
Van Nuys, Calif.

Rolling Out 1960 Campus Favorites

...nett's thailspun. A blend of orlon and wool, this washable shirt is in rich olive and gold striping @ **$8.95**

Terry wears the 100% high bulk orlon cardigan by Pommett. In gold, olive, red, black and brown, it's not only a beauty, but completely washable @ **$11.95**

And in the orlon popover, Dave looks like a million. Again from Pommett, a high bulk orlon popover, fully washable, and in six colors @ **$10.95**

Other knits from **$4.00**

That 100 per cent high bulk cardigan is completely washable – just like Terry himself. I think our biggest problem here was that none of us knew what to do with with our hands.

CAMELOT

43

By the time I got to my junior year at Occidental, the boot was on the other foot. I'd developed my own ideas of how the authority of these rituals could be put to subversive use. Oxy has a large Greek amphitheatre, and a group of us used it to stage a huge initiation ceremony for all the freshmen – first gathering them together for a torchlight parade, and then laying on this whole elaborate, solemn ceremony with music and chanting to indoctrinate them in the 'traditions of the school' – a series of outrageous fabrications, all of which we had come up with the day before.

In effect, we were conducting a large-scale human experiment to see if Joseph Goebbels' propagandist concept of the 'Big Lie' really worked, and somewhat alarmingly I have to report that it does (or at least it did). Our entirely fictitious notions of the college's history and heritage persisted unquestioned by those freshmen for years but, much more disturbingly, also by many in the senior classes who should have known better. How I came to be in a position to warp the mind of an entire generation of students was through the operations of the Bengal Board – an organisation charged with custodianship of that rather nebulous-sounding resource of 'school spirit' (something Goebbels was also very big on). Basically, it was a step on from high school cheerleading, one which happily no longer required us to become honorary girls, but instead involved making huge and elaborate floats for parades using giant wire-mesh frames and huge quantities of *papier-mâché*.

Jumping around and getting everyone enthused is something I've always been pretty good at – it's certainly a knack which has served me well in initial funding meetings with Hollywood studios – and this was my first taste of how much fun you could have by subordinating an established institution to your own more playful agenda (which was pretty much what Monty Python ended up doing at the BBC). The kindred spirits I met up with through the Bengal Board – Art Mortimer and the two Johns, Latimer and Massey – would be my partners in crime throughout my time at college and beyond.

Everything we were doing was for laughs, and we became kind of cool – everybody seemed to want to be worker bees to help put our various schemes into practice. I'm not saying the power went to our heads, but on one occasion where there had been some kind of infraction, I remember sitting looking out of the window with my back to the perpetrator, knowing the backlighting would serve me well. At the moment I swivelled around in my chair, like some college boy Dr Evil, the poor guy was shivering with social anxiety.

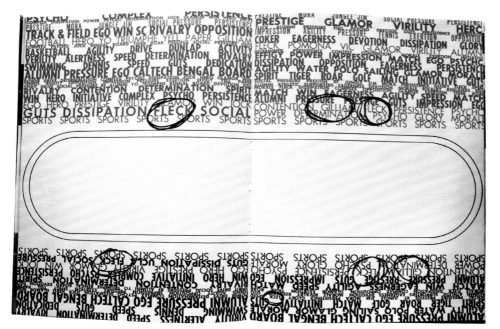

These are the 'words of the year' from a graphic in an old college yearbook. We were just looking for funny things to get people to shout out during a football game, and at one point, when I was on the microphone and trying to get everyone to 'Give me a "Fleck"', my bad enunciation somehow got 1,000 people shouting 'Fuck!' It was wonderful, although I did have a bit of explaining to do afterwards — after all, this was only 1960 and such robust Anglo-Saxon language had yet to become publicly acceptable.

It would be stretching a point slightly to say that after an

adolescence characterised by socially responsible community endeavour, Occidental saw my creativity being set free by the idle rich. But the students there did basically fall into two categories – they were either smart (hard-working scholarship kids like Dick Hallen, the minister's son who was my fresh-man roomie), or they came from the kind of wealthy backgrounds that meant they could buy their way in.

The bulk of the students in Swan Hall, the dormitory where I laid my head for whatever brief interludes of sleep occurred in my second year, fell into the latter category. And although the disadvantageous impact of privilege on character has been well documented, I found myself drawn to the confidence with which these scions of the American establishment carried themselves. Practical jokes were the ultimate expression of their habitual ease, and from the simpler ones – medical students leaving a naked cadaver sitting in one of the quads, or toilet-papering all the trees – to more complex conspiracies to fill a room with crushed newspapers or reassemble a dismantled Model T Ford car inside some-one's room and have the motor running when they came in, I marvelled at the jokers' comedic inventiveness and chutzpah.

If they got themselves thrown out, they could always go to another school, that was kind of the attitude. I wasn't willing to take risks on that level, but I did find my energy and enthusiasm increasingly drifting away from my aca-demic studies towards extra-curricular activities, such as orchestrating a huge campaign to get our little gang's candidate Art Mortimer elected as president of the student body. I remember feeling especially happy about the banners proclaiming 'The People Want Art', and, as if to deliver on that four-word manifesto, we got hold of these huge rolls of butcher's paper and wall-papered the Student Union building with cartoons and slogans and other manifestations of our ungovernable spirit of youthful mischief.

This did bring us to the attention of the dean, but the disciplinary process never had to go further than an uncomfortable chat in his office. And in my last year at Occidental – when Art, John, John and I took over a previously quite serious art and poetry journal called *Fang*, which under our guidance was rapidly transformed into a showcase for scabrous gags and unfettered cartooning – we finally found the right vehicle for our collective sense of satirical *joie de vivre*.

In the years since I'd been caught red-handed 'reading' *Mad* in the garage, my comic book super-hero Harvey Kurtzman had fallen out with its publisher and left in high dudgeon with the bulk of the magazine's best artists in tow. After a couple of false starts, *Help!*, the new satirical magazine he started in New York in 1960, rapidly assumed the same dominant position in my early-twenties consciousness that *Mad* had occupied during my teens. Imitation being the sincerest form of flattery, it seemed our only responsible option was to try to copy it.

Other less blatant sources of inspiration for what we tried to do with *Fang* included the (then) fertile landscape of American kids' TV and the many voices of the great mimic and improvisational comedian Jonathan Winters – who we all loved impersonating. I suppose there's a fairly obvious correlation between a broad comic accent and a cartoon – both take recognisable features and expand them into something else, and both offer you a way of escaping from yourself without having to reveal too much of the real you.

Here are a couple of my **Fang** covers – the first was a kind of Hansel and Gretel thing, with evil dwarves killing rabbits. The other one found me doctoring an old photo to come up with **Fang's** new tooth-inspired logo, which was much less work and therefore obviously the way to go in the future.

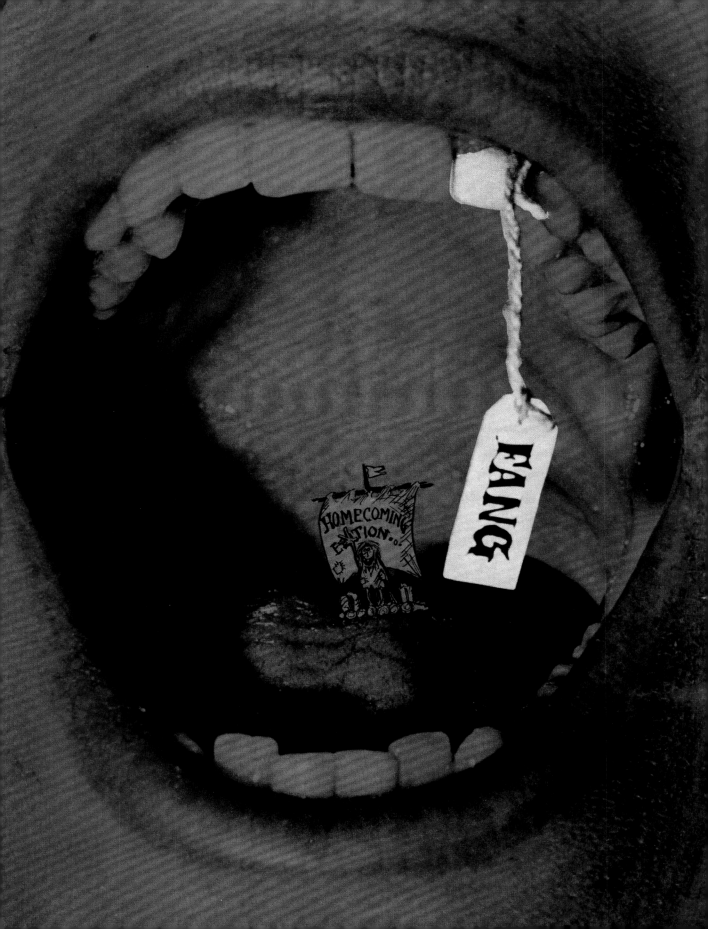

By the same token, one reason students tend to like watching kids' TV shows is probably because even though you know you're technically too old for them, they offer you a link back to the reassuring world of childhood. Thus at five o'clock in the afternoon the whole dorm would settle down to enjoy the many custard pies of Soupy Sales, or repeats of Albert Einstein's favourite hand-puppet show – Stan Freberg and Bob Clampett's *Time for Beany*. It wasn't just televisual comfort food either – kids' shows often tended to be the most interesting, because the adults at the networks weren't likely to be paying attention, so you could get away with murder . . . just as the proto-Python children's programme *Do Not Adjust Your Set* would do when I came to England a few years later.

Fang's most blatant steal from *Help!* were the *fumetti*. That lovely-sounding word – go on, roll it round your tongue – is Italian for 'puffs of smoke', which in this context is a more poetic way of saying 'speech bubble'. The idea came from a wonderful Fellini film starring Alberto Sordi called *Lo Sceicco Bianco* (a.k.a. *The White Sheik*) – which made lustrously cinematic hay out of the Latin vogue for romantic photostories – and Harvey Kurtzman's stroke of genius was to apply the medium satirically.

He'd always wanted to make films, and this way he could mirror the ambition and scope of a major Hollywood production on only a tiny fraction of the budget. As we soon discovered when we started doing them in *Fang*, *fumetti* were effectively stop-motion movies: a great cinematic training ground, not only in storytelling but also in making sets and costumes, and finding locations and actors. I loved creating these films in still form so much that I almost didn't graduate.

I abused my editorial power by giving the lead role in our *fumetti* to Susan Boyle – not the singer, but the girl in my year who I was mad about. But she never seemed to get the message, even when I made us a joint 'electrical' plug costume for a fancy-dress party. Everyone else was quite – ahem – shocked that I would do something so blatant. (I was the male plug, and she was the socket: who said true romance was dead?) The symbolism didn't elude her, it just didn't translate into action.

Alert readers who have speculated that the sexual revolution had yet to reach the campus of Occidental College have certainly put their finger on it (which wouldn't have been allowed in those days). The single-sex dormitory doors clanged shut at ten, and it was a real adventure just to sneak out and get a snog. As frustrating as this was at the time, I don't think it was a bad thing. I went back

HOMO-SIDE STORY

FANG GOES HOLLYWOOD AND PRODUCES
A TRULY EXTRAVAGANT SPECTACULAR IN
THE BEST OF FILMLAND TRADITIONS,
AND ALL FOR THE AMAZINGLY LOW PRICE
OF $5.99 (PLUS TAX)

13

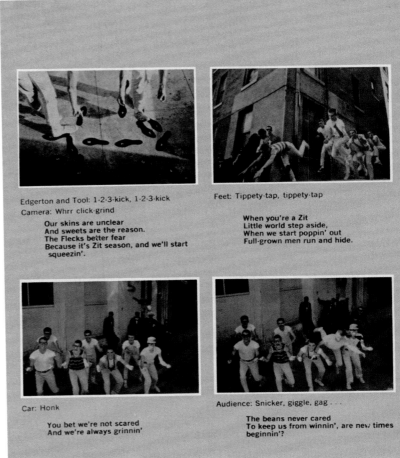

Edgerton and Tool: 1-2-3-kick, 1-2-3-kick
Camera: Whrr click-grind

Our skins are unclear
And sweets are the reason.
The Flecks better fear
Because it's Zit season, and we'll start
squeezin'.

Feet: Tippety-tap, tippety-tap

When you're a Zit
Little world step aside,
When we start poppin' out
Full-grown men run and hide.

Car: Honk

You bet we're not scared
And we're always grinnin'

Audience: Snicker, giggle, gag . . .

The beans never cared
To keep us from winnin', are new times
beginnin'?

'Homo-side Story' was John Latimer's idea — it was all good, gentle fun in a way you probably couldn't get away with now. We'd be out on the streets of LA shooting with all the paraphernalia of actual film-making (including as many extras as we could talk into it) except the movie camera and the sound.

The area around the old downtown site of the Angel's Flight funicular railway — as seen here — was one of our favourite locations, because we could get on with what we wanted to do in the reasonable expectation that no one would bother us. It's subsequently been redeveloped out of existence, so good luck to anyone planning to make a mildly homophobic remake of West Side Story there today.

years later to get an honorary degree, and by that time all the dorms were co-ed. Of course everyone was getting laid, but a lot of clever people were throwing their lives away by getting hitched too early too. I said to the students in my speech that if I was running the place, I would make it so Victorian that they'd all hate me . . . but in the end having to outwit me in order to give in to their basic instincts would make them stronger, cleverer people.

As sheltered and carefree as my four years at college must sound (and do feel) in retrospect, I wasn't living in a *Brideshead Revisited* bubble. I think one of the reasons my parents were so tolerant of my plummeting academic grades was that I never came whining to them for extra money. And the lessons I learned in the course of the motley assemblage of holiday jobs that helped me pay my way through college would prove just as enduring as the things I was being taught at Occidental.

My dad got me work humping stuff around on building sites, and I also worked in a butcher's shop for a while, inevitably at the very bottom of the food chain – when you found yourself cleaning out the big barrels of salt beef (from the inside), you knew the only way was up. I also used to have to go into the walk-in freezer, which was always tricky because if you didn't pay attention you'd find yourself impaled on one of those spikes that the meat hung from. A job in a restaurant posed more danger to the diners than to me, as I was basically there to swab floors and clean up messes, but when the salad boy was off, they'd make me do his job as well, so one minute I would be down on the floor, scrubbing away with some awful disinfectant, and then somebody would say 'salad with vinaigrette', and I'd leap up and with my filthy hands scoop up the lettuce, throw it into the bowl, and put the dressing on. I've often wondered how many customers died from that.

I also found gainful employment at the post office, where the game was to see how far away you could stand from the sorting cubicles and still throw the mail into the correct section, and as a shipping clerk in a factory which made beauty-salon furniture, packing huge lounge chairs and hoisting them onto the trucks (I loved the fact that – Archimedes-like – I could lever these wooden behemoths into their motorised receptacles single-handed). At this time I was also becoming a real freak for Russian literature in general and Dostoevsky in particular, so I'd sit there huddled among the crates with my little packed lunch reading *The Brothers Karamazov* – when the Soviet invasion finally came, I was going to be first in line to welcome them: 'Comrade, I know your books, as well as your language.'

While the long-promised communist takeover

stubbornly refused to materialise, the job that would impact most explicitly on my subsequent creative endeavours was on the assembly-line night shift at the Chevrolet car plant – going in at eight in the evening and working through until five the next day. The nightmarish production lines that often cropped up in Monty Python animations were certainly inspired by this experience. Not so much because the repetitive and regimented nature of the work itself gave me any particular problems – Sisyphus was always my favourite classical character – but more because the pressure to keep up with the pace of the line did interesting things to your mind.

The belt moved at fifty-two cars an hour – slightly less than one a minute. Since I'd got that red and green 'numbers hidden in the dots' test wrong, and

A 1959 Chevrolet Impala – look at the size of the windscreen on that baby!

as a result was deemed to be slightly colour blind (a vital attribute in any fine artist in waiting, as I'm sure you'll agree), the only job they'd trust me with was washing the right-hand front, side, and rear windows inside and out, to remove the inspector's grease pencil hieroglyphs. Unfortunately, in this particular era of brashly expansive mid-century automotive design, that meant covering a hell of a lot of glass.

There was no way I could finish inside and out in just over a minute. While my genial workmates (most of whom seemed happy to work through nine hours of darkness in return for the freedom their wages bought them in the next fifteen hours of daylight) were off enjoying a tea break, I could often be found way down into the next person's section, drops of falling ammonia solution mingling with the sweat on my brow, as I struggled in vain to catch up.

It was probably on one of these conscientious missions down the line that I discovered the painful truth that what I was doing was absolutely pointless. As soon as I'd cleaned my windows, off they went around the corner where another inspector would dirty them up. I wouldn't have minded stepping in at the end of the process – giving that windscreen the clean of its life and sending it out into the world so everyone could say, 'Yes, it's sparkling wonderfully, I'll buy ten of those.' It wasn't just a question of ego – well, not entirely – all I wanted was to be able to take pride in a job well done.

The processes of industrial mass-production were not the only aspect of the student employment market that seemed to conspire against an individual's God-given right to take satisfaction in his work. The most white-collar of my temporary employments, a mail-room gig in the office of Welton Becket, LA's most prestigious architects (the first of many professional opportunities contacts made at Oxy would bring me – remember, it's not what you know, it's who you know), was no less disillusioning. It seemed progress up the social and/or economic ladder was no insurance against having to compromise your principles.

That firm was working on what became the new LA Music Center concert hall, and Dorothy Chandler – the department store heiress and wife of *LA Times* proprietor Otis Chandler, who was a big noise on the board of the orchestra – was constantly coming in and tinkering with the models, so that you'd see these amazing designs being constantly corrupted. I started to feel that maybe the way Welton Becket got to be number one architect was by bending with the wind that was coming out of the arses of their clients. I was young and idealistic then, so this kind of thing made me crazy.

Although I was only dimly aware of the way the cards were falling at the time, in retrospect it was becoming increasingly clear that only the corruption-free environment of show business could provide me with the kind of morally pure working environment I was looking for. It wasn't so much that I knew where I was going, but that I knew which doors I didn't want to walk through. So I declared I would only do work I had complete control over and never work just for money.

My first step in that direction, on leaving Chevrolet in a fit of artistic pique, was to get a job for the rest of that summer with a children's theatre. Designing and building sets, painting myself green and pretending to be an ogre was much more fun than washing windscreens for a living, and the relatively small amount of experience I accumulated there enabled me to somehow blag myself an improbably high-powered position for the next summer as 'drama coach' at Camp Roosevelt – a select summer dumping ground for the children of Hollywood A-listers in my favourite San Bernardino mountains, up above Palm Springs.

The vertiginous physical terrain I already knew and loved, but in 'professional' terms, I was massively out of my depth, having no formal theatrical training of any kind. In some ways, Camp Roosevelt would set the pattern for the rest of my life – go in at the top, then work my way down. It was also enormous fun. This was the place where my Hollywood Jewish friend-making could really get into gear, as gentiles were outnumbered by approximately ten to one, and I became known as 'Gilly the Goy', after the last two words of an innocent question about a potential problem with the catering – 'What are we going to do about the [orange] juice?' – were misheard by one of my fellow camp counsellors as '. . . the Jews'.

Everything went swimmingly

for the first six weeks or so, until I gradually began to sense that the lavish production of *Alice in Wonderland* that I had promised to deliver as the centrepiece of the final parents' visiting day of the summer was far too elaborate to actually pull off. My ambitious plans foundered on the lack of any organisational infrastructure to help translate my vision from two dimensions into three – imagining the whole thing was the easy part, the difficult bit was the reality of actually doing it without the facilities, time, money, or basic talent to make it happen. Whenever I'd start to get something going, these Hollywood brats would have to go off horse-riding or for an archery lesson – so they were not at all like grown-up actors in any way.

Where better to experience the first real catastrophe of my career than *in loco parentis* for the temporarily abandoned children of such Hollywood big-shots as Hedy Lamarr, Danny Kaye (whose charming daughter Dena has remained a good friend of mine to this day), the director William Wyler (whose son behaved like a little shit but ultimately responded quite well to discipline) and composer Ernest Gold (whose son Andy would end up playing the guitar riff and arranging 'Heart Like A Wheel' with Linda Ronstadt)?

I ended up pulling the plug in the final week before the show. It's such a weird thing to establish yourself within a community and then feel like you've let down everyone within it. The scars run deep … even unto today when I often wake from a dream of the fear of repeat failure on whatever my current project might be.

Nevertheless, my over-riding memories of that summer of my junior (i.e. third) year at Occidental are still happy ones. At weekends, a few of us counsellors sometimes got to escape down to Palm Springs, where one of our number's

These rough drawings are all that remain of what could have been – had it only gone ahead – one of the most disastrous summer-camp theatre productions of all time. I think it's safe to say that my loss was Lewis Carroll's gain, but looking at them now I can still feel the formative trauma of this last-minute cancellation gnawing at my guts.

stepmother turned out to be the divine Debbie Reynolds, who had now married a shoe magnate (the yet more seductive intervention of Liz Taylor having done for Debbie's first marriage to Eddie Fisher) and whose second home was a sleek, desert-modern house with a fabulous swimming pool.

The idea of being in a movie star's home,

swimming in her pool and even – in a potentially calamitous show of youthful exuberance – bouncing on her bed, was thrilling beyond anything I had ever previously dreamed of. Perhaps it was for the best that I didn't know at this point that some years later I would get to dance with Debbie. The excitement would have been too much.

I was certainly starstruck. But the funny thing about preparing to graduate from college in the America of the early 1960s was that my yen for Hollywood glamour and the high-minded ideals of making the world a better place that had first carried me to Occidental did not at that point feel fundamentally incompatible. The swearing-in of President Kennedy in January 1961 lent a newly youthful lustre to the highest office of State, and JFK's launch of the Peace Corps later on that same year even made the idea of doing worthwhile things in far-off lands briefly fashionable.

The crusading atmosphere of the all too short-lived Kennedy presidency was another notable instance of theoretically archaic imagery pervading the American pop culture of my youth. As the optimistic post-inauguration spring of 1961 turned to summer, the original cast recording of *Camelot* – Lerner and Loewe's Tony Award-winning Broadway musical adaptation of T H White's compendium of Arthurian legend – was America's number one album for months on end.

The name of King Arthur's legendary court would become posthumously entwined with the memory of JFK from the moment his widow mentioned his love for the show in a *Time* magazine interview shortly after his death, but before that it was more of a subconscious linkage. That show was the vehicle for a veritable bus-load of strange attractors as far as I was concerned. Richard Burton played the chief Grail-seeker and Julie Andrews (whose own alluring cameo in this book is still a little way off) his Guinevere, but it was the show's less famous but similarly well-regarded director, Moss Hart, who was about to provide the cue for my next move.

APPLICATION—
ROTARY FOUNDATION FELLOWSHIP FOR INTERNATIONAL UNDERSTANDING
Academic Year 1962-1963

Before preparing this application the applicant is requested to read the instructions on page 6, and is required to read the folder, "Information for The Applicant." Copy can be obtained from sponsoring Rotary club.

Name in full:

Terry Vance Gilliam
(Do not use initials, underline family name)

Name by which you prefer to be called   Terry

Permanent home address:

8638 Tyrone Ave.
(Street and Number)

Panorama City   California
(Town or City)   (Province or State)

U.S.A.
(Country)

Proposed major field of study   Political Science

Name and location of institution of higher education for which Fellowship is desired. Applicant *must* indicate five choices, *not more than three in one country*, any one of which applicant must be willing to attend. For purposes of the Fellowship program, England, Scotland, Wales, Northern Ireland, and Ireland are considered as one country of study; also, students are not interchanged between Canada and the United States of America. Before listing any universities, the applicant should carefully investigate courses of study, requirements for admission, and the language used, and he must have positive knowledge that they conduct graduate courses in his field of study. The applicant is required to give *specific reasons* for listing the universities on the application.

In order to insure the widest possible geographical distribution, Rotary International reserves the right to designate any one of the five universities listed, or another institution of higher education, as the one at which the Fellowship is to be made tenable. Well-known universities are too frequently selected because applicants do not know that good departments exist in other and sometimes smaller, less well-known institutions. It must be understood that the applicant is less likely to receive a Fellowship for study at a large, well-known university unless his reasons are particularly good.

1st Choice   University of Hong Kong   Hong Kong
              (Name of Educational Institution)   (City)   (Country)
Reason   The fact that it is located in one of the most turbulent and crucial
          areas of the world will, I think, provide an enlightening education.
2nd Choice   University of the Philippines   Quezon City   Philippines
              (Name of Educational Institution)   (City)   (Country)
Reason   Again an important area - also a very fine staff and program

3rd Choice   Panjab University   Chandigarh   India
              (Name of Educational Institution)   (City)   (Country)
Reason   More needs to be understood about India - this school has courses
          that will help reach that end.
4th Choice   University of Cape Town   Cape Town   Union of South Africa
              (Name of Educational Institution)   (City)   (Country)
Reason   A great many good courses in African history, culture, politics,

5th Choice   Agra University   Agra   India
              (Name of Educational Institution)   (City)   (Country)
Reason   Besides being in a different part of India, it offers a different
          study and examination system]]
          s

Of course Vietnam ~ a.k.a the War Corps (e) ~ would soon change all that.

But in the meantime, enough of my missionary instincts had survived my dwindling prospects of academic success for me to still be applying for postgraduate study abroad in my final year at Oxy. My desire to travel to exotic destinations — Hong Kong, the Philippines, the Punjab, anywhere — seems to have been more clearly defined than my sense of what I should actually do once I got there. Maybe I was expecting to put bras on the natives.

He

Life was moving SO FAST that it felt like the city was setting a beat

Chapter

4

Help!

I found graduating from Oxy quite depressing. It wasn't my final slump into academic mediocrity that troubled me – that was a done deal – but rather the prospect of breaking up the *Fang* gang. We'd had such a grand time doing that magazine – taking it up from three issues a year to six, and sweeping the whole student body along with us – and now those days were over. I had absolutely no idea of what I was going to do next, so for the first few months after leaving college, I took the stop-gap option of another eight-week summer-camp counselling job, this time up in the Sierra Nevadas (where Burt Lancaster's daughters were our highest-ranking Hollywood progeny). It was there that I read the book *Act One* – the memoirs of the aforementioned theatrical eminence Moss Hart – which would give me the plan of action I so urgently needed.

$400 for two months less valid state and federal employment charges didn't seem like such a bad deal with food and lodging thrown in…
and Camp Trinity did live up to its 'party ranch' sobriquet to the extent that I finally managed to divest myself of that possession which no self-respecting twenty-one-year-old man – even one who had gone to college on a missionary scholarship – would wish to carry with him too much further over the threshold of adulthood. This landmark was passed in the company of one of my fellow counsellors, I hasten to add, not one of my impressionable young charges. No names, no pack-drill beyond that, though – who do you think I am, Zsa Zsa Gabor?

In later years, once I'd been lucky enough to get the chance to direct movies of my own, I would learn to identify a mysterious – sometimes magical and sometimes disastrous – process whereby 'the making of the film becomes the story of the film'. But I would never have found myself in the director's chair (a largely metonymic furnishing concept in itself, as you're generally spending too much of your time rushing around in a panic to sit down all that much) without an approximately equal and opposite propensity for imagining my way into pre-existing narratives. This staple resource of the child's imagination is one I have adapted to become the motor of my adult life. The big question I have never quite been able to answer is, 'Am I driving the car, or merely hitching a lift?'

It never feels like I'm in control of the direction the traffic is going in, and yet somehow it always ends up reaching some kind of destination, and more often than not the one I originally intended. Reading Moss Hart's autobiography at Camp Trinity in the summer of 1962 was one of the most influential events of my whole life. So complete was my identification with the character of the director of disastrous summer-camp drama productions who somehow progressed to co-writing Broadway hits alongside his hero George S Kaufman that it motivated me to pursue my own goal of working for Harvey Kurtzman with single-minded dedication. I've never thought of myself as a particularly ambitious person, and yet those who have read that book more recently than I assure me that I actually twisted its narrative framework quite considerably to fit the requirements of my own professional advancement.

Either way, it's a great book. And the story of the callow youth who suddenly found himself in a creative partnership with his hero had enough plausibility to sustain me through Harvey's rejection of my initial Hart-inspired overtures. I'd cheekily sent a couple of copies of *Fang* to the *Help!* offices in New York while I was still at Oxy, and he'd been very positive about them (to be honest, it was kind of him not to sue us for copyright infringement), but when *Act One* inspired me to contact him again to raise the possibility of my heading to the home of *Help!* – rapidly becoming a mecca for a new generation of what would later be known as underground cartoonists – Harvey did not exactly encourage me. His reply was roughly along the lines of, 'Don't bother – there's a million people in this town with no jobs. Why would you want to join them?'

When I refused to take his no for an answer, he agreed to meet me at the Algonquin Hotel in NYC – a key location in Hart's story: the former home of the distinctly non-Arthurian Round Table of literary wits Dorothy Parker, Robert Benchley, George Kaufman *et al.* Surely this had to be a good omen? So it proved, as just as I walked in through those most elegant of revolving doors, Harvey's now former assistant Chuck Alverson was – if not physically, then at least in career terms – on his way out.

The Algonquin Hotel, scene of my auspicious first meeting with Harvey Kurtzman.

I'd gone there with no expectation of getting a job, but I'd saved enough money working at Camp Trinity to buy a bit of time, and I just wanted to give myself a chance to make something happen. The first time I stepped out of the station at Times Square, the impact of the looming tall buildings hit me right in the guts. That's the fundamental difference between LA and New York – the former is flat, while the latter is way over your head. People didn't generally look at the best part of the buildings – which was the tops – because their gaze was glued to the pavements, but my neck was always craning upwards. I think that's why so many of my films (*Brazil* and *The Fisher King* being the obvious ones, but it applies to *Baron Munchausen* and *Time Bandits* as well) ended up having a vertiginous aspect – because it's taken me decades to process the overwhelming impact of my first arrival in New York.

Knocking on the door of that suite in the Algonquin

was no less of a headrush. Inside that room were all the famous cartoonists I'd grown up admiring (or at least so it seemed to me at the time – Willy Elder, Al Jaffee and Arnold Roth were definitely there). And what were this pantheon of the cartooning gods working on? Why, a salacious spoof comic for *Playboy* called *Little Annie Fanny* – just as Zeus had decreed they should be. Harvey had popped out for a minute, but when he did turn up, he was a lot smaller than I expected (perhaps inevitably given the superhero status I had accorded him) – this little brown nut of a man, vibrating with compressed energy.

As if this scenario was not already idyllic enough, Harvey offered me Chuck's job more or less on the spot. This was beyond luck, it was destiny. OK, so the $50 a week he was going to pay me was $2 a week less than the dole would have been, but as excited as I'd been by the dream of working on *Help!*, the reality was even better. Life was moving so fast that it felt like the city was setting a beat – every morning I'd wake up and New York would say, 'Ramming speed: *Boom! Boom! Boom!*'

Chuck Alverson – who hadn't been sacked, he just had other things to do such as working for the *Wall Street Journal* – kindly took me under his wing and let me sleep on his couch for a while until I got a place of my own. At one point I found myself rooming with a bunch of air stewardesses who wanted to act but in the meantime would come in at all hours of the night from long-haul flights. Then I got my own room in an avariciously subdivided mansion block right up by Columbia University.

It was fully 8-foot by 8-foot, with a basin and my own toilet somehow crammed in. There was just enough room for a bed and the desk I shared with a pet cockroach (who loved paint and would come out to sniff the plate I used to mix the colours on), so I'd move everything onto the bed when I had work to do, and then back onto the desk when it was time to sleep. Whenever I sat down to work, the cockroach would come scuttling out from his quarters in the desk (which were proportionately a good deal more spacious than mine) to get a lung-full – if cockroaches have lungs – of whatever noxious lead fumes were on offer. I would later pay tribute to our interspecies friendship in one of my first

My old Fang buddy John Massey, moon-lighting in deep water as a **Help!** cover star.

extended animations, *Story Time*, but for the moment I certainly appreciated the company.

Living in New York wasn't exactly lonely, but it did teach you how to be on your own. I was doing a lot of communicating at my desk and in the office, but the only way to speak to anyone back home was to send a letter to my parents or friends and fix a precise time for them to call the public phonebox outside the apartment. Then I'd be there to pick up the receiver at the appointed hour, the operator would ask if I was willing to accept a collect call, I would generously say 'Yes', and the company running the box would inadvertently pick up the tab. It was a black day for American students when the telephone companies got wise to that little scam.

Happily, working for *Help!* kept me too busy to rack up many hours of solitary reflection. Given that Harvey mostly operated from his home out in Mount Vernon, my job was mainly to oversee the day-to-day running of the magazine's office with the head of production, Harry Chester. Essentially, I was Kurtzman's representative on earth, and it was my job to deal with pretty much anything that came up. I also spent a lot of time in the city library, because we were always looking for engravings and paintings that we could put silly cap-

tions on. All the stuff *Private Eye* still does now – that started in *Help!*

I'd arrived in New York in the autumn without anything other than California clothes, and then winter hit. My blood had thinned down considerably since my Minnesotan childhood, and my excitement at how like Humphrey Bogart I was going to look in my first trench-coat quickly turned to chattering teeth as the icy wind whipped through the thin cotton. At one point I even got hold of a sun-lamp in a doomed bid to restore some

On the rare occasions when I actually had enough money to buy a drink, New York City's strict laws ensured that I was usually asked for ID to prove I was over <u>*twenty-one.*</u>

Such was my desperation to get served that I even resorted to a goatee. Alcohol hadn't been a big thing for me when I was in college. I never liked the taste of beer and was good at resisting peer pressure by telling people who tried to bully me into getting drunk – 'C'mon Terry, bolt it down' – to go fuck themselves. But my sophisticated new metropolitan lifestyle required the occasional alcoholic beverage, and I was damned if I was going to be 'carded' every time I ordered one.

California colour, and somehow managed to burn my closed eyelids. The logic of the situation was clear: the next time I used it, I kept my eyes open. Oh the pain! I woke up in the middle of the night totally blind, unable to prise open my eyelids. It was like someone had poured a beach into my eyes.

It's always been my default setting to think that the

way I see the world is just normal, and all the other people are cooler, smarter and hipper than me. In New York in 1962–3, this was incontrovertibly true, and not just of Bob Dylan – who had Suze Rotolo to keep him warm as the two of them walked down a snowy Jones Street in Greenwich Village on the cover of his second album. Not only was I impressed by everyone, but I also knew I looked – and sounded – way too young to be in the responsible position of Assistant Editor, so I'd put on a deeper voice when I spoke to people on the phone, and then say, 'I'll send someone round', before going to pick up the delivery myself . . . 'You got a package for Mr Gilliam at *Help!* magazine?'

On 28 August 1963, **Help!** sent me down (in full Zelig mode) to take photos of the cartoonist Paul Coker at the march on Washington, where Martin Luther King made his 'I Have a Dream' speech. As far as the famous oration itself was concerned, being there was a bit like that speech scene in LIFE OF BRIAN – 'Speak up!' – but there was a great atmosphere down on the mall. Look how cool everyone is in their suits and hats (luckily I'm behind the camera, so you can't see how badly I'm letting the side down in fashion terms). It certainly was a very black sea that we wandered through on that day, but no one was anything other than positive towards us — Martin Luther King didn't tend to bring out the anger in people. It was the same the night my friend Baltimore Scott took me up to the Harlem Apollo to see a stellar bill featuring Richard Pryor, Billy Eckstine and The Supremes — I was pretty much the only white face in that crowd (just as Scotty's had been one of the few black faces at Occidental), in fact I was the lightest thing around to the extent that moths were fluttering around my face. It was certainly an amazing night out. There were parties there of three or four different generations — from grandmothers to small children — even though Richard Pryor wasn't what you'd call a family entertainer, even then.

and now a commercial announcement . . .

"Buy Gillette Blue Blades or I'll kick your ass."

Every day was a new adventure.

From the civil rights struggle to the beginnings of the feminist movement, it felt like the John Birch Society version of America was no longer having things all its own way. The old system was being ripped apart with the shape of its replacement very much up for grabs, and the offices of *Help!* were as good a place as any to feel the wind of change in your hair, as Harvey's elite cadre of *Mad* veterans were now being joined by a new generation of young cartoonists such as Robert Crumb and Gilbert Shelton – creator of the *Fabulous Furry Freak Brothers* and *Fat Freddy's Cat* – many of whom had cut their teeth in *Fang*-style college humour magazines such as the University of Texas at Austin's *The Texas Ranger*.

Even at this early moment in his thespian odyssey – and channelling Groucho Marx as he undoubtedly was – Woody Allen's naturalistic acting style leapt off the page.

University had become a place where you escaped the army to play around for four years, and Harvey Kurtzman gave a lot of these well-educated pot smokers who would later light the touch paper for the underground comics explosion (including me, although I was never much of a pot head) their first national outlet. He was such a conservative guy in real life – he didn't really drink or take drugs – that his status as Godfather of the Underground probably came as something of a shock to him, but in political terms, given his stalwart opposition to McCarthy (I remember him launching a devastatingly sharp and angry attack on the witch hunts in *Mad*) and his very humane response to the horrors of the Korean War (the gruesome pre-Vietnam warm-up that nobody talks about these days), it actually made perfect sense.

Harvey lived quite a cloistered existence for such a smart guy. So when I'd be off out on the prowl around the clubs of Greenwich Village, in search of suitably switched-on-looking people willing to take bit parts in *fumetti* for the measly $15 a day we were offering, I'd sometimes come back with a big name who was new to him. Judy Henske was one such – Judy was this incredible tall, funny folk singer who was playing a lot on Bleecker Street at the time, and eventually became a good friend of mine. When I asked if she fancied doing a day's photo-story acting for *Help!*, she agreed, on the condition that she could bring someone along with her.

That someone turned out to be Woody Allen, who while not yet making films of his own was already a well-known stand-up comedian on the New York club circuit. His *fumetto* – 'The Unmentionables' – was scripted by my *Help!* mentor Chuck Alverson, who would later co-write *Jabberwocky* and a first draft of *Brazil* with me. *Fumetti* were the perfect training ground for would-be film-makers (Henry Jaglom was another of our extras who went on to do great things on celluloid). You were framing shots and bringing storyboards to life, even if these were motion pictures without any motion – and the meticulous attention to detail of Harvey's film parodies would be very influential on my own later efforts in the cinematic sphere.

Where Fang's fumetti were entirely no-budget affairs, Help! had the cash to take us to the Adirondacks or Fire Island (before it went gay) for lavish location shoots like these.

And if an actress needed carrying or help finding her way into the scene (which they often did), what choice did a conscientious Assistant Editor have than to oblige?

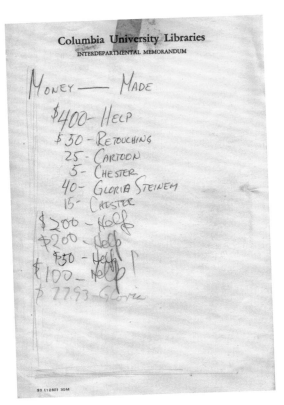

MONEY —— MADE

$400 - HELP
$30 - RETOUCHING
25 - CARTOON
5 - CHESTER
40 - GLORIA STEINEM
15 - CHESTER
$200 - HELP
$200 - HELP
$50 - HELP
$100 - HELP
$27.93 - GLORIA

My income may have increased slightly, but the basic principle of my household accounting system – save every last cent for the important things that you want to buy (note stolen stationery,) – had remained unchanged since childhood. There was progress in other areas, though. Not every man can boast a payment of $40 for services rendered from the glamorous feminist pioneer Gloria Steinem. Gloria had been Alverson's predecessor in what became my job as Harvey's assistant and was still writing funny picture captions for *Help!* at the same time as becoming the global face of feminism. This was an aspect of her career she tended to keep quite quiet about later on, so when she came forward to speak warmly of Harvey at the time of his death, I thought, 'Good for you.'

Gloria was certainly an impressive character – smart, funny, good-looking. Men loved her but women didn't seem to be threatened by her, which is quite an unusual combination. It was a measure of how good she was at getting people to do things that I once helped her complete the production of a lavish coffee-table-type book about being cool on the beach, for which she had somehow elicited a foreword from the celebrated liberal economist (and well-known hater of beaches) J K Galbraith. She was also involved with an organisation whose brief was to bring people over from behind the Iron Curtain and show them life in the West which subsequently – although she did not know this at the time – turned out to be run by the CIA.

My own film-making ambitions had begun to coalesce by this time. I was somehow managing to set aside almost half of my meagre weekly wage to save up for my first Bolex camera, and spent months denying myself even the luxury of a five-cent packet of chewing gum in the interests of realising my vague dreams of auteurhood.

One of the themes of my New York years was
the wonder of discovering foreign films – whether they be Ealing comedies, Kurosawa or Buñuel – and realising that not everyone in front of the camera had to look like Rock Hudson or Doris Day (or Jerry Lewis and Dean Martin, come to that). Or even be filmed in colour. I'd devour Chaplin retrospectives, and come out of Eisenstein films in a reverie thinking, 'Wow, *angles*.'

Obviously my secret life as a commie *manqué* – as opposed to a commie monkey, which is probably what Senator McCarthy would have called me –

The Outsider's Newsletter was another satirical magazine I contributed to – an offshoot of the better-known Monocle, put together by the same people, Victor Navasky and Richard Lingeman. It had a harder, newsier edge than Help!, more along the lines of Paul Krassner's underground press staple The Realist, and this cover was in honour of the controversial visit to New York by South Vietnam's then de facto first lady Madame Nhu, in the autumn of 1963. Her hatred of Buddhists was one of the causes of all those monks setting themselves on fire – hence the petrol can and cigarette lighter.

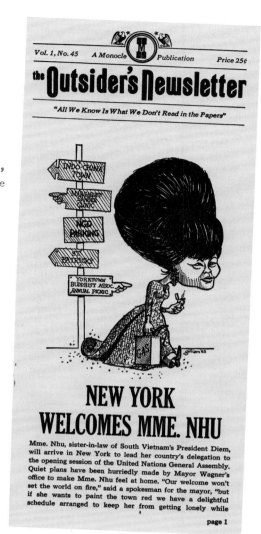

made old Sergei particularly appealing to me. In fact, Eisenstein's *The Film Sense* is probably the only technical book on film I have ever read. He combined storyboards with camera moves, which I found very instructive, although a certain reluctance to take direction could already be discerned on my part, even in the company of such an illustrious teacher. I remember taking strong exception to his theory that if a scene is visually rising from left to right, then the music has to go that way too.

I did briefly try going to film school – it was an evening course at New York's City College, and I went once a week for a month – but that was the one place where I felt like the more laid-back attitude to life inculcated by my West Coast adolescence really counted against me. I just found that, coming from California, my general attitude towards life was quite different from the New York kids, who were very aggressive and always grabbed the equipment. After a few of those kinds of run-ins, I just thought, 'Bugger that, I'm not going to hang around here.'

Then I worked as a volunteer for a while in a studio that did stop-motion photography (dancing cigarette packs, that kind of thing). It was through an actor friend, Jim Hampton, who'd been in some *fumetti* and played the role of the trumpeter in the TV show *F-Troop*. Ted Nemeth, whose studio it was, said, 'Well, we don't really *have* a job here, so we can't pay you,' but I told him I didn't care. I just wanted to be around all this stuff – handling the equipment, moving cameras, even sweeping up if that was what they wanted me to do.

It was really important to me to understand film-making's physical manifestation, and when Mary Ellen Bute, Nemeth's wife, began work on an adaptation

HELP!

of James Joyce's *Finnegans Wake*, I also got a valuable early lesson in doomed adaptations of unfilmable literary classics – a field in which I would later come to be considered something of a specialist.

Green as I was, I still knew I had a contribution to make. One day they were trying – and failing – to get a shot with a kind of crown effect, using upturned chairs on a round table. Understanding the spatial relationship between different bodies is something I've always been good at, and this was just a matter of simple physics – if you want that thing to look like it's turning, you've got to either go around it yourself, or find a way to make it actually turn. The more clearly I explained that the alternative strategy they were adopting was never going to work, the more they struggled to get the message, until finally they had a 'Who the fuck are you to be telling us what to do?' moment.

Dave Crossley took time out from his busy sexual schedule to write *Help!*'s Madison Avenue-style brochure for the Ku Klux Klan for me to illustrate. Thanks, Dave.

'Who the fuck am I?', I dutifully asked myself. 'I'm the person who knows how to do this when you don't!' was the devastating comeback (at least, in the safety of my internal dialogue). At that point, my informal paying-my-dues cinematic apprenticeship effectively came to an end. From then on, I knew all I needed to do as far as film studies were concerned was go to the movies – that's always been enough for me – get myself a camera, write some little stories and get together with some friends to try to shoot them.

Happily, as I gradually found my New York feet, I'd begun to get another gang together. Well, two-thirds of it was the old gang (i.e. me and my old *Fang*-buddy Art Mortimer, who had eventually followed me in making the big move to the East Coast), with Dave Crossley, one of the *Texas Ranger* crowd – a talented writer who was inexplicably irresistible to women – joining us as the third man.

<u>Help!</u> baldly imagined The Beatles in middle age. Sadly, destiny had different plans for the group's long-term future.

I moved out of my old eight-by-eight room, said a fond farewell to my pet cockroach and ready supply of Columbia University Library notepaper, and joined Art and Dave in an Upper East Side flatshare, which – somewhat miraculously given how cheap it was – offered us the eye-catching calling card of a Madison Avenue address (at 71st Street to be precise). Never mind that it was basically a two-room apartment with three very small beds in the bedroom, one of which Dave was perpetually banging away in.

Art, Dave and I held a lot of good parties in that flat, and were planning to have another one on what turned out to be the night of President Kennedy's assassination. Although not so widely remembered for this reason, 22 November 1963 was also the occasion of my twenty-third birthday. You know those mornings where you wake up late thinking, 'Great, it's my birthday', then you turn on the TV and think, 'Whoops'?

Everyone still came over and got drunk anyway, but it was more like a wake. Whatever the rights and wrongs of some of the things JFK was doing, there was a horrible sense – just as there would be five years later with the deaths of Martin Luther King and Bobby Kennedy – of, 'They've killed our guy.' It was hard to believe that there'd been this charismatic young leader with all this energy who seemed to be changing things, and then all of a sudden, he was gone.

In a strange way, I think that only energised people to push even harder. Also, The Beatles stepped into the breach to cheer America up. 'I Want To Hold Your Hand' came out just a month after the Kennedy assassination, when much of the country was still effectively in shock, and the Fab Four's first trip to the US was just a few weeks later in early 1964. I'm sure part of the amazing excitement they generated was down to that – it was as if they'd picked up the mantle of youthful change out of Dallas's blood-stained dust.

By the time John, Paul, George and Ringo

hit New York for the first time, I'd finally saved enough to buy that first Bolex camera. Art Mortimer had spent his money on a motorcycle, so I rode pillion up to Park Avenue where The Beatles were staying to film the crowd breaking through the barrier. The British invasion was on, and from that point forwards, we sort of became awash with England for a while.

Richard Lester's 1960 Spike Milligan and Peter Sellers short *The Running, Jumping & Standing Still Film* had been one of the formative influences on the way The Beatles conducted themselves (both in public and on film), and was

This is a contact sheet of the three of us fooling around out the back of the basement flat on West 83rd Street. I'm not sure if we were trying to put together a storyboard for a 3-minute short that never happened, or perhaps this is a homespun fumetto that never quite got finished. Either way, you can see the kind of shit-hole this place was, and the pith helmet testifies eloquently to our encroaching Anglophilia.

the reason they hired Lester to direct *A Hard Day's Night* and *Help!* Along with the *Goon Show* recordings that were belatedly becoming available in America on state-of-the art long-playing records, this ground-breaking 11-minute film (made by an American cineaste in Britain, lest we forget) also helped set the tone for our Madison Avenue household's first forays into film-making.

I'd never seen anything that felt so free. Famously budgeted at just £70 (including a fiver for the rent of a field) Lester's frenetic and fun-packed *jeu d'esprit* was a far cry from the more studied and sombre work coming out of New York's experimental scene of the early sixties. I must admit I never really liked Andy Warhol's stuff – I thought it was pretentious bullshit – but I didn't mind a bit of Stan Brakhage. And I was shocked on seeing some of Stan Vanderbeek's work again a few years ago – especially 1964's *Breath Death*, which I saw soon after its original release at the Thalia (the ultimate art-house cinema, which made a cameo in Woody Allen's *Annie Hall*, when Diane Keaton takes her new boyfriend to see *The Sorrow and the Pity* there) – by how many of the ideas for my later cut-out animations I borrowed (to put it politely) from him – the tops of heads come off, feet go in mouths, it's the same shit, I just (oh, alright then . . .) stole it – but not consciously, your honour.

But all that would come later. When Art Mortimer, Dave Crossley and I got together to fool about and make little silent movies – putting on top hats to make a speeded-up Victorian melodrama, with a sympathetic girl of our acquaintance agreeing to lie down in sled tracks in the snow and be 'tied to them', like a damsel in distress – it was Dick Lester who was the presiding spirit.

a sketchbook
report·
by
Robert Crumb

HARLEM

It was amazing how fast Bob could
draw – he was so brilliantly focused
on what he was doing that, as we
walked around Harlem, work of this
quality just seemed to be appearing
out of nowhere on his sketch pad.

HEY EMILY HONEY!
LEN' ME YO' CHILLUNS...
AH'M GOIN' FOR MAH
WELFARE CHECK!

I also remember us trying to do some stop-motion animation of

surreal little stories by drawing on spacing leader we got out of film company trash bins.

Sadly, none of these formative works seem to have survived, but it was fun doing them at the time. We'd get up on a Saturday morning and, depending on what the weather was like, we'd write something accordingly, and go out and shoot it on a 3-minute roll of film (all we could afford).

Guerrilla film-making experiments aside, *Help!* was still occupying the bulk of my waking hours. Even though the magazine began to falter financially as the early sixties turned to mid-, Harvey retained his happy knack for attracting the brightest new cartooning talent from all across America. One such fresh-faced out-of-towner was Robert Crumb, who in order to make the bold move to New York left behind the security provided by the Indianapolis greetings card industry. In years to come, Crumb would be rightly celebrated for the intensity of his engagement with various aspects of Black American culture, but when Harvey sent him uptown to draw in Harlem for the first time, he was still on distinctly unfamiliar territory. Luckily for him, he had *Help!*'s famously streetwise Assistant Editor to show him the ropes.

It was obvious from very early on that Bob was going to be a star. As well as the notebook that he always carried with him, there usually seemed to be a crowd of acolytes in tow. The funny thing was, he seemed to think I was the cool one. OK, I might have been slightly more sharply dressed, but he was the one getting the girls.

In mid-sixties Harlem, the spectacle of two white men sketching and taking pictures (never mind eating an apple) was always going to be greeted with a measure of suspicion, so obviously, Bob and I felt slightly nervous — that's probably why my focus isn't too great on these shots — but we were having fun and probably radiated a certain goofy innocence. Either that or everyone was convinced we were narcs and decided to leave us alone for that reason.

New York had at least one more crucial formative encounter in store for me. My *fumetti* press-ganging missions into Greenwich Village were still a big part of my *Help!* duties, and when I came across a tall, angular Englishman called John Cleese in a struggling student revue, I sensed he'd have what it took (i.e. a willingness to work for $15 a day). The original *Beyond the Fringe* theatre show had been a huge success in New York, but *Cambridge Circus* – a slightly rickety vehicle for the next generation of Footlights graduates, including Bill Oddie, Tim Brooke-Taylor and a certain Graham Chapman – did not strike quite such a chord with American audiences. I think all the participants were

Behold Christopher Barrel, returning dutifully home to his wife, Wilma Barrel — with a case of ennui. Look at him. This sort of thing happens to a man. Too much sameness, too much tedium, too much everything everyday, and then the ennui sets in. Some survive, some never get out of it and some never notice; but to some there is An Occurrence . . .

CHRISTOPHER'S PUNCTURED ROMANCE

BY DAVE CROSSLEY
JOHN CLEESE AS CHRISTOPHER BARREL
CINDY YOUNG AS WILMA BARREL
MARTIN IGER, PHOTOGRAPHER

15

enjoying themselves well enough (coming straight out of college to perform in Greenwich Village couldn't be bad, could it?). John was the one who stood out, though – as he always did – and we became friendly quite quickly.

I think it was Cleese's fearlessness as a physical performer that was most striking at that stage – we'd be riding the subway together, and he'd suddenly start doing very freaky movements with his arms and hands, magnificently oblivious to the reactions of his fellow travellers (and the New York subway wasn't necessarily somewhere you wanted to be making enemies at that time).

What amazes me about this slightly warped tale of a man's burgeoning passion for a doll is how prescient it was in terms of John's later life, though this particular blonde American Barbie didn't end up costing him quite as much as some of the later ones.

In the spring of 1964 I was determined to do everything in my power to get myself passed unfit for military service.

Chapter **5**

Army Dreamer

hile JFK's inferior replacement

president Lyndon Baines Johnson was getting his feet firmly under the White House table, things were definitely hotting up in South-east Asia. Like all sensible Americans of my generation, the Vietnam War ranked quite low on my list of desirable holiday destinations. The first time the shadow of the draft really loomed over me – in the spring of 1964 – I was determined to do everything in my power to get myself passed unfit for military service.

I made sure I didn't sleep properly in the week leading up to this potentially fateful face-to-face encounter with the military-industrial complex. I drank heavily. I took up smoking – something I'd never done before – and generally did anything I could think of to completely waste myself. The night before the draft interview, we had a huge 'going off to war' party in our basement flat on West 83rd Street, and I stumbled out of bed the next morning and made my way to the place where you had to queue up to get drafted.

The first thing you have to do is take the physical – cough, bend over – and by the time the long queue had snaked me round to the main guy you had to give the paper you'd been sent in the post to, I could barely stand up, I was so fucking gone. Obviously it was nothing they hadn't seen before (we were all looking for a way out ... pretending to be blind, gay, mad, whatever it took), but the unique feature of my case was I'd arrived a month early. For some reason – probably not an unconscious desire to do deeds of heroism in far-off lands – I'd somehow got the date wrong.

When the formally scheduled day of my appearance at the draft board finally came around, I couldn't face repeating the whole smoking and drinking rigmarole – it's not like the authorities were going to take any notice of that anyway – and was duly deemed fit to serve my country. For me, as for many of my college-educated peers, joining the National Guard seemed the best option. Setting aside the whole danger issue, if you'd been lucky enough to come out of college and get a good job, the last thing you really wanted to do was disappear off to Saigon for two years. Not that you'd automatically have to, as the Viet Cong hadn't really started to bite yet, but going to war was a definite possibility.

The National Guard on the other hand restricted the initial leave of absence from your actual life to a more manageable six months of basic training, followed by monthly meetings and ten annual fortnight-long summer camps to keep you up to speed. So I signed up for what was disparagingly known by more combat-ready regiments as the 'Silk-Stocking Brigade' – its regimental offices conveniently located on Park Avenue, just a few blocks from the flat on Madison – and was sent down to Fort Dix in New Jersey for half a year's intensive indoctrination in the essential principles of grunt-dom.

Check out my US army dog tags – it seems I was still a Presbyterian.

Luckily, Fort Dix wasn't too far from New York, so I could get weekend passes home to keep as many of the pigment-covered plates of my old life as possible up in the air. Unfortunately, there was no perfumed training enclave for the effete skivers of the National Guard – we were all out there on the ranges together, and most of the other guys were proper shit-kickers who just couldn't wait to get out there and kill some 'gooks'. I'm not being disparaging about my fellow draftees: I realise that for someone from a tougher background than my own, the army offered opportunities to earn respect and broaden your horizons that might well not have been accessible in civilian life. Also, some people really thrive on the order and rigidity of the military – attentive readers will not be surprised to find out that I was not one of them.

Any inclination I might have had (which was infinitesimal) to subsume myself entirely in the business of soldiering would certainly not survive the absurdities of basic training. I just found the whole thing very hard to take seriously. Even when we were out there in the wilds of the Garden State on full-scale military manoeuvres – having to 'take that hill' and all this kind of thing – I'd be running around like a kid playing soldiers, shouting '*Boom!*', '*Bang!*' and '*Taka-taka-taka*' (my best shot at a convincing machine-gun sound).

'What's wrong with you, Gilliam?' an exasperated commanding officer would ask. 'C'mon, these blanks are practically silent,' I would reply. 'If you're going to fire a gun, it should at least make the right noise.' Obviously I was taking the piss, but I was also trying to make this foolishness as entertaining as possible for myself and others, and as a result soon found myself widely acknowledged as a bit of a joke.

For the duration of my basic training the Fort Dix Post became an unlikely outpost of the underground comics revolution.

One thing you discover fairly quickly once you put on a uniform is that if you have any kind of talent, the army loves it. And I soon found ways to elude as many of the more onerous duties of military life as possible by reverting to high school and early Oxy type as a theoretical promoter of social cohesion through the medium of cartooning.

When I was working (if you could call it that) on the *Fort Dix Post* newspaper, the colonel and his wife had raised money for a new chapel, and he wanted me to go and do a drawing of it that they could use in the *Bugle*. I dragged this out for I don't know how long – certainly a week or two of sitting in the post library, which was all I really wanted to be doing.

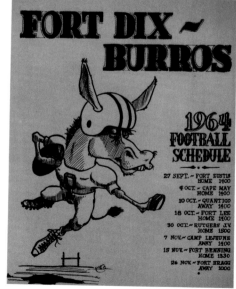

When it comes to swinging

the lead, there's no better prop than a pencil, and my immediate commanding officer – who was a man I found it quite hard to salute, because he was a few years younger than me, and somewhat dumber – was kind enough to hand me another 'get out of the firing-line free' card. He'd seen me sketching one day and wondered what I was doing, so I showed him some of my

You know what they say, you can take the cheerleader out of the man, but you can't ...Oh no, sorry, that can't be right.

drawings and he asked me to do a portrait of his fiancée. Everyone else was outside crawling around in the mud simulating the terrifying impact of heavy machine-gun fire, and I was inside in the barracks, drawing the lieutenant's wife (from a photo – a charcoal drawing from life would have been pushing even my luck).

He was going crazy for this picture, he wanted it so badly, but I just kept him at bay by insisting, 'It's got to be great,' until he finally uttered the fateful words: 'Gilliam, the great is the enemy of the good.'

This was a lesson I steadfastly refused to learn in my subsequent cinematic career (even after enduring the ordeal of screening a film I'd made for the Weinstein brothers – 'It's really good, Terry, it's really good . . . but it needs to be great.').

The lieutenant liked the result so much that he got me to do one of him as well, and drawing him in a sequence of different unflattering guises became a reliable source of hilarity in the barracks. One night I was turning him into Napoleon and regaling my fellow raw recruits with what I was fairly confident was a very comical impression of the man himself (the lieutenant, not the little general) when I noticed some of my audience looking behind me with fearful expressions. It turned out he had snuck up the fire escape to get a surprise glimpse of the artist at work on his portrait, and was now so embarrassed that there was no way he could punish us. Does this kind of power (on my part, not his) make someone a better person? I wish I could say it did.

There was one lesson basic training taught me

that it took me a long time to unlearn, and that was how to skive. It was something I'd never really done before, having previously been an active and industrious youth. But by the time I got back to civvy street and was trying to get energised to do things again in my old creative milieu, I suddenly found I had a whole armoury of new default responses – avoiding, shirking, those kind of -ings – to over-ride.

I wasn't born to duck and dive, but the army had brought out my closet malingerer. This inner opportunist had been seen at his most brazen in my single-minded pursuit of no-cost military dental treatment. It all started innocently enough, when I had a wisdom tooth that became very infected, so the Fort Dix dentist pulled it out. I knew that once one went, the other one probably would too, so I asked him if he could extract that for me as well, but he refused on the grounds that as yet there was nothing wrong with it.

That night I went back to the barracks and systematically ground my teeth – just clamped them together and twisted – until my whole mouth became so inflamed that the dentist had no option but to go in and finish the job for me. I've always been very pragmatic about such things, and free dentistry is too good an opportunity to pass up in America. Some might see the principle of natural justice at work in the nasty case of mumps which subsequently put me in the infirmary with a temperature of 104, and a sadistic arsehole of a corporal who still had me up out of my sick-bed cleaning the latrines to save him from doing it, but that would not be my interpretation.

The National Guard summer camp, which I had to attend for a couple of weeks in 1965, was even more of a joke than the basic training had been – at least first time around we'd been thrown in at the deep end with people who were actually going to be soldiers. Now we found ourselves being bossed around by a lot of older part-timers who liked the idea of becoming officers to make up for the fact that they hadn't got to serve in the Korean War.

Joseph Heller's *Catch-22* (first published in 1961) was required reading for reluctant draftees like me. That book really captured the tragic foolishness of the whole business – you'd be out in some god-awful place and guys would actually be dying because they'd skived off to hide in the grass where tanks were doing their exercises. Or someone would get positioned on a distant outcrop of rock and the commanding officer would forget they were there, so they'd eventually wander in the next morning, freezing cold and hungry. At this point you realised why so much of what you learn in the army is about projecting a coherent show of capable authority – because of the desperate need to conceal the reality of institutional incompetence.

Someone once worked out that the amount of money they were wasting on trying to turn people like me into soldiers was upwards of a hundred thousand dollars. And all the time this was happening, the war was getting worse, as the shocking reports being filed daily by journalists like the *New York Times*' David Halberstam were making only too clear.

Luckily for me, I was able to take advantage of that military susceptibility to absurdist logic that Joseph Heller so astutely noted. As the situation in Vietnam continued to worsen, and the gossamer threads of *Help!* magazine's administrative structure finally began to fall apart, I decided to head off to Europe for a while. I wrote to the National Guard and told them that I was being relocated and the magazine was sending me across the Atlantic to run a new bureau for them, so unfortunately I wouldn't be available to go to the monthly meetings and summer camps.

Happily, the army had a system in place for just such eventualities – what they did was allocate you what's called a 'control group'. Mine was based in Germany, but as I hitch-hiked around Europe, I found myself staying longest in Lindos on the Greek island of Rhodes, where my former *Help!* colleague Dave Crossley was now living (Pink Floyd had a house there too at one point). Once all my correspondence with the army was going through Rhodes, I wrote to them again saying, 'Our European office is here in Lindos – which unfortunately is a long way from Germany, so I won't be able to attend the meetings . . . *blah, blah, blah.*'

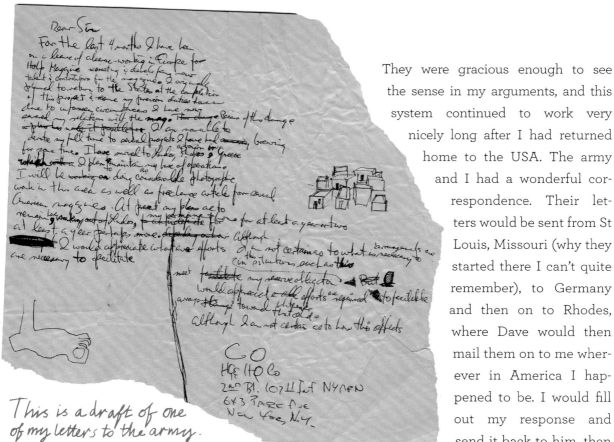

This is a draft of one of my letters to the army.

It is — quite literally — a tissue of lies, but note significant doodles of rustic Lindos dwellings (right) and what would later come to be known as a 'Monty Python-style' foot (bottom left).

They were gracious enough to see the sense in my arguments, and this system continued to work very nicely long after I had returned home to the USA. The army and I had a wonderful correspondence. Their letters would be sent from St Louis, Missouri (why they started there I can't quite remember), to Germany and then on to Rhodes, where Dave would then mail them on to me wherever in America I happened to be. I would fill out my response and send it back to him, then he would stamp it in Rhodes and send it on to the control group in Germany, then they would send it back to St Louis. I think that's what they call 'the circle of life' . . . or even Catch 22 in reverse – either way, I couldn't lose!

As for how I came to want to leave New York – the city that had given me so much excitement, and made all my Moss Hart-ian dreams come true – by the latter half of 1965, that same adrenaline mood which I'd found so captivating on first arriving in the city had become something I couldn't really deal with any more. That early morning drummer was beating time far too quickly for me.

I'd never fallen prey to the delusion that often takes hold of New Yorkers that there is no world outside of Manhattan. I used to really enjoy going home to LA at Christmas. There was a scheme where people would fly across the country and want their car delivered, so if you were willing to do the drive, you could go from East Coast to West (and back) for the price of the fuel. My and John Latimer's (he too was now in New York) record for the journey from George Washington Bridge to the California border was fifty-two hours, which basically meant driving without stopping – we'd pull into a petrol station and one of us would run in to grab snacks and pay while the other filled up the car and then gunned the engine.

We smashed up quite a few cars in the course of those journeys. One time in Missouri I lost control of the wheel at 80 mph and went straight into the dip that divided the road, tearing out a great chunk of earth in the process. On another occasion, when I and a different group of friends decided to go through North Texas on Route 66, the car got out of control in an ice storm (who knew they even had those in Texas?) and

Mortimer, Latimer and Gilliam prepare to head west in someone else's undamaged (as yet) glossy-finned beast.

skidded through a petrol station, just missing the pumps. We couldn't get out at first because the door on one side was blocked by the pole holding the big Chevron sign – that's how close we were to a spectacular Hollywood ending.

Such good luck seemed to be worth pushing on a transatlantic basis. So when the fast-moving allure of New York began to coagulate into a creeping sense of claustrophobia, as *Help!* plummeted into a financial abyss and none of my diverse portfolio of replacement activities – automotive comics (Hank Hinton's snappily titled *Car-Toons*), greetings cards, dot-to-dot puzzle books, even a brief period as Managing Editor of *Ripley's Believe It or Not!*, which I can't actually remember – could quite fill the gap, it was only natural that I should succumb to the lure of the continent that inspired Disneyland.

'Is this the only world that's out there for me?' was the kind of question I was asking myself on an increasingly regular basis as my twenty-fifth birthday loomed. There had been girls in my life (although never as many as in Robert Crumb's). The mid-1960s was an exciting time to be a young single man in New York – mores were changing, and the difference the pill made to us is hard for people who grew up taking it for granted to understand – so I do have some happy memories from the roof-top of that Madison Avenue flat. But there was no one I was serious enough about to want to stay in America for. It was time to escape to Europe.

The Beatles weren't the only siren voices calling me to England in

1965. Herman's Hermits and The Dave Clark Five (who at one point were bigger than the Fab Four – well, I suppose there was always one more of them) added to the chorus. And by the time I'd booked my passage on a 'student ship' – a crappy ocean liner that charged something like a hundred dollars to get you from New York to Southampton in eleven days – the song I was dancing

The thing you learn by travelling on your own is that people are incredibly generous and interested in someone from another country, especially if you make a **big hand** to carry with you. My enlarged appendage always got a laugh, even from people who didn't pick me up.

the night away to was The Rolling Stones' '(I Can't Get No) Satisfaction'.

Once I'd run around the ship to see if there were any girls on it that I fancied and discovered that there weren't, Mick and Keith's disingenuous lament (after all, if they weren't getting any satisfaction, what hope was there for the rest of us?) became the theme song of the voyage. Dancing yourself insensible did seem like the best way to get through those interminably tedious days with nothing to look at but the grey circle of sea. And when we finally docked, there was a magical surprise waiting for me – not the kind the Rolling Stones would have been looking for, but none the less welcome for all that.

Disembarking from that ship in Southampton,

I remember carrying my bags off the gang-plank and feeling something very different to the rush of alarming novelty that is meant to overwhelm you on arriving in a new country. What I felt was new alright, but it was a feeling (possibly illusory, as some of the scurvier denizens of Southampton's dockside could no doubt have demonstrated had fate given them the opportunity) of, for the first time in my life, being totally safe – safe from people who might want to hit me, or do things to hurt me.

It wasn't like I'd been a victim of systematic bullying throughout my child-hood and am now going to lurch unexpectedly into *A Child Called It* territory, far from it. But one of the weird things about America – and I think I always found this a bit strange unconsciously, even before I'd lived anywhere else – is the feeling you get there that if someone doesn't approve of you, there's a good chance they're going to pop you one. It's probably just that go-ahead American attitude which dictates that guys who don't like you feel they have to do some-thing about it.

I'd only been on the receiving end of this national propensity a couple of times when I was growing up. Once, when I was thirteen or fourteen and got separated from my parents – in central LA, down by the Coliseum – a group of slightly older black kids came along and started saying things like, 'You're the guy who called my brother a bastard.' It was one of those incidents where you're thinking 'This is ridiculous, they just want to hit me', and then they do.

Another time at a school dance, a gang from south-central LA turned up to deal with a rival group from our neck of the woods. All the lights went off and – *Boom!* – the main doors smashed open. Suddenly the dance floor was full of kids with knives and chains who were 'looking for someone'. Luckily, that someone wasn't me, but a sense of America being a dangerous place to live was something I never really shook off. So when I got to England and suddenly didn't feel threatened by anyone – even if this was just as a consequence of being somewhere new and not knowing the rules – I just thought, 'This is fantastic.'

The more I've pondered this divergence in transatlantic threat perception – especially from the perspective of abandoning my ancestral homeland to forge a new life amid America's erstwhile colonial oppressors – the closer I've come to ascribing it to the fact that people in England seem to have a much better sense of personal space than people in America. They don't feel entitled to invade your territory the way Americans do, at least that's how it's always felt to me – perhaps they just scratched that itch sufficiently with the whole British Empire thing.

So I pootled happily around England, savouring my newly enhanced sense of security and well-being. One weekend, while I was staying at some crappy London B&B, I was heading off to Hampton Court for the day when I realised that Shepperton Studios was also around there somewhere (well, eight miles away). So, having found my way to the old gatehouse and seen the closed faces of the guards on duty, I detoured through a neighbouring garden centre, climbed over a fence at the back, somehow made my way across a moat-like stream and eventually managed to gain entrance to the studio where so many films I'd loved had been made. It was all shut up for the weekend, so there was no one there to stop me strolling around the standing sets on the back lot and editing rooms, just getting the feel of the place, before walking blithely out past the guards on the gate. If my 1965 self had only known I'd end up making the studio segments of *Jabberwocky* there, a decade or so later, I could even have essayed a cheeky, 'I'll be back.'

When you go abroad on a budget, it always pays to get a list of friends' contacts to sponge off, and it was through this useful document that I found myself having Sunday lunch with someone's parents in Tunbridge Wells. I asked them, 'How often do you get up to London?' And they said, 'Maybe once every year or two.' To an American, the insularity of this (England's capital being only about thirty-five miles away) seemed very exotic and quirky.

There was something about London when I first arrived in the late autumn of 1965 – it wasn't quite a cartoon version of itself, but there was certainly a medieval simplicity to the social hierarchy. The place was still uptight enough to be interesting. Businessmen in the city still wore bowler hats. There were still walls to be broken down and cocks to be snooked, whereas by the time I returned a couple of years later, everything had burst into flower.

The English as a people were kind of a surprise to me. I'd assumed we'd speak the same language for a start, but my first attempt to communicate with a cockney waitress at a Lyons Corner House soon relieved me of that particular delusion. The general atmosphere of diffidence was something to get used to, but in a way it came as a relief after the rapid-fire aggression of New York. There was an occasional undercurrent of anti-American prejudice as well – especially when I tentatively dropped in on *Help!* tribute publication *Private Eye*, where it was made fairly clear to me that a recommendation from Harvey was not going to be enough to overcome the social handicap of coming from the land of the free.

Strongly opposed as I was to all the shit America was doing in the world, it was still a shock to find myself defending my homeland against people who assumed it – and by extension I – was an instinctive warmonger. Once I left England and started to make my way around Europe, I started to encounter even more challenges to the assumptions I'd been brought up with, i.e. that the American way of life was the good one, and in foreign policy terms we were just there to help.

To be able to run from one culture to another, discovering all these different ways of looking at things, gave me an extraordinary sense of freedom. People were travelling more by 1965, but the 'hippie trail' hadn't really got going as an idea yet – Graham Nash wrote 'Marrakesh Express' the next year, but no one would let him release it till 1969. This was the time before things were named – the Garden of Eden period, when we didn't know what the apple was called, but it sure tasted good.

We might have heard of Ken Kesey and his Merry Pranksters, but it was taking the rest of us a while to catch up. In our own minds we were probably still more intellectually aligned with the beat generation of Kerouac and Ginsberg – the past always being easier to cling on to, whereas the future can only be understood once it's actually happening. The civil rights and anti-war protest movements had been well underway back home before I left for Europe – people were motivated and angry – but the full flowering of hippiedom (which some might say dissipated the political engagement of the early sixties anyway) was still a way off yet.

In the meantime, I was really enjoying myself. Whether I was randomly bumping into an old friend from New York in a café in Dean Street, Soho; swimming in the Aegean on Christmas Day, 1965; or jumping in the back of a Spanish pick-up truck and sleeping wrapped in just a sheepskin – my ramblings around Europe were the epitome of picaresque.

A three-quarter-length suede coat – bought on my travels and costing 200 Turkish lire – would make a great impression on my Monty Python colleagues when I wore it to our first formal meeting two years later. I wasn't very interesting, but my coat was.

I'd started off with a thousand bucks in travellers' cheques, and it was just a question of making that last as long as possible. I did anything I could to keep going – in Spain you could make a bit of money by selling your blood for transfusions. In Istanbul if you hung around the right Aladdin's cave-type hutch in the bazaar you could become a 'ten-per-center' by drawing in fellow Western tourists in return for a percentage of the take.

I was never quite alone. There always seemed to be somebody around, and nobody had the fear that people have now. I remember meeting this beautiful blonde Swedish girl who had hitch-hiked down to Istanbul. She said a guy in a truck had made a half-hearted attempt to grab her once, but that was as far as it had gone. There was also Lucille Rhodes, a friend from back in New York who I'd agreed to meet in Gibraltar (she accompanied me to Tangier). When I got to Florence I bumped into Danny's daughter Dena Kaye, who was there as an exchange student, so we hitch-hiked up to Bologna together to sample the cooking.

*The photos I took on this trip were the first I ever tried to develop myself – the **Help!** ones always used to get sent to the Lab.* These test prints are pretty crappy, but they do capture some of the excitement I felt at finally encountering the artefacts and architecture – and people – of Europe for the first time.

I like the body positions on this one, which is right in front of the cathedral in Florence. When you've only got thirty-six Kodachromes in a roll, all the photos have to be considered, not like that digital shit where you can just keep hammering it. I suppose it's the difference between a rifle and an AK-47 – you've got to make the individual shots count rather than just pulling the trigger and hoping you get something.

If you've lived for large parts of your life fantasising about Sleeping Beauty's castle, there's inevitably going to be an element of disappointment when you actually get to visit real ones. But my European trip was the next step on from those childhood jaunts to Stoney Point – a chance to appreciate the incompleteness of something, where your imagination begins to fill in the gaps. I love ruins for that reason – they're like broken statues, sometimes you get a more vivid sense of the bits that are missing than the bits that are still there. And stepping off the edge of Europe into the souks of Istanbul, Morocco and Tangier was another new dimension, with all the bustle and the narrow spaces.

By the time I was heading back northwards to Spain from Morocco, I'd got bored of hitch-hiking and decided to try buying myself a motorbike instead. I had to waste a couple of weeks monkeying around in Gibraltar while they got it ready, then the moment of total freedom finally arrived. I drove off into Spain at night and within an hour, maybe less, I'd hit an Alsatian which ran out in front of me and got spread out all over the road (at least, I did – the dog jumped up straight away and bolted off, apparently none the worse for the experience).

Luckily, the crash happened right in front of a bar, and a few of the locals were kind enough to come out and drag me inside. Where I'd landed my arm was basically raw meat, and my hip was painfully swollen as my pockets were full of loose change from my travels, which had created a kind of mincing-machine effect on impact with the road surface. First they got a bottle of some fiery Iberian liquor and poured that on to cauterise the wounds.

This quarter of Istanbul, which was all mud
streets, has been pulled down since and
rebuilt in a less characterful fashion, but
looking back at these pictures I can see how
they informed the sense of scale and visual
drama I'd be looking to create once I got
into film-making.

This serious-looking Florentine character
seemed to have turned up fourteen years early
for a LIFE OF BRIAN crowd scene. I wasn't
quite sure what was going on, but there were
a lot of nuns around so I assumed some major
bishop or cardinal was floating through.

I can say without fear of contradiction that my
screams woke many a sleeping baby. Then they
found a doctor who was drinking (presumably
heavily) in the back room. He bandaged me up,
and said I'd be OK.

So I staggered off back into the night, re-
aligned the bike where the frame had got bent
out of shape, and resumed my journey. Apart
from my arm and hip, the front headlight was
the main casualty of the accident, which meant
trying to stay as close as possible to any car
which came by so I could use their front beams
to follow the course of the road. It was blacker
than a Hollywood studio executive's heart that
moonless night, and inevitably just about everyone else driving through the wilds of Spain
was going at speeds higher than my infernal –
and quite seriously damaged – machine could

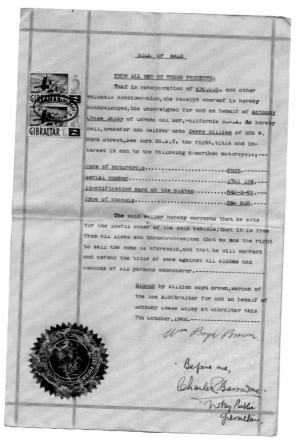

The contract of ill-omen – I've signed a few of these in my time.

93

manage, so it was a constant struggle not to lose control and go flying off the road once my four-wheeled help-meets had left me eating their dust.

As the night went on, that bike (which was a Putsch – although the name would have made more sense without the t and the c) started to take on genuinely satanic properties. Every so often it would stop, and I'd invariably have to push it up a hill. Then, when I finally made it to my destination – which was Malaga – I was heading along the main drag, momentarily feeling pretty good about myself as I passed the crowded bars, when it broke down one more time, so I had to ignominiously push the demon bike past the cool, not to say smug, revellers – grunting and staggering – to the youth hostel, with everyone thinking, 'What a putz!'

After a week reading old Mickey Spillane paperbacks at a house on the beach near Alicante, a bit further up the coast, my wounds had finally healed enough for me to consider getting back on the bike. I came off again on a wet corner on the way to Barcelona – not as badly this time, but when I finally got into the city, the wheel got stuck in a tram-track in rush-hour traffic. All these cops were blowing their whistles and shouting as I ploughed on, afraid to slow down, and once I finally got the wheel out of the groove, I knew I had to get out of there, so I just raced on out of the city without stopping at any red lights.

By now I'd become obsessed with this bike, which must have been prophetically possessed by the spirit of Don Quixote, because it seemed to be doing everything it could to humiliate me. Apart from anything else, it was always running out of petrol – which might not sound like the Putsch's fault, but I can assure you it was. This thing was a demon sent to destroy me – I'd drag it into a garage and the fucking petrol cap wouldn't come off. Once I reached the next youth hostel after Barcelona I just said, 'That's it – this bike must die.'

I went out early in the day and hid it on the cliff top, covered in brush and bamboo. When night fell I got all the guys and girls from the hostel to march up with me for the act of sacrifice, but the infernal machine got the better of me one more time. The petrol cap I'd never been able to loosen had now come undone of its own accord. Most of the fuel had leaked out so the grand explosion I'd planned to impress everyone with was now not going to happen. Luckily there was just enough fuel remaining to get a fire going, so I pushed it off the cliff with just enough aplomb to save face.

What I hadn't reckoned with was that this was an area where a lot of smugglers operated and the Guardia Civil were always on the look-out for their signals. So the minute the bike went up in flames suddenly there were police all over the place. Everyone ran like mad and I remember hiding in a clump of bamboo for over an hour until the coast was clear, then hitching out the next morning having resolved never again to buy a two-wheeled conveyance from a Gibraltarian.

By the time I eventually ran out of money, I was in Paris – living in a freezing cold place on the West Bank for eight francs a night, with no means of financing the return journey across the Atlantic that I found myself increasingly ready to make. Luckily, I managed to persuade René Goscinny (a small man composed largely of concentric circles who was co-creator of the immortal *Asterix the Gaul*), whom I'd met through *Help!*, to find me some work, and he gave me two pages of his magazine *Pilote* to fill up with jokes about snowmen. I sat there and drew until I had enough money for a flight back to New York. Here are the icy fruits of my labours . . .

There's no business like snow business.

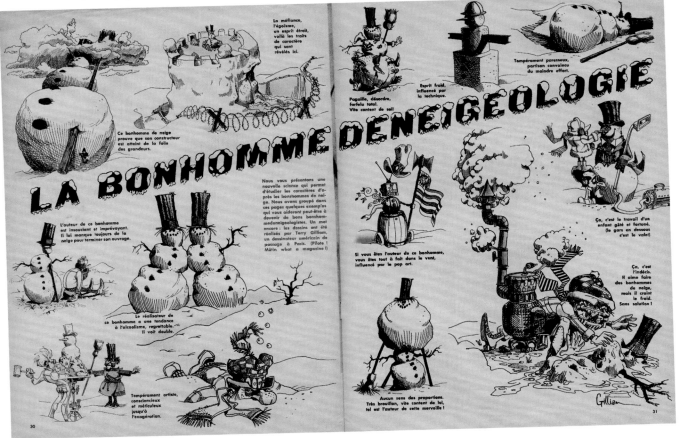

Other people at the agency were trying LSD...

Chapter **6**

There's a Riot Going On

For the first few weeks after I got back from Paris in early 1966, Harvey Kurtzman kindly put me up in his Mount Vernon attic. I think he and his wife Adele were quite intrigued by the little rat's nest I made up there with all the exotic fabrics I'd brought back from my travels in Istanbul and North Africa. I love handmade carpets – there's something about the process of weaving that I find immensely fascinating – and the Islamic tradition whereby they always leave a deliberate flaw in the rug because only God can make something perfect also really speaks to me. I've certainly tried to stay true to that principle in my own work.

Adding to the textural *smörgåsbord* on offer in my temporary home was the Turkish coat of destiny – yet to acquire the painted sun on the back, which would ultimately catch fire in the jealous imaginings of my Monty Python colleagues – and a ratty fox-fur lining for some other garment I'd hauled back with me, which I'd taken to wearing as a stand-alone wrap. By the time my ahead-of-its-time wardrobe of ethnic carpet samples had seen me through the last cold days of winter 1966, I'd confirmed that for me living in New York now fell into the been-there-done-that category.

Looking back, I think my decision to move back out west to LA wasn't so much about heading home as clearing the decks – checking out what America still had to offer me – because I'd been so fascinated by Europe that there was definitely unfinished business for me on the other side of the Atlantic. As it turned out, with my customary *Zelig*-like (or should that be *Forrest Gump*-ish?) subliminal acuity, I'd picked a great time to be moving to the West Coast, although in the end even the noisy counter-cultural climax of 1966–7 would not be enough to drown out London's siren lure.

In the meantime, Hollywood was definitely a factor as far as my going back to Los Angeles was concerned. A girl who'd worked with me throughout the death throes of *Help!* had got married and moved out there to work in films, and she introduced me to the great Ealing director Alexander 'Sandy' Mackendrick, as there was some possibility of me getting an acting job in what turned out to be his final film, *Don't Make Waves*. Somewhat to my shame, the fact that Tony Curtis was going to be in the movie was far more impressive to me than Mackendrick's amazing pedigree as the man who gave us *The Ladykillers* and *Sweet Smell of Success* – it's always been like that with me and directors, the things they've done never connect up as tidily in my mind as an actor's body of work.

Like thousands of other young Americans, I was letting my hair grow longer at the time – prompted, inevitably, by The Beatles. Joanne Crump, a friend from Oxy, had done the honours for me the last time I'd had a trim, using the cover of *Rubber Soul* as a reference. After spending so much of my life with a crew cut – which it turned out was what the role in the film demanded – I, sadly, had to say no to the part to preserve my new-found *à la mode*-ness.

My refusal to make this modest tonsorial sacrifice can probably be taken as an index of my lack of commitment to a possible new career as an actor. But in the increasingly polarised atmosphere of mid-1960s America, small personal decisions such as whether to wear your hair short or long had started to have major ideological significance.

There was a weird line drawn in the sand at around this time – which wasn't just about the length of your hair, but also about the way it was cut – and there was no option but to choose a side. With the Vietnam War on the right and John Lennon on the left, I was never in any doubt about where my loyalties lay. And the sense of security and freedom that I'd enjoyed in Europe (and especially England) rapidly gave way to a high probability of being vilified on the streets of Los Angeles as a harbinger of drug-addled revolution and a betrayer of American values.

Luckily for me, it turned out that if you moved in the right circles, having hair like a girl's could actually enhance your employment prospects, as well as throttling your nascent career as a matinée idol while it was still in its foetal stage. On first moving to LA, I'd done bits and bobs of freelance artwork – carrying on cartooning for various magazines, while working on an illustrated book called *The Cocktail People* with my friend Joel Siegel. Then, when Joel got a job at a big advertising agency called Carson/Roberts, he took me in with him for an interview. There was a creative executive, Ken Sullet, there who'd worked with the great parodist Stan Freberg on his ground-breaking early sixties comedy album *The United States of America, Vol. 1*, so that really impressed me. The good vibrations were mutual. It turned out they had a vacancy for a token long-hair – as so many American media companies did at the time – and I fitted the bill nicely, so they hired me as Joel's visual accompanist.

I'd not been back on the West Coast long before I found myself that little house on stilts up in Laurel Canyon – an address which had yet to become the shorthand for gracious rock-star living that Joni Mitchell *et al* would turn it into. At this stage it was just a little place in the hills where a bunch of hippies hung out – the closest you could get to living in the country while still being effectively in the middle of LA. It was great up there, though. You'd walk outside in the morning and the air would be lovely and clear. Then you'd look down the road and there would be some girl in a white shift, dancing in the dew, and you'd think, 'Fuck! This is magical – Camelot may be dead, but the faerie kingdom lives on.'

That wasn't the only echo of the past that would be my future. I also attended the first Renaissance Fair, where people were wearing crushed velvet and mead was being drunk and it was all very medieval (basically it was *Jabberwocky* waiting to happen). Obviously mead was not the only mind-expanding substance that was freely available in the LA of 1966–7. I once picked up this beautiful girl hitch-hiking, who I impulsively decided to stay with in Laurel Canyon for a while. She turned out to be a complete acid-freak – when I asked her why she was looking so intently off to one side, she just said, 'Oh, that tree flew away.'

I used this sign to mark out my own bit of territory at Carson/Roberts – not only was this strategy more civilised than the way a wolf would do it, it also allowed me to demonstrate the very au fait-ness with 1960s popular culture that had made me such a shrewd appointment.

Other people at the agency were trying LSD,

and a lot of them seemed to be having really bad trips and getting quite seriously fucked up, so I decided to give it a miss. I think being a few years older than many of those around me (most of whom seemed to be in their early twenties) probably helped keep me on the relatively straight and narrow (or as close as my mind has ever got to that).

I'd always been quite good at resisting peer pressure, and this propensity would serve me just as well once I was on the receiving end of the blandishments of Hollywood as it did during my (relatively) abstemious 1960s. These two strands of self-disciplinary DNA had in fact been woven together as early as my teenage years, when I would shock high school classmates with my disdain for drive-ins. There are plenty of places you can drive the car to if you want to make out . . . if you're going to watch a film, then watch the film. (I know what you're thinking: 'What were those crazy Presbyterians thinking, giving this guy a missionary scholarship?')

Mrs. T. Gilliam, a chronic dieter, hasn't had a slice of pie since 1961. Good news, Mrs. Gilliam. Now Tillie Lewis has Low-Calorie pie fillings.

Mrs. Gilliam?

Cars have always been synonymous with freedom in America – environmental consequences notwithstanding – and a steady income from Carson/Roberts enabled me to channel my burgeoning Anglophilia into the purchase of a secondhand Hillman Minx convertible. It wasn't long before the opportunity arose to give vent to that Anglophilia in a less mechanical context. While working at the agency, I kept hearing about this Cambridge-educated English journalist called Glenys Roberts, who was kind of legendary for being hot and smart. One weekend, my friend Chuck Alverson and his buddy from the *Wall Street Journal* asked me to join them on a trip to Tijuana, where Chuck was doing a piece on bull-fighting, and it didn't take long after the latter's girlfriend joined us for me to realise that she was the woman I'd been hearing about.

This was a trip that was full of signs and portents. First off, one of the bull-fighters was the legendary El Cordobés, a man to whom I'd been told by many people I bore a striking resemblance. My European travels had taken me to Granada on a weekend he was fighting there, and I was constantly being stopped in the streets by people who thought I was him. Now I'd finally caught up with the great man in Tijuana, he certainly wasn't a disappointment. At one point, a bull leapt the barrier the *toreros* hide behind and somehow got stuck upside down. No one seemed to be able to shift it until El Cordobés leapt in, grabbed the bull by the tail (rather than the horns) and somehow hoisted it out.

Later on, in another fight, one of the picadors' horses got its guts ripped out

I think this one was Joel's idea.

El Cordobés
—can't
see the
likeness
myself.

and someone had to run over with a bit of corrugated cardboard to cover the mess. Then the mules who were there to pull the dead bull out of the ring refused to go through the gates. It was all getting increasingly strange and gruesome, as a dark and portentous cloud seem to hover lower and lower over the bullring, and everyone seemed to be going slightly mad. All the while I was sitting next to Glenys, clutching her closer and closer. Perhaps she was subliminally seduced by my alleged resemblance to the star of the show (El Cordobés, not the bull), but whatever the reason, in the course of that bullfight, the man from the *Wall Street Journal* was effectively usurped . . . not immediately, but with fairly instantaneous effect.

Within a month or so, she had moved in with me in Laurel Canyon, forcing out my room-mate, Mike Drazen. Glenys had previously had a fling with Danny Kaye, so she already knew of my friend Dena. It's funny how certain names keep cropping up at different stages of your life for apparently random reasons. Our next-door neighbours in Laurel Canyon were my old Woody Allen facilitator Judy Henske and her husband Jerry Yester (who was in a band called The Association and had once been asked to be in The Monkees). Across the way lived the charming and erudite Derek Taylor, who was the PR man for The Beatles, and later became a great friend of mine when I was working with George Harrison at HandMade Films.

My first desk, which was positioned in an aisle at Carson/Roberts, had just been vacated by Gayle Hunnicutt, a Texan beauty who quickly became a well-known actress, eventually marrying David Hemmings, moving to England, kids, divorce, marriage to columnist supreme Simon Jenkins, and then . . . And then . . .

All of which probably makes me look like a chronic name-dropper, but I never deliberately sought anyone out for that reason. It was just a matter of the people you bumped into along the way and ended up getting on well with. It was the same with places – I never thought, 'It's all happening in New York/ LA/London . . . I should go', there was always a specific reason for me to need to be wherever I was, and it was only then that good luck kicked in.

One of the most exciting aspects of that time was that no one really seemed to know who anyone was going to end up being, let alone where the next happening destination was to be found. Accompanying Glenys on journalistic assignments as a semi-official press photographer, I found myself in all sorts of interesting situations.

I remember one piece she wrote for *Los Angeles* magazine about all the artists and musicians living in the various LA canyons – 'When the surly smog lies low over . . . Los Angeles, the canyon dwellers stay at home and smile.' In retrospect, it might have been in our best interests as local residents to keep quiet about that, but either way, one of the canyon dwellers I was commissioned to photograph was a charming hirsute provocateur called Frank Zappa, whose wife and kids I later got to know quite well, after Frank's sadly premature death.

Not all my chance meetings of that era went quite so smoothly. One of the biggest accounts Carson/Roberts worked on was the toy makers Mattel, and I was deputised to deal with Kenny Handler – the son of the owners of the company, upon whom the original Ken doll was modelled (his sister Barbara was the template for Barbie). I'd been a little surprised to be asked round to the house in the evening to discuss whatever project he had in mind, but when he informed me that his wife was 'out for the evening', he did so in such a way as to leave me in no doubt that Carson/Roberts had stitched me up – I was to be the token sacrifice.

For some reason Glenys and I turned up at the studio round the corner from Sunset Boulevard just as Frank and his Mothers needed some extra voices for a party sequence, so we ended up being on <u>Freak Out!</u> and <u>Absolutely Free</u>.

I was often told that I had a certain appeal for those who were 'batting for the other side', and to be honest I didn't really know how to deal with it. The first stirrings of gay pride might have been being felt in San Francisco and New York by that time, but homosexuality was still seen – by me, if not by everyone – as quite an alien and threatening phenomenon. I realise that must seem a bit naive for a man on the cusp of his late twenties, but I think I'd probably lived a rather more sheltered life than I liked to admit. People would talk about

jerking each other off when they were growing up as if that was something everyone did, but I would have no such memories to contribute to the group discussion. And even on the odd occasion when participation in heterosexual orgies had been arranged, my timid participation had been far from that of the fearless libertine I fondly fancied myself to be.

Kenny was subject to no such inhibitions. At the time, he was using the family fortune to try to build himself a cutting-edge impresario persona – based on the rather more illustrious examples of Brian Epstein and Andrew Loog Oldham – and he gaily regaled me with tales of how he, the Handler, handled his various dubious musical protegés. I remember there was one band called The Oranges of Hieronymus Bosch, who were inexplicably failing to make it until Kenny told them to go out onstage wearing no underwear. From that point on, their household-name status was assured. Still more memorably, the Ken doll went on to become the popular gay icon it still is today.

I had a fair number of wild schemes of my own

at this time, which failed to quite get off the ground, including a sequence of still-born illustrated book projects for the publishers of *The Cocktail People* (which made Joel and me all of $12, each!), an unfeasible nightclub venture, and perhaps most ignominious of all, a children's TV show called *WC Clown*. This was a joint advance on what we vainly hoped might be the soft underbelly of children's TV by Siegel, myself and our mutual friend Irv Sepkowitz (who did eventually become a successful TV executive, helping negotiate Larry Hagman's contract to stay on in *Dallas* after the 'Who Shot J R?' cliff-hanger), built around a character shamelessly based on the great W C Fields.

In our pitch document, we cockily took down what we perceived to be one of our main rivals by asking, 'Who needs *Sesame Street*?' The answer to that question turned out to be 'everyone does'. I never mentioned this to Jim Henson when we became friends in England, years later. He reciprocally neglected to inform me that he was a Christian Scientist. He'd probably still be with us if he hadn't been, because he didn't get down to the hospital when he should've because his faith forbade it.

New showbiz gods were coming along at an amazing rate at this point in history, although music was as yet far ahead of film as a harbinger of the flower-power *zeitgeist* – I still had to get myself a second-hand tux from somewhere down on Melrose Avenue in order to attend my first Academy Awards as a photographer with Glenys representing the *London Evening Standard* (it was an old 1930s one in which I did look pretty snappy, though I say so myself). The dress code would be very different for the Monterey Pop Festival, which my Laurel Canyon neighbour Derek Taylor helped organise in the summer of 1967.

The first great outdoor rock festival had all of the good things you'd expect of such a momentous event and very few of the negative associations of mud and murder which would later accrue (respectively) to Woodstock and Altamont. I definitely picked the right one of those three gigs to have a photographer's pass for. Two of my most vivid memories of Monterey are of seeing Tiny Tim drifting around ethereally and of being stunned by the sheer androgynous decadence of Brian Jones and Nico, who were parked in the VIP section in matching antique lace. For a fabric enthusiast like myself, the impact made by that glamorous and diversely doomed pairing was probably as much of a revelation as any of the amazing music I heard that weekend.

Monterey Pop stars – Jimi Hendrix, Ravi Shankar, The Monkees' Micky Dolenz and Big Brother & The Holding Company with an as-yet unsigned Janis Joplin.

If the crowd is going one way, my instincts have always tended to be to go in the other, but as far as the rapidly coalescing sixties counter-culture was concerned, I wasn't so much going in the opposite direction as standing still while everyone else moved. In the increasingly self-satisfied aftermath of Monterey, I did start to wonder if some people were maybe losing the impulse to think for themselves a bit, and just being swept along by the wave.

On the one hand, I was thrilled by the ensuing chaos – it was fantastic to see all the changes that were happening and the way society was opening up. On the other, in any kind of situation which is in a state of flux, there will always be those who are taking full advantage, whatever form such predation might take – from drug-dealing to more legal but no less pernicious forms of exploitation – so that you suddenly get that feeling, 'Uh-oh, this is different now, and I'm not sure I like it any more.'

What was making me crazy

was the way every new idea that appeared would be instantly picked up by Madison Avenue – or Carson/Roberts, or anyone else thinking, 'We could sell something with that' – and turned into an ad. Who was the evil genius doing this? Why, there he was in the mirror.

In my own defence, I was as caught up as everyone else in the innocent euphoria of the times. So if there was a lot of confusion and disappointment involved when I started to suspect that everything was being compromised, it wasn't so much the naming of the animals that was the problem as the misuse of those names once we'd come up with them. Like when that ultimate symbol of automotive radicalism the 'Dodge Rebellion' was first unveiled – 'OK, be wild, but be it in a Dodge.'

Suddenly everything was being commodified, and once an act has to have a particular object attached to validate it, then it isn't the same act any more. I think what it ultimately comes down to is not being able to be sure of the line between what you're really experiencing and what has been programmed into you. These days I'd call this a 'Philip K Dick moment', but at that point I had yet to read any of the visionary books Dick was churning out at an astonishing

Even the Daguerrotype guys were doing selfies.

pace just up the California coast in San Francisco. As it was, I'd just be walking along the beach in Venice or Santa Monica – hand in hand with the woman I loved, the waves lapping and gulls crying – not being sure if this seemed wonderful because it actually was wonderful, or because I had seen so many ads that said it was.

Working in the advertising industry is not conducive to the survival of idealism – with regard to advertising itself, as much as life in general. There was one huge campaign we did for a brand of split-pea soup, which Joel and I had a lot of fun with and put a great deal of creative energy into. 'Save our Soup' – that was one of the slogans. Unfortunately the whole campaign was a complete disaster, because the company had failed to get the soup onto the shelves of the supermarkets in the areas where the ads were running – it was like screening a trailer for a film that never actually came out.

If you are unable to control the urge to add water to Andersen Soup – Call this number immediately!

000-0000

One call may save your soup!

You see, Andersen Soup was not meant to have water added.

Unlike ordinary soups, Andersen is simply made as thick and rich and delicious as the Andersen Soup Guys know how.

And they know good soup.

Then it's sold to you. It's perfect the way you buy it. So, control yourself.

Fight the Dread Water Urge!

Remember, you're not alone in your fight. There's Water Anonymous to help you. There to talk you out of adding water and destroying Andersen's delicious perfection.

The gimmick was that you didn't have to add water to it, and we did some very funny radio commercials where people were calling up as if to Alcoholics Anonymous admitting they couldn't stop sneaking down in the middle of the night to do just that.

Another Carson/Roberts account I worked on, which put down useful markers for future trauma, was Universal Films. There's nothing in the *Cahiers du Cinéma* about making ads for cheesy exploitation flicks being perfect training for the budding *auteur*, but it certainly worked out that way for me. Apart from encouraging you to break other people's films down to their constituent parts in your mind, it also teaches you not to be too precious. I remember Joel and I being very pleased with a tag line we came up with for

I couldn't find Madigan, but King's Pirate and The Perils of Pauline occupy a similarly illustrious place in the cinematic pantheon.

a Don Siegel (no relation) cop drama called *Madigan* – 'Once he was happy . . . now he's *Madigan*' – and that was one of our good ones!

By the end of a year or so at Carson/Roberts, my standards were slipping. I'd arrive late in the morning – maybe 11-ish – then go out for lunch at 12.30, and not come back for a full three hours. In short, my inner malingerer was stirring into slothful life – it was just like being in the army, but without having to draw charcoal portraits of my boss's fiancée – and it became a race to see which would come first: me quitting or being sacked. While the judges were still waiting to call that photo-finish, a sequence of three interlocking incidents was initiated that would irrevocably change my relationship with the land of my birth. America, the country I'd called home for the first twenty-seven years of my life, was about to become somewhere I visited rather than lived.

The first heartbreaker was the end of my love affair with Disneyland. The beginning of the big break-up was when they closed down Tom Sawyer's

Island after dusk, which had been unchaperoned with caves that were open at night, where people used to have a much more interesting time at night than perhaps they were meant to. But the clincher was when Glenys and I went to Anaheim on a press trip to check out the new ride they'd just opened. Somewhat resonantly in terms of later relationships in the film business, the name of that ride was *The Pirates of the Caribbean*. My disillusionment with Disney bound together for all eternity with Johnny Depp's lapse into big-budget self-parody – *Boom!* How the circles close!

We were there with another couple who were covering the story for *Newsweek*, and the four of us were dapper young professionals who couldn't have been any more legit had we been there on the express orders of Richard Nixon himself. But when we arrived at the special place where the special people enter, we were told that the head of security would have to come down and vet my hair, because the guy on the gate who looked like an FBI agent had put in an alarm call.

As I waited, seething, at the gate, I became aware – for the very first time – of the barbed wire around the entrance. Of course it had always been there, but you didn't see it when you came in with the normal people, and such was the bliss that place prompted in me that my imagination would have probably vaulted the barbed wire even if I had noticed it. It was only on the privileged fringes that the subliminal Auschwitzness of the place started to become apparent, especially when we were informed that we weren't going to be allowed in because 'the company has a grooming policy'. Apparently it was in place for our own protection – to stop the ugly short-haired deformed people inside from attacking us (or words to that effect).

The idea for *Brazil* was born out of several different moments

of extreme alienation (it was a breech birth) and this was definitely one of them. Another was the Century City police riot of July 1967 – a lesser-known but similarly brutal foretaste of what was to come at the Chicago Democratic Convention of 1968 and on the campus of Kent State University, two years later.

Century City was the old backlot of 20th Century Fox and, apart from the Plaza Hotel and what was left of the studios, it was basically wasteland. But LBJ was on his way and the demonstration was in full swing by the time Glenys and I stopped off there, donning our newshound hats on the way to a party. Helicopters were circling ominously overhead, there were snipers all along

the roof, it was just the right atmosphere for an anti-war demonstration. As usual, the police had been primed to expect commies, drug addicts and sexual degenerates, but the crowd was actually very sedate ... there was the odd hippie accoutrement, but it was mostly just respectable people, expressing their opinion about a war that was spiralling out of control.

The hardy souls on the front line were handing flowers to the cops, and then a group of them sat down and starting singing, 'We shall not, we shall not be moved ...' That was the only signal the police needed to activate their battle-plan. All these cops on Harley Davidsons just drove straight into the crowd, paving the way for another phalanx of whatever the cop equivalent of infantry is, who just charged in from behind the flower-bedecked front line, laying about them on all sides. It happened so quickly that all I remember was being hoisted by the hair and smashed down on the ground.

Everyone's trying to run and suddenly you're in the middle of this maelstrom of bodies and shouts and screams. The helicopters are coming even lower to intimidate everyone with their *whump-whump-whump* noise, and when you look in the eyes of the cops, you can see they're so hyped up they're just crazed.

Luckily, Glenys and I managed to scramble back up on to our feet and get the hell out of there, more or less unscathed and miraculously in time for the party. I remember us seeing ourselves on the TV later on, because the ginger-haired girl who'd been standing next to me was being pulled out of the *mêlée* on the news. But this does seem a little bit convenient, and my memory – like most people's – has a tendency to tidy up around the edges of a story and smooth the occasional transition, so let's say that whether this actually happened or not, it is *narratively* true.

Either way, the media reporting of this event was even less reliable than my memory of it. For the whole of the next week the *Los Angeles Times* was full of bullshit about this serious disorder that had been deliberately started by left-wing agitators. But people were out on the streets selling the *Free Press* – which Michael Douglas was one of the backers of – telling a completely differ-ent (and much truer) story, about how the demonstrators were lawyers, doctors and teachers who had been subjected to a systematic assault by the very people who were paid to protect them.

My small contribution to the public debate was this poster of a notorious incident where a disabled man had been mistreated by the police during the riot.

By the end of the week, the *LA Times* journalists were all in revolt and it was one of those rare occasions when the truth wins out because people at the top realise how bad their bullshit is making them look. That weekend, the full story of the police riot was finally allowed to come out, and it did feel like, 'Yes, you can change the world – something was wrong here, and now people's determination to make it right has actually triumphed.' Enthused by my participation in this victory for the forces of truth and justice, I decided to leave the country more or less immediately.

The sheer hypocritical stupidity of the Vietnam War – and the frustration of experiencing this wonderful new world of freedom at the exact moment that our political system was marching blindly down this other path – was driving me nuts, and Glenys was homesick and wanted to get back to London. So she and I got in a car with Harry Shearer (later to be well known as Spinal Tap's Derek Smalls and the voice of *The Simpsons*' Mr Burns, but at that point just a buddy of mine, as one of Joel Siegel's fellow alumni of the UCLA humour magazine) and drove east to get a flight out of New York.

If I'd needed any more evidence – which I didn't – of the increasingly divided and inhospitable nature of the country we were planning to leave, that car journey would provide it. We opted to take a northerly route so as to visit the Expo 67 in Montreal on the way. And during a brief stop-off in one of those motel towns in Wyoming or Montana, we went into the drugstore to buy something, and suddenly it was, 'Uh-oh, the long-hairs have arrived.' The moon-faced, in-bred ones didn't like us. It was like a chilly northern version of *Deliverance*, or a less druggy *Easy Rider* – neither of which film had been made yet, so the whole alarming situation was very prophetic, at least in cinematic terms.

An old woman screamed abuse at us in the street for a while, so we took refuge in a café and were trying to have as inconspicuous a meal as possible when a group of menacing-looking guys came in and sat in the booth next to us. After a while, one of them got up and asked, 'Who do you think you are – Jesus? Maybe we ought to

This standard-bearer seemed to have lost track of exactly what he was fighting for.

have Christmas early this year . . .' I think he probably meant to say Easter, but the disruptively long-haired presence of myself and Harry Shearer had caused him to get his Christian commemorations in a twist.

Is it too much to ask you to believe that the song playing on the jukebox at the time was The Beatles' 'All You Need Is Love'? Because that is the way I remember it, and the dates do tally. There was definitely a black couple in another booth smiling at us a little sheepishly, as if to say, 'It was our turn for several hundred years, and now it's yours.'

We got the waitress to call the cops, because it really didn't look like we were going to get out of there any other way. By the time the sheriff and his deputy had arrived and we were giving them the whole 'We're just passing through and don't want no trouble . . .' routine (to which they responded with a less than entirely reassuring, 'We don't see a problem, son'), a hostile crowd was starting to gather outside, and we had to run the gauntlet of a lot of bumping and shoving to get back to our car. After a short chase through the town we eventually got back to the motel, hid the car and piled all the furniture up against all the doors and windows before sneaking out of there at dawn. If America wanted me to stay, she had a funny way of showing it.

...swinging LONDON was paradise on earth

Chapter **7**

London is the Place For Me

Where my first trip to London had been all about savouring an unfamiliar sense of security, coming back there in the August of 1967 was like arriving at a costume ball. People looked *extraordinary* – I didn't understand how they could be affording it, until I went to Biba and saw what good value for money that place was – and the juxtaposition of the flamboyant clothes and hairstyles of the young with the enduring formality of their elders only made the overall effect more striking.

How you dressed at this time sent a very clear message about who you were and what your attitude to life was. My clothing seemed very plain compared to the eccentric opulence of the natives, but I suppose like all island societies the Brits were desperate for novelty to insure them against their own insularity. Either way, for a craver after hierarchical clarity such as myself – 'That's a king, that's a knight, that's a peasant . . .' – swinging London was paradise on earth.

It was also exciting to be free of accountability for all the

destruction America was visiting on the planet. Occasionally someone would try to make me – Jesus-like – responsible for the sins of my people, but they knew I'd abandoned my country for a reason (I had decided I was better as a cartoonist than a bomb-throwing anti-war protester, thereby saving the lives of many rioting American policemen), so they never gave me a hard time for too long. The one person who didn't seem too pleased to see me was Glenys' husband – this was hardly surprising as they weren't quite divorced yet, although it had obviously been some time since they'd been a happy couple.

I was still sending cartoons like this pre-Nietzsche Jesus home to the US to keep myself in bus tickets. I am not yet me!

He was a successful sports journalist who described me, rather unflatteringly, as 'a monosyllabic Minnesota farm-boy' – a verbal barb which I have managed to blunt over the years by repeating it constantly as if I'd thought of it myself. Under the circumstances, I couldn't blame Glenys' soon-to-be ex for taking a dislike to me – to him I was like some GI who'd come over and stolen his woman with a couple of packs of nylons and some chewing gum.

It's fair to say that my entrance into English society was not at the basement level. Glenys knew a lot of people, and they were a smart and well-connected crowd, one of whom let us stay for a while in an apartment they owned in South Kensington. For my first few weeks in England – before I could start to get some work together – I was effectively a kept man.

The first place we rented together was in Ovington Square in Knightsbridge, just a couple of blocks west of Harrods. You walked in off the street, through the main house, and straight into an artist's studio, which was wonderful. The only catch was having to share the place with a large extended family of fleas. We had to get the whole place fumigated, but our tiny squatters were horribly resistant to all the toxic chemicals we could throw at them. The only way to get rid of the fleas was to catch them individually and break their little backs – but then, who hasn't had house guests like that?

I had a bunch of artwork with me and ran around London

knocking on people's doors, showing them my portfolio and saying, 'This is what I do – any chance of giving me a job?' One of the first people I went to see was the animator Bob Godfrey – later best-known for the brilliant children's TV series *Roobarb*, but at this stage he'd caught my eye by making a film about DIY animation. Any form of cartooning was interesting to me – from the primitive flip-books I used to mess around making, to the arty European animations I'd obliged my New York friends to sit through at the Thalia cinema – but I had no clear plan of action to move into that field.

Like Harvey Kurtzman before him, Bob turned me down flat at first. But his studio – which was on Wardour Street in Soho, near where the Marquee Club used to be – was the only place I knew, and when years later I started renting his animation camera, we quickly became firm friends. It was quite a chaotic environment, but – again like Harvey – Bob was a magnet for a lot of talented people.

This was a very exciting time for someone who was interested in animation to be hanging around in Soho. The Dog & Duck was the pub all the top guys used to hang out in (maybe they liked the cartoony name). If you were lucky you might see one or both of the two great British–Canadian animators of the time in there – Richard Williams (the man behind the cartoon sequences in *The Charge of the Light Brigade*, who later ended up doing *Who Framed Roger Rabbit*) and George Dunning (who did The Beatles' *Yellow Submarine*).

The key that opened the door to me masquerading as one of their number was the discovery of the airbrush. Airbrushes had fallen out of favour among illustrators in general and at that stage were most likely to be used for touching-up pictures of vacuum cleaners in sales catalogues, but from the first time I held one in my hands, I knew they were for me. At the risk of trying to present myself as the Chet Baker of the airbrush, it was like being the guy who picks up a trumpet and finds he can play it straight away.

I wasn't working completely in isolation, airbrush-wise – a Miles Davis and a Dave Brubeck of the medium already existed. There was a guy called Bob Grossman who used to do cartoons for the left-wing San Franciscan magazine *Ramparts* – he did really wonderful stuff. Once I'd bought my own I taught myself the rudiments of airbrushing technique by working backwards from pieces I had spotted in various magazines – 'the only way he can have done this is by drawing it, then cutting this out and spraying a bit here and a bit there . . .' – it was pretty scientific stuff.

Alan Aldridge was also famous at that time for his work with The Beatles and others on the London psychedelic scene. He was really good, technically, but there was something about his stuff that wasn't quite to my taste, which was lucky, because it meant I could dismiss him airily – or airbrushily, in this case. At that time, he was thought of as the Great British airbrusher, but his work seemed to go out of circulation for a few years, until his daughter put on a really brilliant exhibition at the Design Museum a few years ago and then everyone saw it afresh.

The greatest virtue of the airbrush is its capacity to give softness to an image, but it has equally well-developed capacity to fuck up irredeemably at the very last moment. You're doing all this beautiful work and then it sputters and you have to clean the head and start again. The other striking contrast is the one between the (in an ideal world) roundness and serenity of the finished painting and the incredibly noisy industrial process that creates it – it's more like working on the Chevrolet assembly line than in the New York Public Library. The brush runs off a generator, so you've constantly got a noise like a small helicopter landing in your ears, and you've got to control the spray very carefully because the slightest mistake and the whole thing will be ruined. It creates quite an unpleasant atmosphere for anyone else who happens to be in the area, but the results can be spectacular so their suffering is more than justified. At least, I always thought it was.

In terms of bread-and-butter employment, I was spreading myself thinly around as many different magazines as possible. Around this time Glenys was made editor of a weekly news magazine called the *Londoner* and briskly informed me, 'Come on, you're the art director.' This wasn't quite as brazenly nepotistic a move as it looks on paper, as she'd been brought in to apply her American experience in the hope of making the magazine a bit punchier and zippier, so having an actual Yank on the staff – especially one with such *Help!*ful experience in the field – kind of made sense.

The office of the *Londoner* was aptly situated in a small square Samuel Pepys once lived in, just off Fleet Street – at that time still in its pomp as the epicentre of British print journalism. We'd get the trusty old Routemaster bus to work, and when you got off it, you really knew you were arriving somewhere. The trucks would be lined up outside the big newspaper offices with their great rolls of paper going in one end, and then the newspapers would come out the other. (OK, I realise I may be simplifying this process slightly, but that's what cartoonists do.)

119

I loved the bustle of it all

– the pubs would be open all night long so the printers could slake their notable thirsts, and there was all this groovy modern stuff happening even as all these remnants of different earlier civilisations piled up around you. The shape of the streets and the scale of the buildings really spoke to me – where New York had been overwhelming, London was much closer to human size.

I would walk into the City

of London at the weekends and wander around in a Dickensian reverie, irrespective of the actual Dickensian significance of the location in which I found myself. Now the streets are crammed all the time, but then the City was a ghost town on Saturdays and Sundays – it felt like the whole place was yours. I'd go across the bridge to the house Christopher Wren lived in when he was building St Paul's (near where the Globe theatre is now) and walk down to Shad Thames, which was still a working docks at that time and not just a bunch of cool little lofts.

The places which are mostly just names now (or relocated miles out of town to grim new spaces between ring roads) – Billingsgate, Covent Garden, Smithfield – were all still vibrant hubs of street life. Floral Street was called that for a reason. And if you were feeling especially cultural and went to the opera, you'd come out picking your way through lorries unloading fruit and veg, and the streets would be jammed solid with hard-working porters.

I realise that to those who are too young to have experienced it for themselves, this costermonger-tinted vision of England's capital might sound like the nostalgic ramblings of a superannuated animator, but the London I live in now is not the place I was so excited to find myself in as 1967 rubbed itself lasciviously up against 1968. From the late sixties even into the seventies, London still functioned like an ancient city. Things were still being made here, there was a properly mixed economy. But then suddenly – and I suspect Margaret Thatcher had a little something to do with it – nobody needed craftsmen or factory-workers any more. It was all service industries with nothing to actually service.

The same thing happened in Paris when Les Halles was demolished. Some developer presents the city council with a neat-looking model made out of cardboard, and all of a sudden the old fluid interplay of the market, the church, the cafés and the whorehouses is overthrown by a new tyranny of straight lines. Just as I willingly forsook my Americanness for an Eton mess of pottage (does anybody actually know what a mess of pottage smells or tastes like? I don't know if I've ever stepped in one), so the great cities of Europe sold their souls for civic redevelopment.

The collateral damage to be incurred in the construction of these new tidied-up urban spaces was beyond the darkest imagining of my blissfully innocent late sixties self, as I savoured the gossipy camaraderie of a time when Fleet Street was Fleet Street and women (and men) were glad of it. In those days everybody knew the people they were competing with – it really was a different world to the glumly diasporic existence of what remains of the British national press today. El Vino's was the place where journalism could really flourish – somebody would overhear a drunken conversation and say, 'Wait, I'm working on a similar story ...'

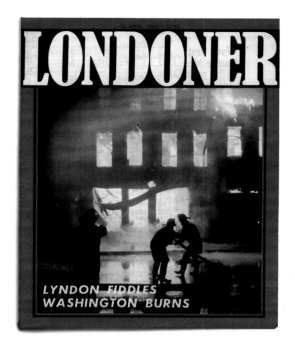

THE LONDONER,
13 April 1968:
The New York Times,
The Times London,
the Angling Times
– We beat 'em all.

In those circumstances, it was much more difficult for politicians to play divide and conquer with the fourth estate. That's why I think the break-up of Fleet Street – a historic event for which again we have Margaret Thatcher to thank, although her Australian friend Rupert was the instigator – has been such a disaster. Everyone is very full of how much more 'connected' everybody is in the digital age, but I'm not fully convinced of the value of that connection. OK, so you can read someone else's article very easily on your laptop, but what was published might only be half of what they know, while the other half that you'll never find out about because you're not getting pissed with them in El Vino's any more might've contained the solution to the problem you'd been trying to crack for weeks.

The discipline of old-school print journalism certainly seemed to agree with me. Under the pressure of the *Londoner*'s weekly turnaround, I found myself gladly breaking off diplomatic relations with my inner malingerer, and instead embracing the protestant work ethic of the endlessly encroaching deadline – a template which would serve me well in the frantic and industrious few years that were to follow. I got a real kick out of the weekly rush on the train to get all the artwork up to Darlington where the magazine was printed, then staying there overnight to pick up the first finished copies, hurry back down to London and distribute them to the conveniently located desks of all the main editors in Fleet Street.

When things worked out well – which they generally did – it felt as if the dramatic political events of the period were flowing through us, like the time the Washington rioters of 1968 were considerate enough to torch America's capital at exactly the right moment for our press deadline, so we managed to get colour photos on the *Londoner*'s front page before anyone else in the world.

My own next personal banner headline would be generated by another unlikely recruit to the realm of hard news. I'd stayed in touch with John Cleese since watching him alarm usually unflappable New York subway travellers with his maverick arm movements, and he'd gone on to work at *Newsweek* magazine for a couple of years before becoming an instantly recognisable satirical fixture on British TV. When I asked him if he could think of anyone in that seemingly impenetrable fortress who might be interested in inviting Gilliam's Trojan horse in for a quick ride around, he suggested a producer called Humphrey Barclay.

The WE HAVE WAYS OF MAKING YOU LAUGH team. Check out my jelly shoes – pretty groovy, I'm sure you'll agree. Michael Palin's wife Helen hated them so much she wouldn't let me in the house with them on.

Just like my other mentors, Messrs Kurtzman and Godfrey (a firm of solicitors you might think twice about entrusting with a complex financial transaction, but boy, could they draw!), Humphrey took a while to see reason. I chased him for a couple of months, leaving messages that were never returned, and in the end I think he picked up the phone by mistake. I talked him into buying a couple of comedy sketches I'd written – which I don't think he was even that keen on – for a subversively grown-up kids' show he was producing called *Do Not Adjust Your Set,* starring some young comic writer/performers named Michael Palin, Terry Jones and Eric Idle. I think Humphrey took pity on me, being an amateur cartoonist who liked what he saw in my portfolio.

As fate would have it, he was also putting together a show
that would prove to be the ideal outlet for my capacity to dash off a rough and ready caricature in double quick time. *We Have Ways of Making You Laugh* was a new TV panel show that – while not destined to foreshadow the longevity later achieved by *Have I Got News for You* – did provide me with a handy leg-up into the world of British small-screen comedy. The idea was that my fellow panelists, among them Eric Idle, Dick Vosburgh, Jenny Handley (daughter of the much loved war-time radio comedian Tommy Handley), Barry Cryer, Katherine Whitehorn, Benny Green and Frank Muir, the host, would say witty and erudite things, while I would finish off a series of caricatures (which I had generally prepared partly in advance, because it is possible to have too much spontaneity). These could then be displayed as the relevant guests entered to (hopefully) unanimous wonderment on the part of viewers and studio audience.

The fact that the show went out live made it quite
a pressurised gig, and by the end of the first episode the adrenaline was really pumping. The audience seemed to have loved it, and we went out on a high with some kind of group song, only to walk off backstage and find out that no one outside the studio had seen the show, because the engineers had gone on strike without telling anyone. Since no copy was ever made, it is possible for me to assert without fear of contradiction that this show was a unique landmark in the history of British comedy. Strangely, the remaining shows in the series – the ones which were actually broadcast – did not attain quite the same exalted standards. But they did feature what would turn out to be the pivotal moment in my entire career.

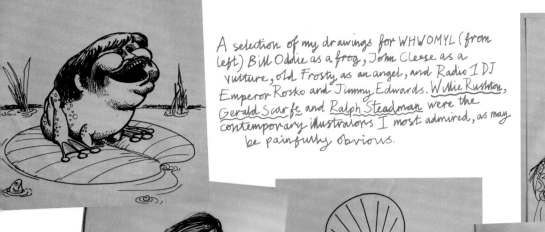

A selection of my drawings for WHWOMYL (from left) Bill Oddie as a frog, John Cleese as a vulture, old Frosty as an angel, and Radio 1 DJ Emperor Rosko and Jimmy Edwards. Willie Rushton, Gerald Scarfe and Ralph Steadman were the contemporary illustrators I most admired, as may be painfully obvious.

People were always coming into the office with half-finished material. So when Dick Vosburgh said he'd spliced together a sequence of Radio 1 DJ Jimmy Young's slightly painful punning links (Radio 1 had only launched the previous year and the asinine patter of its DJs was still considered a bit of a novelty), but didn't know what to do with them, nobody turned a hair when I said I'd like to have a go at turning them into an animation. They probably thought I'd done plenty of that kind of thing in America and was a highly trained operative in the field, rather than the speculative first-timer I actually was.

I was given two weeks to do it – and four hundred quid. So I just got some head shots of Jimmy Young blown up, airbrushed a body on and made him speak by wiggling his mouth. When you're trying something for the first time, you can sometimes achieve a wonderful blend of naivety and pragmatism – not really knowing what the obstacles are enables you to find a way around them by sheer beginner's luck.

Of course I wasn't working completely from scratch. I'd had a fair amount of experience of appropriating visual imagery from various sources while working at first *Help!* and then Carson/Roberts. And the experimental animations I'd sat through at the Thalia cinema in New York had certainly expanded my ideas of what the medium could and should be. Having grown up in the Walt

These rapidly sketched-out storyboards – all that seems to remain of my Jimmy Young cut-out experiment – not only helped establish me in a new career as an 'animator', but also established the methodology for later adventures in live-action film-making.

When I'm doing these little sketches, it's almost like they're writing the film for me: it's not quite automatic drawing, but a line will sometimes jump-start me in an unexpected direction.

Disney orthodoxy of beautiful, ornate, meticulous cell animation, the starkness and even crudity of Borowczyk and Vanderbeek was a punky breath of fresh (or foul – depending on your point of view) air.

Faced with the impossibility of competing with Uncle Walt on his own painstaking and expensive turf, my logical next step was to get as far away from him as possible. But I wasn't going to just slavishly copy the DIY daredevils of the animation avant garde either (or at least not consciously). What I ultimately came up with was a new kind of hybrid that spoke inarticulately to both traditions without the commitment to do either one properly. Of course, I didn't realise this was going to happen when I was working on the Jimmy Young thing – at the time that was just a one-off, a bit of fun.

As soon as my first animation was broadcast, things began to happen very quickly. The reaction (both publicly and professionally) was huge and – in terms of people offering me work – pretty much instantaneous. I wasn't thinking, 'At last, this is my big break.' It was more a question of, 'I seem to have found a way of doing this, so if everyone wants me to, then I might as well.'

First, Eric Idle asked me to do some animations for the second series of *Do Not Adjust Your Set*. That was when I did *Christmas Card*, which was the first time I used Bob Godfrey's camera. I'd come across this incredible collection of Victorian Christmas cards in the basement of the Victoria and Albert Museum, and basically all I did was copy a lot of them, cut them up and put them back together with a lot of jokes and a bit of a story.

Peace at Christmas

The idea of taking images out of their original contexts was at the heart of what I was doing, and the new technique I'd hit on more or less by accident quickly began to generate its own momentum. In the seventeenth century, Puritan iconoclasts used to painstakingly snip out representations of God or the Holy Spirit (which they considered sacrilegious) in pre-Reformation religious artworks. My approach was – you will not be surprised to hear – a good deal more frivolous. I'd find people in serious situations – soldiers in war-time, politicians on the campaign trail – and liberate them by putting them in a dress or making them do something ridiculous.

I'm not sure that I could ever have got started in a world where everything is copyrighted and you've got to pay for all of it.

The more solemn and even humourless the original character, the more potentially funny he or she was. I'd always be laughing if I could find a picture of someone and put them in such an incongruous setting that you'd forget who they actually were. That's how I ended up with formidable 'Rivers of Blood' demagogue Enoch Powell selling 'whiter than white' washing powder in *Beware of the Elephants* – it was the perfect way of bringing the brash commercial language of Carson/Roberts to bear on the political situation in my newly adopted homeland. Harold Wilson also turned up in the same cartoon – these are historical figures who aren't thought about too much now, but I like to think I immortalised them in an appropriately respectful spirit.

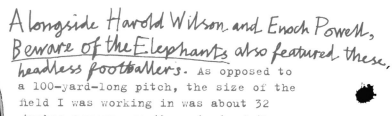

Alongside Harold Wilson and Enoch Powell, *Beware of the Elephants* also featured these, headless footballers. As opposed to a 100-yard-long pitch, the size of the field I was working in was about 32 inches across, so the extent of the physical task involved was to corral and manipulate all these little pieces of paper beneath a 2-foot, 8-inch piece of glass. The essential tools of your trade are tiny pieces of Sellotape folded over themselves to make little circles so they're essentially double-sided, but with the bulk of the stickiness padded off with your fingers first so the adhesive isn't too strong. You want just enough to hold everything in place without so much as to actually stick it. Beyond that, the key to everything is carefully edging round every individual bit of paper in black, because obviously all the pieces you're using are cut-outs, and that little bit of white edge which catches the light beneath the glass will give the game away. That's the one useful thing I've told all the animation students I've ever spoken to – 'Get your marker pen and black out those edges.'

WHITE ON TREES?

The sole-ful street from THE ALBERT EINSTEIN STORY was a blatant instance of cut-and-paste shoe-booting – 'For each piece of footwear, there is an equal and opposite piece of footwear...'

It was also around this time that I started doing some work with Marty Feldman, the break-out star of the BBC's hit satire series *At Last the 1948 Show* (some of the other cast members also went on to do good things, they just needed to find the right collaborators first). On the strength of that, he got first his own BBC show, *It's Marty* – which I did a couple of animations for – and then in 1971 his own big American series for ABC, of which more later.

In the meantime, I had transatlantic concerns of my own to deal with, as the draft threatened to come back to haunt me. With the Vietnam War still stubbornly refusing to be over by Christmas, the army began closing down the European National Guard control groups and sending them back to the States.

Suddenly the epistolary distance-keeping strategy which had worked so well for the last few years no longer seemed to be equal to the task. *Cool Hand Luke* was out in cinemas at the time, and that film ends – spoiler alert – with Paul Newman dying, a tragedy I was very keen to stop befalling me at that time (although by a neat twist of fate, in later life Paul and I would end up going on a number of fiercely enjoyable but potentially life-threatening car and boat rides together).

It was nip and tuck for a while as to whether I'd have to return to America and be shipped off to become cannon fodder, but luckily for me, this crisis point was reached just as I'd begun to make a bit of a name for myself in Britain. So I got myself a lawyer, and we persuaded a series of the people I was working for – from *Nova* magazine to Rediffusion – to write letters to the US army saying that not only was I essential to the well-being of their organisation but also that, if forced to return to the United States, I would instantly become indigent and a burden on American society.

These letters were so persuasive that I ultimately joined the elite ranks (and from what I understand, there were literally five or six of us) of those National Guards lucky enough to earn themselves an honourable discharge from the US armed forces. The fact that I earned this by acting dishonourably pretty much from the beginning is an irony Joseph Heller himself might have appreciated.

My fellow traitors will not fail to notice that by the time I left the army I had progressed to the rank of private first class, not second class – I had really worked my way up through the system.

Chapter 8

Interstellar Overdrive
(Take 6)

**S**o I finally shrugged off the hand of Uncle Sam's press-gang from my collar in the same year I started working with several of the men who were soon to become my co-Pythons. If a divine power had made a New Year's resolution at the start of 1968 to show me the nature of the good fight I was meant to be fighting, she could hardly have done a better job of it.

On the face of it, my new partners in crime would be a respectable bunch – old-fashioned-looking Oxbridge graduates without a tie-dyed acid casualty amongst them. Appearances can be deceiving, but because they were satirists, they weren't necessarily counter-cultural by inclination. The key to the British idea of comedy was people not being afraid to be ridiculous – everything didn't have to have a higher social purpose. The point of the exercise was just to get everyone to laugh at silly things, rather than to pursue any particular political agenda (although to be fair it probably is much harder to waterboard somebody if you have a good sense of humour). But in a weird way, they couldn't afford to dismantle the existing system, because then there'd be nothing left for them to have fun taking the piss out of.

I was less conservative than the others in this regard. They were subversive, but they had that typically sneaky, passive-aggressive British way of undercutting the system – which was much gentler than the blunt American attack I was used to – whereas my messianic delusions ensured that I was quite happy to bring the whole thing crashing down around us. It's possible some of my fellow Pythons-to-be might have been slightly fearful of me as a result, and I – reluctant as I would've been to admit this at the time, or indeed for many years afterwards – was rather intimidated by them.

There was no doubt in either my or their minds as to who was the barbarian at the gates and who were the superior beings. It was their use of language that gave them power over me, especially the ones from Cambridge. They had this really well-honed banter, which I was in awe of. It began with being at university together, and by the time I came into their orbit, they'd had years of writing together in various different combinations to sharpen it up still further. Of course, everything they found funny was within certain bounds and based on particular common references, but I didn't know what those references were, so I'd be blindly banging around and crashing into things, like the proverbial minotaur in the crockery retailer's.

This rapidly became my unique selling point within the group. Because compared to them (they were so incredibly precise in their verbosity), I must have seemed like some kind of force of nature – a creature that hadn't been neutered by language. I could come in with a big hammer and smash everything up – being the son of a carpenter, I'd hammer in the morning and hammer in the evening – and with so many egos and superegos around, they had a vacancy for an id.

Some of the violence in my Monty Python animations would come from my frustration at not being able to express myself as clearly as everyone else, and some of it evolved naturally from the limitations of the technique itself. But before those two forces could start to pull me in the same direction – as I strove to unify the verbalisation of my lack of verbosity with the visual articulation of my technical inarticulacy – there were a few uncomfortable social preliminaries to be got through.

If you want chapter and verse on the hour and day everything happened, you'd probably be better off reading Michael Palin's diaries. But Eric Idle has ascribed the motivation of 'sexual jealousy' to those of his fellow Englishmen who gave me a slightly frosty reception at first, and while it would be immodest of me to agree with him in public, by the time of our early meetings, I had certainly learned to make my transatlantic otherness work for me more successfully than I was doing on my initial arrival in the UK.

Pachyderms – shock-troops of the unconscious.

In the many accounts of these formative encounters that clog up the voluminous Python chronicles, my Turkish suede coat – on the back of which I had by now painted a large sun (shame to waste a canvas of that grandeur) – does seem to get more than its fair share of attention. And I was still with Glenys at the time, who I think some of my soon-to-be colleagues were quite impressed by. But like any self-respecting mould or lichen, I took a little longer to grow on them.

Eric is the one of us who has always been the most drawn to the new and the exotic and the flamboyant, so he was my buddy right from the off, but Terry Jones and Michael Palin – those two little Oxfordians in the corner with their nasty rodental faces – took a bit more convincing. Now, forty-five years later,

Mike, Terry J. and I all live within five minutes of each other, so I must have made some progress in the intervening decades, and to be fair it was actually Terry J. who established the initial template for my contribution to the group that eventually became Monty Python.

The main creative dilemma we were grappling with was how to bring together all the different material we were planning to write without succumbing to the alternate tyrannies of either constructing a linear narrative or having to hobble each sketch with a traditional ending. Terry had very much liked the 'stream of consciousness' element in *Beware of the Elephants*, when it went out as part of the second series of *Do Not Adjust Your Set*, and argued very strongly that the show (which was soon to be christened as below) should have the same free-form feel.

Honeycomb and box collage from *Monty Python's Flying Circus* series 4 opening titles – as you build up the different layers, you can start to get shadows. Sometimes you have to prop up particular pieces of paper with tissue, so that when you squish them all down, hopefully all the shadows will have gone.

The collective decision to pursue this goal by using my animations as links between the sketches was one that would have happy consequences for all of us. The others were liberated from the dominion of the conventional punchline, while I was given a specific task, which was at once thrillingly clearly defined and infinitely variable. I would be given a series of specific starting and ending points, and everything in-between would be up to me.

This arrangement suited me for a number of reasons. First, because nothing sets you (or at least me) free creatively like having a set of limitations to explore. Second, because my mind tends to work really well that way – making the kind of big connective leaps where this triggers that off, and then that goes there – whereas if I've got too much choice then I'm lost, because I want to

Max Bygraves' 'You Need Hands' had long been the cut-out animator's anthem.

explore all the possible options at once. Third, and perhaps most importantly, the fact that I essentially worked on my own helped define my role within the group as an outsider with a specific contribution to make.

The meetings where we got together to discuss which

material should and shouldn't be used were – necessarily, but perhaps more so due to the nature of the personalities involved – very strategic affairs. The factions within the group weren't set in stone, but would dissolve and reconstitute along a series of different fault lines – Oxford (and Occidental, the Os often stuck together) against Cambridge, the *Do Not Adjust Your Set* veterans versus the rest, people whose names were Terry standing up bravely against people whose names weren't Terry – according to the issue in hand. Luckily for me, given first my spectacular lack of aptitude for power-play of this type, and second my complete inability to present my ideas verbally, the fact that I was responsible for the only section of the show into which no one else had any direct input excused me from most of the political in-fighting.

My fellow Pythons used to be quite tactical, both in terms of their own contributions and their responses to those of others, for instance not starting with the material that was dearest to them, and/or allotting their laughter as much as a reflection of current alliances as the virtues of the material itself. Because I lacked the need for such manoeuvrings, I actually became quite useful to the group as the genuine laugher – like a comedy-writing version of the mystery shopper. If I thought it was funny, then the chances were it actually was, because I had nothing to gain by taking sides.

Eric's theory – which I think is a good one – is that we were all slightly mad in different ways, and as a consequence we added up to a single effectively mad personality, which operated in a strangely functional way. I think there was certainly a good work ethic established right from the off, and the fact that each of us had done the odd thing that the others respected helped band us together. There was also a lucky chemical balance between me bringing a bit of fresh brashness and brutality to people who, while not exactly old lags, had certainly done their time in the satirical trenches with David Frost.

The great thing about making the first and second series was the necessity to just churn stuff out. With success and the extra resources that brings, you can second-guess yourself to death, but when you simply have to produce 30 minutes of material

The solo photo (left) was taken so I could be grafted onto early Python PR pictures, which always tended to get taken while the others were rehearsing somewhere, and I was stuck at home working on the animations. At first I got a bit pissed off seeing all these publicity photos with only five people in them – note my ill-suppressed howl of delight at a rare moment of inclusion (above) – but ultimately I realised that the lack of visual images of the American interloper only added to my mystique. In terms of my being a cut-out animator, I suppose title dictated presentation.

in double-quick time, that really frees you up. For instance, if you've ever wondered why all the characters in those animations tend to hop everywhere, that's because it's much quicker and easier to do than making them walk or run.

One of the fundamental appeals of animation is that the restrictions of everyday mortality do not apply. People can be squished and stomped, and still bounce back up – like in Tex Avery cartoons. It's almost a glimpse of eternal life. We're free from the limitations of what God made, and in terms of the world I'm working in, I actually become God.

There's a famous early animation from the 1920s called *Out of the Inkwell* by the Fleischer brothers, which I stole a lot from. The animator draws a clown, but it's like the sorcerer's apprentice in that the character escapes his control and takes on a life of its own. People knowing how much that cartoon meant to me might assume I identified with the animator, but I actually wanted to be the cartoon. And so my schizophrenic life began . . .

That demolition of the fourth wall is essentially what happened when I was doing the Python animations. I'd be throwing all-nighter after all-nighter to get the work done, and at some point in the early hours of the morning, the story would just start making itself. One object would suddenly find itself juxtaposed

If you want to kick down the doors of perception you need a BRONZINO foot.

with another one in a relationship that immediately made sense of something else, even though I didn't necessarily quite know what.

When that euphoria kicks in, I'm like a junkie. It's great, and it's flowing and where does this stuff come from? Wow. I'm riding the tiger – let's *go*! A lot of it is about trying to block out the more sensible part of my brain – the controlling part that tries to be rational, that tries to explain. This is a place artists have sought to travel to by many different means. It doesn't really matter how you get there – from straightforwardly blotting out the super-ego (who is the last caped crusader you want on the scene when you've got a deadline to meet), to the various mind-games of the unconscious, which the surrealists pioneered – but I never bothered with any of that stuff: I always found exhaustion worked best for me.

This 'Man-Bird' image from the late 1970s could just as easily come from ten years before, which testifies to how little room for creative evolution my cut-out technique allowed me (or threatened me with).

Lack of sleep, lack of time, lack of money and lack of talent – these are the key contributory factors which collude together to define the *oeuvre*. And the same methodology would ultimately carry me on into film-making. When things are really coming together (as opposed to falling apart) on a movie set, I actually feel like the waves of some kind of ocean are carrying us where we need to go, and I'm just the guy holding on to the tiller.

Obviously the idea that one's actions are being directed by some kind of invisible external force can be a dangerous one to give in to. ('That's why I had to kill and mutilate all those nuns, because the voices told me to . . . it can't have been me because I'm a really nice guy.') But I suppose that's what being an artist is really: a kind of controlled madness. That's why we're allowed to wander the streets doing the shit that we do.

There was a fair amount of wandering the streets involved in my Pythonian endeavours. While the others would be shut up in rooms together writing, rehearsing or filming, I'd be off truffling out images to take to a place called Atlas Photography just off Regent Street. I'd go roaring in there at night with old engravings from Dover art books all earmarked with little markings and

dimensions, then they'd blow them up as required for me.

It didn't matter where the pictures came from – obviously it helped if they were out of copyright, but it wasn't necessary to think too strictly in those terms, so if I found myself a wonderful face in a Richard Avedon book, I would just think, 'I'll have that.' My karmic pay-back for this carelessness with the copyright of others would come a few years later when Atlas shut up shop. All the negatives of the photos I'd had taken were stored there, and someone threw out the whole lot without telling me. Not since the fabled destruction by fire of the Great Library of Alexandria has there been such a loss to humanity.

In the meantime, I totally enjoyed that whole hunter–gatherer aspect. The *Flying Circus* was my passport into the BBC, which was a wonderful institution to have the run of at that time,

There was a wonderful saucy innocence about those Victorian babes, which was like an antique porn version of the whole McGill postcard NO SEX PLEASE, WE'RE BRITISH thing.

because it was having a very free moment (as our presence there probably testified). It still had that old-fashioned structure, which allowed you to just get on with things. The whole bureaucracy of middle managers, which came in with the John Birtisation of the place in the nineties – when everything suddenly had to be accounted for and given a price – would have made a show like *Monty Python* impossible.

If I needed photos or film footage of anything, I could just walk into the Hulton picture library on Marylebone High Street and whatever I wanted was available to me. There was a very serendipitous quality to some of the connections that would randomly crop up. I'd go in looking for First World War vehicles and come out with something . . . completely different.

John Cleese's old *Frost Report* colleague Ronnie Barker's collection of Victorian nudes were also a constant source of pictorial sustenance. Ronnie had appeared on *We Have Ways . . .* once, and I'd been over at his house afterwards, and he said I could use what I wanted. Ronnie himself was a lovely person – there was a maturity about him that was unusual in one so talented – but I think it's possible I tested even his patience slightly by using his nudes all the time. Especially as I probably never thanked him properly. Now he's dead it's probably a bit late, but still, thanks for all the naked women, Ronnie.

Once my stars had made it off the cardboard casting couch, the next stage was to get the locations right. The cinematic parallels here were no less marked than they had been while doing the *fumetti*, except that this time the whole process was completely under my control. I had a special cabinet, which was my equivalent of the scenery dock in the old studios at Shepperton that I'd sneaked into on my first visit to England – where they'd have the Roman wall, next to the Egyptian doorway. It gradually filled up with skies, seas, buildings, rural backdrops, people and animals, all of which I was at liberty to mix and match until I found something I liked. Then it was just a question of cutting them out, colouring them in with felt-tip markers and away we'd go.

The camera-operators I worked with at BBC TV Centre tended to

be young guys who were happy to play around until we'd got everything lit right and my envelopes full of disembodied heads and legs could be marshalled to my satisfaction. The sound effects I'd add later on my own. Another advantage of animation over live action is that the sound doesn't have to be naturalistic – you can make the voices and the effects as grotesque as the imagery. I'd always loved the way that after watching, say, a Chuck Jones cartoon, it would sometimes be the noises rather than the images that would stick in your head. And this was also a great opportunity for me to make my own DIY tribute to the many voices of Jonathan Winters – whose comedy I'd loved as a student at Oxy – as well as the amazing Bob and Ray radio shows which I'd listened to religiously while working for *Help!* in New York.

When putting my head under the blanket wouldn't quite give my voice the right quality, or the kitchen utensils weren't quite cutting it as massive steel girders, I could always call upon the BBC Sound Effects Library and its amazing arsenal of 33-rpm records. You didn't even have to sign them out. It was run on an honour system, where they trusted you to bring everything back, and there were only a couple of guys working in the whole department, so the cost of doing it was much less than the cost of running that BBC department now, what with the endless reams of paperwork and the numbers of paper-pushers needed to push them around. The rest of the Pythons helped out a lot too. Once the show was up and running I'd corner them in a corridor and get them to perform my dialogue into my little tape-recorder, which I could then incorporate into the next batch of animations.

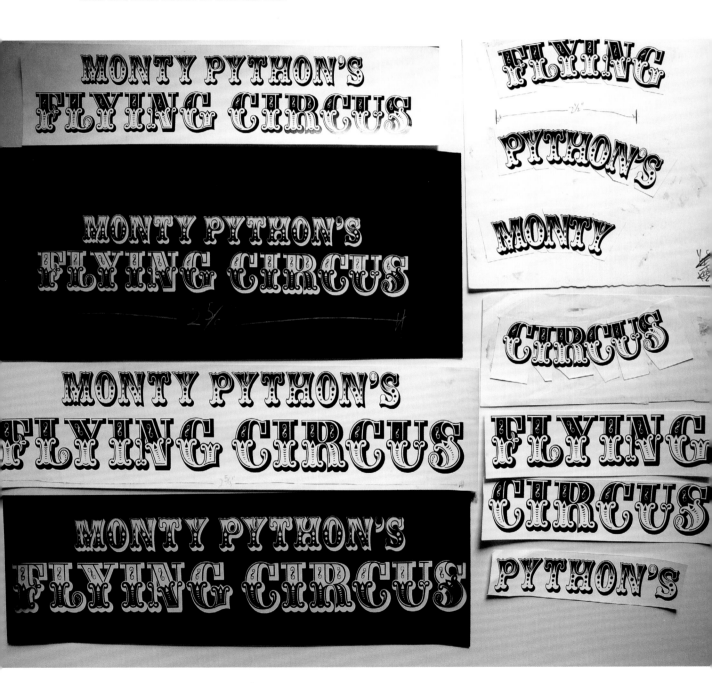

Carnivalesque lettering.

It was very exciting to be part of a group and see something we were working on gradually coming together – especially for me, because the other five had all known each other previously, whereas I was the foreigner who'd come all this way to suddenly be in this place where people actually got what I did. I was happy to be the butt of their jokes about my linguistic infelicities, on the understanding that we seemed to share the same comedic world-view. Whether this was actually true or not, I felt it was, and nothing gives you confidence like the feeling that you've found your audience.

This feeling of euphoria was magnified once I got to see people actually watching my animations. Shooting the debut series of *Monty Python's Flying Circus* had inevitably been quite a fragmented and uncertain business. Even by the time we got to the first recording at BBC TV Centre at the end of August 1969, no one – least of all any of us – quite knew how the whole thing was going to fit together. It was only when the animations came in that you understood the context for much of the other stuff. (Or was it the other way round?) And because a lot of the people on the show had been seen before, but the cartoons were kind of the fresh thing, once the first series started to go out, a lot of the spotlight with regard to what was new and exciting about it seemed to fall on me.

George Melly wrote a wonderful piece comparing me to Max Ernst – thank you very much, I'll take it! But by the time I was getting asked on *Late Night Line-Up* with Mike and Terry J. to be interviewed by Joan Bakewell, I was actually starting to panic a bit. I'd never dreamed of scaling such heights, and I just thought 'I've got to get my feet back on the ground', so I ran off to Morocco for a couple of weeks, where I was reasonably confident no one would know who I was.

I'd always known I wanted recognition – that monster was never not lurking within – but suddenly I was breathing the rarified air of *Late Night Line-Up*, and this did slightly terrify me. It's much easier not to sell your soul when no one wants to buy it, and I've always been afraid my resolve might weaken if I ever gave it a chance. In fact, that fear has probably been the only thing that's protected me from myself, along with the benevolence of my inability to secure myself a bottomless-pocketed patron . . . my armour is thick.

The danger of becoming a successful person is that you're then supposed to be able to replicate whatever it was which brought you that success. And the requirement to be able to do it again can start to feel like a terrible pressure.

Harry Nilsson might not be the best example of this, but he is someone who I would say had it all – to the extent of almost being a genius – and yet the biography I was reading recently showed him falling into a spiral of drink and drugs that felt like a direct by-product of his achievements. That's why I've worked so hard over the years not to become too consistently successful – because it's safer that way.

When I started cropping up in village idiot roles,

it wasn't so much a conscious decision to bring me into the fold but rather a product of me getting bored. I would work away all night on my own then come in with my cans of film and see everybody else having a good time, so I started putting on whatever costume nobody else wanted to wear and being the knight with the rubber chicken. None of the others knew whether I had any skills as a performer – they hadn't seen my Chekhov, or my green-coloured ogre at the children's theatre – and whereas I always had (and still do have) a tremendous admiration for their gifts as actors, my own ambitions in that area never extended beyond chipping in with the odd peculiar grotesque.

There was a painful time on one of the Python shows where I was given the role of an American dialogue coach. I was just supposed to jump in and say 'No, it's OK' in a very strong American accent, but it kept coming out British. This might seem strange to anyone who's heard me talk recently, but how I spoke then was very different to how I speak now, because the longer I've lived here, the less English I've tended to sound.

In my early years of living in this country, every time I opened my mouth I was expecting people to say, 'Why don't you just go back where you came from?' Not that they actually would, but it was definitely an anxiety that was there in my head. In those circumstances, it was only natural that the process of linguistic osmosis, which always takes place when you spend a lot of time with people, should speed up a bit as far as the other Pythons were concerned.

I'm sure the same thing happened to them when they were at university. They all came from different parts of

Jester's cap and bells, optional; non-speaking roles a speciality; Michael Palin knee attachment, model's own.

143

the country originally, but by the time they left Oxford and Cambridge, Received Pronunciation had all five of them in its grip. Enunciation was the thing I struggled with, whereas the Pythons were incredibly precise in the way they spoke. After a certain amount of time in their company you'd inevitably find yourself (or at least I would) talking a bit more crisply, and next thing you know you're spitting those 't's out really clearly, like you're in *Brief Encounter*. But then when you're not working with them so much any more, your unconscious just says 'Fuck it', and you can revert back to your inner Minnesotan farm-boy.

By the time the Flying Circus was properly up and running, Glenys and I had moved down the route of the number 14 bus from Ovington Square to a flat near Putney Bridge. *Python* was only paying standard BBC money at that stage, but it was already nice to be able to pay the rent. The flat was in a modern block and we were always bumping into Kenny Everett – then a Radio 1 DJ and producer of The Beatles' 1968 Christmas single – who lived on a floor below us. He was a very funny guy, who never complained about the noise as my studio door became the punch-bag for my deadline-related frustrations (eventually there wasn't much more than a hinge left).

It wasn't just my neighbours who were on the up. I'd bought myself a Morris Minor convertible for £35 before Python began, and I upgraded to a Triumph Spitfire when the BBC payments started to roll in. But when Glenys and I split up shortly after *Python* started, she got the Triumph and I got the flat (although she did also come back and take the vacuum cleaner).

The other important possession I got to keep was the Siamese cat that defeats the Killer Cars in the *Python* animation. It was just called 'Cat' – I never asked him his name – but I remember my dad being over from America and holding him up for the photograph I took, '… as he rampages through London'. Siamese cats are really smart – a fine example of the breed. John Cleese had his sibling, so it was kind of a Python-esque dynasty.

Although I didn't see it this way at the time, Glenys and my break-up was the best thing that could have happened to both of us. She ended up marrying – and having a daughter with – Dougie Hayward, tailor to the stars (and alleged inspiration for Michael Caine's Alfie) and working as a feature writer for the *Daily Telegraph* and then the *Mail on Sunday* (where she still writes the occasional article mentioning me in studiedly neutral terms to this day). And I was left footloose and fancy-free at exactly the right moment to meet my wife-to-be Maggie Weston, who was working in the *Monty Python* make-up room – a form of employment a teenage Lon Chaney impersonator like myself had no option but to find irresistibly attractive.

Maggie, my wife, did the make-up on the Python shows and then on all my films up through Munchausen. She is the one of us whose nomination got me into the Academy Award ceremony.

COUPLES

by John Updike from his novel, Couples, to be published in November by André Deutsch at 30s.

John Updike, thirty-eight, and a Harvard graduate in English, draws heavily on his poor childhood in Shillington, Pennsylvania for material for his novels, which include The Centaur and Rabbit Run, and on his two years on the New Yorker for his humour. His sixth novel, Couples, concerns a group of people involved in a black mass of community sex.

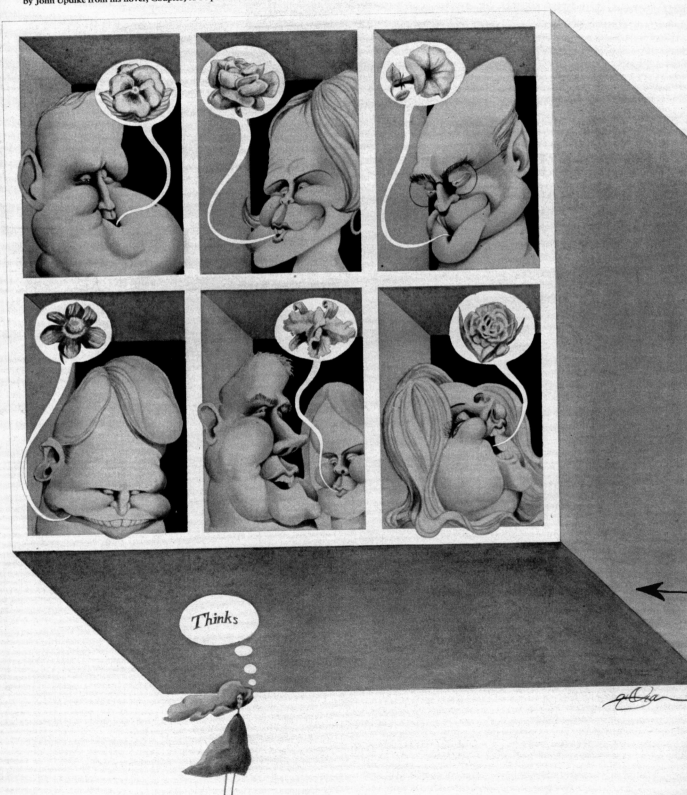

TERRY GILLIAM

What more auspicious location could we have found for some of our early trysts than the very Torquay hotel that ended up being immortalised by John Cleese and his then wife Connie Booth as *Fawlty Towers*? I remember swimming in a hotel pool with Maggie late at night, her willingness to join me for a dip happily unaffected by the despotic proprietor's unwarranted criticism of my table manners. This was definitely a good omen. I'd actually gone to a fortune teller with Connie a few years earlier on my first ever location trip with Python (both being Americans, we had no option but to be pals). Although the self-styled seer was good on our immediate futures (insisting we would be 'heading North' for 'a reason to do with films', which was dead right, as we were soon on a shoot in Bradford), she made no mention of the extent to which our diverse destinies would ultimately be shaped by Devon's rudest hotelier.

This was one of the highlights of my swiftly abandoned career as a magazine illustrator... accompanying a piece by John Updike for the beautifully designed magazine **Nova**. The book was called <u>Couples</u>, so I isolated them all in seperate boxes, with their own flower for company as a tribute to their bitchy but fragrant language.

There was certainly an element of 'us against the world' about MONTY PYTHON on tour.

Chapter

9

Performance

One of the mutual interests that brought Maggie and me together was our love of leather. She'd done a fair amount of work with various kinds of hide – whether making belts or learning to use dyes – and obviously I had my extensive sheepskin coat-painting experiences to share with her, so several of our early dates involved the pursuit of skin, as we made frequent return trips to a really good leather place on Old Street where you could buy animal hides to make things with.

Some time after the second series of *Python* finished – in early 1971 – we went on another escape-from-success trip, this time camping in Greece. I returned home to find a letter from Stanley Kubrick asking me to do an animated title sequence for *A Clockwork Orange*. Unfortunately, he needed it done within a week – a time-frame too constricting even for me – so that didn't happen. A few years later, Kubrick contacted me again when he was preparing *The Shining* to see if I could help him find an art director who would work the way he wanted – i.e. with a catalogue of lintels and door frames from which Stanley could choose, before expecting his lucky employee to have a perfectly realised set drawn in something like fifteen minutes.

Perhaps unsurprisingly – this methodology was just about workable for animations, but would be a much taller order in three dimensions – none of the art directors I approached with Kubrick's proposition wanted to go within a mile of it. I wrote Stanley a postcard saying 'Sorry, I did try . . .', but heard nothing back by way of a thank you. That'd teach me to try and do something for my *Paths of Glory* hero.

One set of titles I did get to do was for Samuel Z. Arkoff's CRY OF THE BANSHEE with Vincent Price.

The film looked sumptuous but was actually made very cheaply by recycling all the costumes from *Anne of the Thousand Days*. In the same environmentally friendly spirit, I went to town with my felt tips on a bunch of Albrecht Dürer engravings. Why should I learn to draw like him when I could just cut them out and move them around? I wasn't stealing from him – it was an act of respect and love . . . plus he was long dead and therefore out of copyright.

My own chance to find out how many different ways there are to upset and disappoint people as a film director would come as a side-effect of the endlessly proliferating *Python* virus. In the early days, there was nothing we could do to upset people, however hard we tried. Pretty much everything we did was 'inappropriate', but since no one knew the word yet, we were getting off scot-free.

People were constantly asking us to do things and Eric Idle was particularly good at starting projects and then pissing off on holiday and leaving everyone else to do the work. Everyone else, in the case of *Monty Python's Big Red Book* – the first in a long line of Python publications – being me, Mike, Terry J., and most of all Terry's sister-in-law Katy Hepburn, who was by that stage working as my assistant on the animations.

My earlier experiences in the snark-infested waters of comedy book publishing – with *The Cocktail People* and various still-born successors in LA in the late sixties – had not been positive ones, but my initial reluctance to get involved began to melt away once I realised this was an opportunity to bring some of the sensibility of the American underground comics boom I'd missed out on through being in London to a new British audience. By the time we were on our second volume, *The Brand New Monty Python Bok*, we were really having fun with it – one of our favourite innovations was printing dirty thumb-prints on the otherwise pristine cover so it would make book shops go crazy.

'The man with giant legs' – one example of me having fun in THE BRAND NEW MONTY PYTHON BOK, which the booksellers didn't complain about.

A number of them did insist on returning stock claiming 'this is soiled', and the same mentality of trying to extrapolate from the playful *Out of the Inkwell*-type attitude of the original show would prevail in pretty much all subsequent Python spin-off activities. I had great fun working on some of the albums. After André Jacquemin had recorded the sketches, he and I added the lush FX and atmospheric

A later album cover I did for *Monty Python Sings* – it was my version of the Rolling Stones' logo with the stave turning into a guitar string mouth-tightener.

A version of the artwork also featured on *Monty Python Sings (again)* in 2014.

(again)

production with a combination of his four-track and my two-track tape recorders in his parents' garden shed. I would also like to claim credit for the idea of the three-sided album – 1973's *The Monty Python Matching Tie and Handkerchief* – where side two had double grooves spiralling inside each other, so depending on where the needle came down, you would go into one sequence of tracks or the other. Things were coming together so fast that I'm not absolutely sure it was my idea, but I would like to claim the credit for it anyway.

What was interesting as the show developed was that although each of us had his own specialities and strengths, we were all learning from each other as we went along. So sometimes I'd notice my animation becoming more verbose in an attempt to emulate what the others were doing, but in the same episode there might be a sketch that had picked up trace elements from my cartoons.

As *Monty Python* grew in popularity, the demand for live shows became impossible to ignore. On the one hand, this was exciting because it gave me the opportunity to do more performing, and the custard pie sketch required a level of subtlety I could just about master. (John always thought I mugged too much, but he could keep his arty notions . . . I got laughs, and that was what I thought we were in business to achieve.) On the downside, there was one bit early on in the first stage show where I had to vomit into my top hat and then step forward to give a little speech, and which I would struggle not to fuck up. Thankfully this was eventually dropped.

I found the repetitious nature of performing onstage night after night unfulfilling, but it was fun to be part of the fan frenzy – especially when *Python* started to go international. As our slightly uptight cerebral take on the British invasion pushed out from its initial Canadian bridgehead and eventually into America, we knew we were breaking fresh ground, and it was exciting to be treated like rock stars (although comedy groupies were a very different animal to the rock star variety – far less beautiful, but they had a lot of personality, and we owed them a great debt of thanks for helping us keep our vows of celibacy).

There was certainly an element of 'us against the world' about Monty Python on tour, but our arrival in town was a far cry from the Viking raids of Led Zeppelin or The Who. After the shows, we tended to go off on our own and read our books or write our diaries, rather than hurling ourselves into Dionysian gang-bangs. It was nice to feel like stars for a while, but once you've had a few standing ovations and all that shit, the thrill wears off pretty quickly, unless you're one of those people who needs to hear applause to remind them that they're still alive.

Of the group, I think Eric was the one who liked that kind of approbation the most, which is probably why he still lives in Hollywood. But Monty Python was never about one individual, it was always about the six of us, which I think made the pressure much easier for us all to cope with. The great advantage of hitting it as big as we did collectively rather than individually was that we all took the piss out of each other, and that helped keep us as grounded as we were ever going to get.

Obviously we all ended up trying to prove ourselves on our own in one way or another – with varying degrees of success – but because John was the first one to go solo (when he left the TV show after the third series, although obviously he came back in for the films), I think he suffered a lot. He went higher, faster, than the rest of us, and therefore he had further to fall. The fall has always been the thing I'm terrified of. Hence the low altitude of my flying dreams – Icarus was not my role model. If you just never quite get where you're aiming for, the chances are you won't hurt yourself so badly when you tumble back down to earth.

In Germany again – this time playing a 'Mouse boy' (note Palin in customary 'peering' guise). I had to ride in on my horse twirling my tiny lasso, then as I threw it, we cut to this little mouse which I was meant to be catching and then, woah, I would be pulled from the horse by the teeny rodent. I was quite big on doing stunts but, foolishly, this gun was a real metal one — not rubber, like stunt-men normally use — and landing on it as the horse bolted brought back painful memories of bruises from the demon motorcycle of yore.

PERFORMANCE

153

Dad and Mum were over from America, and I think this was the first time they'd seen their son being filmed, which was a novelty they seemed to enjoy (though obviously my costume was nothing new to them). I like my dad's hat and permanent-press trousers combination – truly the 1970s were the golden age of manmade fibres.

No one could have accused us of flying too close to the sun with our first Monty Python film project. *And Now for Something Completely Different* was essentially a compilation of re-shot sketches from the first two series, packaged up as a film and mostly paid for by Playboy Club entrepreneur Victor Lownes. But we got the chance to show our mettle when Columbia Pictures, the American studio, came to us and insisted we had to eliminate 'Upper Class Twit of the Year' (which was the last sequence), because no one on the other side of the Atlantic would understand it.

In the same way that St Paul became the most zealous of Christians after he'd stopped persecuting them, I – the American – was as determined as any (and more determined than most) of my English colleagues that the Britishness of Python should not be compromised. If we'd watered it down, as some faint-hearts argued we should (exhibiting the excess of in-breeding that led to the loss of the empire – what they needed was some foreign blood to stiffen that old ramrod back), we'd have lost the opportunity to elevate our American audience with something real, in favour of giving them a muddled version of something transatlantic, which all too often became the British way in subsequent years.

When we stood firm, the studio upped the ante by saying that if we left that sketch in as the end of the film, they 'couldn't guarantee its success in America'. This was how they put it, and with that statement they effectively guaranteed the film's *lack* of success.

Although *And Now for Something . . .* failed in the States, it did well in the UK, paving the way for a more full-blooded initiation into the pleasures and pain of film-making. For me, *Monty Python and the Holy Grail* would be a chance to revisit the enchanted medieval landscape of the Gilliam family's garden in Panorama City, where the swords were made from eucalyptus branches and helmets from family-size ice-cream tubs – cut out the slot for the eyes and away you go, but try not to get whacked with a wooden shield, because that really hurts. We were able to call upon a bigger budget now, but not by much.

Terry Jones and I had become very frustrated working on the first film, because we both thought we could do a better job of directing it than the *Python* TV veteran Ian MacNaughton. So when the time came to make *The Holy Grail*, we offered our services to the others as a kind of directorial dream-team. At first, we were full of confidence: 'Of *course* we can do a film.' It was only once the process actually started that we realised how much we still had to learn.

The locations weren't the problem – at least, not at first. Terry J. and I covered the whole country looking for every medieval castle available, and I was happy to find I had a pretty good nose for them. It's hard to describe without trespassing into the dubious territory of the paranormal, but some kind of topographical magnetism – it's almost like a cinematic leyline – did seem to tell me when they were just around the corner. Experiments have been done in planetariums that prove that dung-beetles rolling their shit through the night guide their path by the Milky Way, and that's pretty much how I've worked ever since when it comes to location hunting.

It was inevitable that the rest of the group would have some difficulty coping with the idea of Terry J. and I having any kind of authority over them. But the speed with which the 'them against us' divide opened up took us both by surprise. We weren't even that bossy, but someone's got to tell people where to stand, and in which direction to point the camera. Graham was the worst, because he and Ian had been drinking partners. He used to get really pissed at night and be incredibly brutal: 'Why isn't Ian directing this thing? Ian was great, but this is a shambles . . .'

What made such victimisation especially hard to take was that the rest of us were all working so hard (in our own young, naive and determined ways) to plough on through the endless series of crises with which we seemed to be beset. And yet Graham – the tough guy, Mr Extreme Sportsman, who thought we were all amateurs – couldn't even bring himself to walk across the (admittedly quite rickety) rope bridge we'd got the great mountaineer Hamish

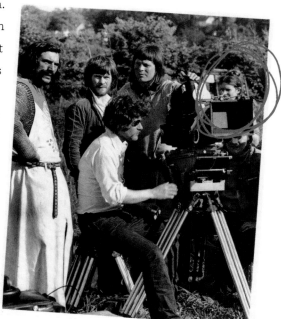

From the facial expressions here, I would guess Terry J. is trying to retain his authoritative demeanour while I query his directorial vision. Note also a rare in-shot appearance by Maggie Weston, the power behind the throne (or in this case, the camera), who had also given me that excellent medieval haircut.

Look at the change in my appearance after just two weeks' filming! Luckily my new straggly wild-man look was exactly the one I needed to play the bridge-keeper.

That's Graham and Terry J. in the armour, Roger Pratt (who went on to be the cinematographer on Brazil and 12 Monkeys) is pointing in a different direction to me, and crouching off to the side, the brilliant cameraman Terry Bedford is ignoring everything I say.

MacInnes (a.k.a. 'The Warden of Glencoe') to set up for us. The answer was simple – the Demon Drink.

When we needed a sheep for the taunters to throw off the ramparts onto Arthur and Bedevere, someone from the art department spotted a dead one by the side of the road, which had people vomiting when they tried to move the carcass. The next morning, Tommy Raeburn the props guy was down by the lake's edge, heroically gutting it and filling it with stuffing. We were making do with what reality was throwing up.

The most urgent problem we had to face came when we discovered that the castles we'd chosen with such care – most of which were owned by the National Trust – wouldn't allow filming. We finally found a privately owned alternative – the one that's out in the water at the end of the film – and on the day we were supposed to be shooting, the guy with the key (who was the son of the owner) had to fly up from London to let us in.

In the TV series, the squishing foot from the Bronzino painting almost became a cue to cut back and forth between the unconscious mind and the world of physical reality. The disruptive interventions I make on screen in *Monty Python and the Holy Grail* – via the Beast of Aaarrgh, or as Patsy, pointing out to the others that Camelot is only a model when they're still trying to play it straight – probably stemmed less from any counter-cultural or surrealist ideology than from my status as the member of the group most responsible for ensuring that what we were filming made sense on a physical level. It was just a way of solving problems.

We only ended up doing that ridiculous thing with the cut-out because we got banished from the real castle, so come on, let's comment on it and admit it's only a model. There's no point pretending this is anything other than what it is. The same thing happened with the Black Beast, when the animator suffers a fatal heart attack – I just didn't know how the hell else to get out of that situation in narrative terms, other than to break the whole thing apart and step outside it.

This certainly wasn't – as some have surmised – a coded message that I'd had enough of doing animations for Monty Python, because at that point I was still going strong. I can't remember exactly how or why I came across the book on images in the margins of medieval manuscripts that was one of the main inspirations for much of my work on *Monty Python and the Holy Grail*. Chance is always waiting for a little door to open so it can sneak in, and finding that stuff wasn't just a red-letter day for me, it was an *illustrated* red-letter day, in which a strange half-goat creature could clearly be seen pissing on a cat.

The basis of it all was that these miserable monks who had to sit there repeatedly rewriting the Bible just got bored out of their minds and started doodling. I loved the way the little characters they'd create – imaginary animals called 'non-descripts' (logically enough, because they hadn't ever been described) – started out trapped in the decorated letters at the start of

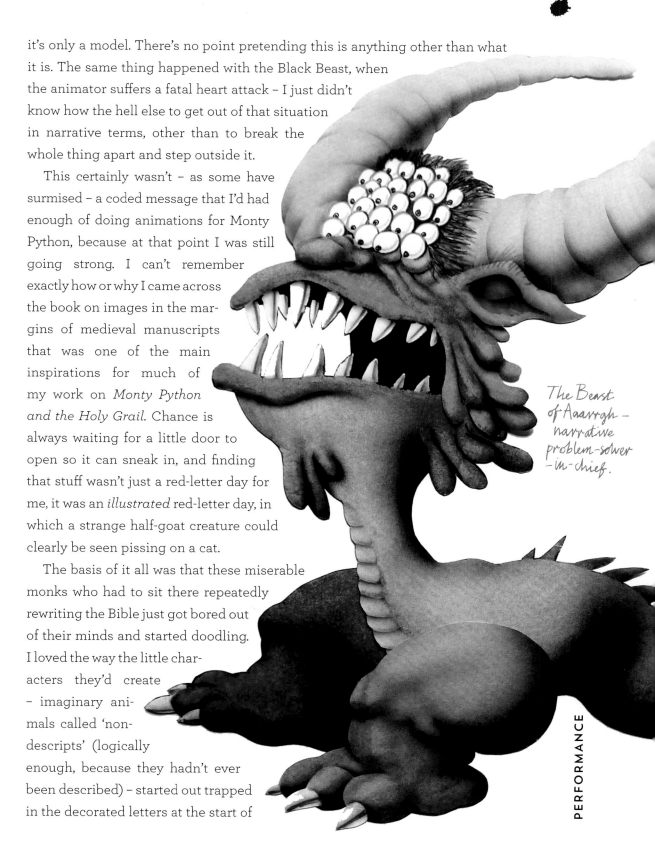

The Beast of Aaarrgh – narrative problem-solver -in-chief.

PERFORMANCE

Sketches for
Pythonian
non-descripts
– not without
good reason
have the
medieval
drawings that
inspired them
been called
'The New Yorker
cartoons of
their day'.

each document and then spilled out along the margins like a guerrilla army. Some of them related directly to the text, but some of them were just fucking around (an illustrative template which readers may already have noted has also been applied as a respectful tribute within this very volume), and half the fun was telling which was which. Basically, these illustrations were the medieval ancestors of *Out of the Inkwell*; conclusive proof, if more were needed, that – at least as far as 'post-modernism' is concerned – there's nothing new under the sun.

The extensive parallels between the way these images flourished on the edge of the main story and my own marginal status within Monty Python (and, indeed, the broader human race) will no doubt be evident to all. But there was also a sense in which they related to the work of the group as a whole – we were all gigglers at the back of the class, the same way those monks had been. And it turned out that conjuring up an army of mischievous non-descripts was a great deal easier than getting my fellow Pythons to do what they were told.

It had been a hard day's knight.

One particular crisis while shooting *Monty Python and the Holy Grail* came when we had to dig a hole to get the camera in the right place to film for a special effects shot that involved animals being thrown over the battlements. The others didn't understand the importance of having to kneel uncomfortably, aligning them beneath the level of the parapet so later I could get a clean matte, and the heated debate which ensued culminated in me proclaiming, 'You wrote this sketch and I'm just trying to make it work!' Then I stomped off in high dudgeon to lie down in the tall grass. At this point it was a good job that we had two directors, as it meant the other Terry could take over while I quietly processed the realisation that perhaps I didn't want to direct Monty Python films any more.

Unfortunately, this one wasn't quite finished yet. The last scenes we had to shoot were the Black Knight stuff, which was done back down in London, in Epping Forest. There was only me, John, Graham and Terry J. left at this point, until Terry and I got in a stalemate about reshooting part of the scene because a background was too dark (he thought it was, I knew it wasn't), so I grabbed Maggie and we drove away on holiday together to head off the serious fight which would have undoubtedly broken out otherwise.

By this stage – unbeknownst to my disputatious colleagues – Maggie had forced me into marriage with the time-honoured 'we get hitched or that's it' manoeuvre. Prior to being confronted with this stark ultimatum, my idea of what being a grown-up entailed had stopped at buying a car and owning my own hi-fi – surely that was sufficient? I hated the idea of a wedding as a public event rather than a private thing between two people, so the deal was that we got married, but we didn't tell anybody. This was how we'd ended up at Belsize Park registry office with Maggie's parents (but not mine, who remained in the dark about it all for ages, as did the Pythons) and her mother's borrowed ring. While I appreciate that this stripped-down ceremony would probably not constitute many other people's idea of love's young dream (I was only thirty-two after all – still little more than a child), the fact that Maggie and I are still together more than forty years on suggests we must have been doing something right.

As a further down-payment on adulthood, Maggie and I had taken out a mortgage on an £8,000 flat on the top floor of Sandwell Mansions on West End Lane in West Hampstead. The first thing I'd done there was start ripping walls out to make space, which left us with a big front room divided by the stud work of the former wall, so you could see through it like a rood screen. We'd painted

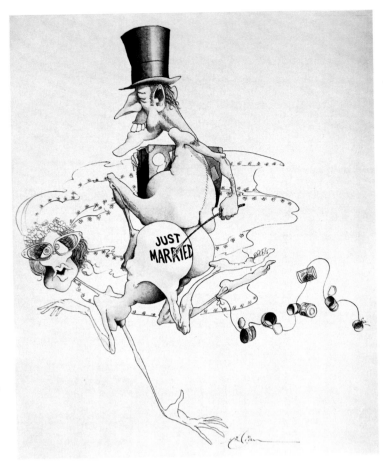

This 1968 illustration for The Londoner turned out to be a prophetic foretaste of the nature of my marriage five years later, albeit with the gender roles reversed.

our entrance hall a waspish shade of yellow which I was very enamoured of, and there was a big skylight from which I hung a rope-ladder, so we could get out onto the roof. At that time I also developed a big thing about shifting rooms by 45 degrees, as there was a light-well at that angle in the corner of the bedroom, so I'd built the sleeping platform out on a diagonal too.

If I could turn anything to take it off the square then I would – I suppose as a reaction against my father having been a Mason. And when *The Holy Grail* went into the edit, my urge to keep things slightly off the straight and narrow expressed itself via me coming back to the edit room to re-cut scenes at night, without Terry J. necessarily knowing.

This is probably as good a time as any for me to make

a full confession. There were times when the film's editor John Hackney came to me complaining that Terry was choosing the wrong shots – he seemed to be making his choice based on his memory of the feeling on the day the scene was shot rather than what was actually captured on film. I agreed with John, and we would go in and swap the shot for one that contained the actual information the scene demanded. The next day Terry never seemed to notice our late-night interventions, but my come-uppance was just around the corner.

We mixed the sound for a first screening for 'the money people' – a somewhat less strait-laced group than that designation normally suggests, as Led Zeppelin, Pink Floyd, Chrysalis and Charisma records (the latter being the label that put out our albums) had all chipped in, partly to support us and partly as a creative tax strategy. Unfortunately, large numbers of people walked out disappointed. This was largely my fault, because I was so intent on creating a realistic atmosphere that I'd over-egged the sound effects to the detriment of the dialogue.

This was the moment of reckoning, as the four non-Terrys – especially Graham, who hated what we'd done with a passion (he'd known we'd fuck up, and now we had) – turned on their two directors. The guilt was shared between us, but if not the lion's share then at least the cheetah's share of it was mine, as I had been the one most responsible for over-cooking the sound. Going back through the whole thing and sorting it all out was a straightforward enough job, but still, it was my worst professional moment since having to cancel the Camp Roosevelt production of *Alice in Wonderland*. In retrospect, I'm curious as to whether the 'sound effects' version was really as bad as we thought it was – I find it hard to believe I could have been that destructive – but sadly there's no way of bringing that one back, not even on Blu-Ray.

Luckily, once all the sound issues were resolved, what we had on our hands was unquestionably 'one of the greatest films of all time'. The New York opening was a big event for me, having left that city eight years before in something less than a blaze of glory. The night before the premiere, we had met some bright, new comedians who within a few months were to become *Saturday Night Live* – Bill Murray, Dan Ackroyd and Gilda Radner. Then the next day someone called us and said you'd better get down here. When we turned up at Cinema 1 on Third Avenue, the queue went right round the block. Astonishing! And there, politely lining up with everyone else, were the soon-to-be *SNL* people.

Equally memorable was watching the audience's reaction when the Black Knight's arms and legs were being chopped off. No one laughed – everyone was gasping in horror. The Vietnam War was really going down the toilet by 1975, and the fact that the humour in the scene lay not in the violence itself, but rather in the Black Knight's attitude to it, was being lost on everyone. Two arms and one leg had to come off before they finally started laughing.

At the start of *The Holy Grail*, I'd enjoyed the idea – and the fact – of Terry J. and I doing something as a pair. But the more we worked together, the clearer it became that we had divergent ideas about the best ways to go about things, and I soon got tired of trying to persuade the rest of the group of the inherent rightness of my approach. I've never been any good at getting my point of view across in those kinds of situations, and tend to subside all too readily into a seemingly random sequence of simian grunts.

I think I'd also started to suspect that comedy wasn't of quite such paramount importance to me as it was to the others. I thought it was just as important to get the mud and the squalor of the setting right, so an exchange like

'How do you know he's a king?', 'He hasn't got shit all over him', could really resonate. As far as I was concerned, if we hadn't managed to make something with a coherently real and gritty feel to it, we'd have been left with just a collection of sketches (like *Spamalot* years later). In short, while the time had not yet come to formally disband the gang of six, there were a lot of other things I wanted to be able to do in movie-making, and it was clear to me the only way to get them done was to go it alone.

I had a couple of false starts, both with a Beatles-y flavour. *A Hard Day's Night* director Richard Lester – who I'd been excited to see in action back in California a few years before, when Glenys and I did a story for the *Evening Standard* about the making of *Petunia*, which Dick (as his friends know him) was filming with Julie Christie – approached me with a script he wanted me to work on. It was exciting to meet the man behind *The Running, Jumping & Standing Still Film*, but nothing really came of it. Then a producer called Sandy Lieberson asked me to direct a musical film called *All This and World War III*, which was going to use a lot of Beatles songs.

Jabberwocky storyboards took 'back-to-basics' to the next level.

Much as I loved The Beatles, I found that idea quite hard

to get excited about. Sandy could see I wasn't happy with it, and asked if there was anything I'd rather do instead. So I swept him off his feet with my in-depth plan for *Jabberwocky* – 'Here's the eight-line poem, we've got a monster, let's go!' – called in my old *Help!*-mate Chuck Alverson (who I'd lured into the Lester project) to co-write the screenplay, and prepared to have a second crack at the world of knights and peasants, but this time without my fellow Pythons getting in the way. (Mike excepted, as he was always a breeze to deal with, so I decided to bring him along for the ride . . . Oh yes, and also Terry J., who was to be eaten by the monster even before the title sequence.)

Right from the off, I found being in sole charge of the director's chair to be more a source of excitement than of anxiety. I like and need a certain amount of pressure when I'm doing a job – it keeps me focused and prioritising, rather than lapsing into a miasma of excess possibility. Make do and mend was certainly our watchword on *Jabberwocky*. Apart from short location shoots at Caerphilly and Chepstow castles, most of the film was shot on the old *Oliver!* set at Shepperton, with a few helpful remnants salvaged from a German film version of *The Marriage of Figaro* to make it look less familiar.

However stretched we were for time, that was no excuse not to prepare Caerphilly.

We bunged the Germans a bit of money not to tear down their set, and then revamped it. No one would've known where it came from once we'd finished with it, and it would have been nice to have been allowed to do the same with the fantastic huge fibre-glass sewer that Blake Edwards had been using on the *Pink Panther* film he was making at the time. But his people kept getting wind of the possibility that we might re-use some of their old stuff and deliberately set fire to it to stop us. That really pissed me off, because it was so wasteful.

We'd have to wait a few years to get some small revenge on Mr Edwards (when he wanted to produce *Life of Brian* and we didn't let him, despite having enjoyed a delightful evening in the company of Blake and his wife Julie Andrews, whose unusually potent sexual allure was lost on none of us in person), but they do say that particular meal is best served straight from the chiller. In the meantime, we had a lot of black cloth to do shadowy recesses with, and I had made a couple of box-windows with very deep reveals that we could throw light through, to give the impression of a thick castle wall. We also had a small number of four-by-eight rubber pieces that we could move around as flagstones, and from that point on the bulk of efforts and financial reserves could go into making Max Wall's throne look convincing.

Far from being intimidating, the presence at Shepperton Studios of 'proper' actors such as illustrious stage and small-screen veterans Max Wall and John Le Mesurier was actually a huge relief, because these people had been trained to respect their director, a novelty which I found delightful. Especially with someone like Max, who was in his seventies by then, but if I said, 'Lie down here and we're going to cover you with a pile of dust,' he'd just do it, whereas too many of the Pythons abjured such physically demanding assignments. I never really blamed them for their obstructive attitude – I think it was just that they knew who I was, so why would they respond any differently? Whereas by the time I was doing *Jabberwocky*, *Monty Python and the Holy Grail* had come out and been quite successful, and Terry Jones and I had our names up on the silver screen right after the words, 'Directed by', so the pros just assumed I knew what I was doing.

Max Wall is remembered now as a much-loved figure, but he'd gone through a bad patch in his life when he'd been widely hated – and effectively black-listed in professional terms – for being known to have had an affair when such things weren't publicly allowed. As a consequence he was quite a sad, lonely guy from

day to day, but in terms of his attitude to his work, he was just a joy. I think he loved the fact that he was suddenly playing one of the leads in a movie, and he and John Le Mes' – who'd long been great fans of each other, but had not previously met – just kind of fell in love, which was why I encouraged them to let their characters develop into a couple of old queens bringing a bit of sweet, funny tenderness to the autumn years of their on-screen relationship.

Harry H. Corbett took a bit more handling, because he was a complicated character and probably his own worst enemy in the long run, but once you'd got the hang of him, he was fine. I've tended to be very cautious about who I've worked with over the years – I've got to feel that they're people I'm going to be able to have fun with, who are really committed to what we're doing and aren't going to pull the kind of bullshit that I read about all the time in other people's biographies. But my personal experience has often been that the guys who are the most notorious for being difficult actually aren't, they're just very intelligent people who have been treated like cattle and respond quite badly to that.

Strangely, the only trouble I got from anyone on that film was one of the lower-echelon actors, who at one point told me he would 'rather show his cock' than pick his nose, which was an important bit of business that was actually in the script. I remember thinking, 'What the fuck is this?' But in my experience (now as then) there's never really any point in getting angry on a film set, and if a scene is going to end up in a lengthy battle and eat up what little time is available I'll just change the script.

One of the most exciting challenges presented by *Jabberwocky* was translating the monster from two into three dimensions. Val Charlton – who'd helped build the fairy boat in *Monty Python and the Holy Grail*, and would later construct the three-headed griffin in *The Adventures of Baron Munchausen* – was my right-hand woman on this job, which inevitably got patched together long after the eleventh hour and after the SFX man had effectively had a breakdown.

Laying down the law to Michael Palin as a director. I find that one of the keys to retaining my actor's respect is to always come on set dressed appropriately for a man in a position of authority.

It turned out that the secret of the Jabberwock was to have the guy in the suit standing backwards, so the legs articulated the way a bird's would. I was obsessed with disguising the fact that a man was inside, but the biggest problem was that the claws were too floppy. We ended up shooting them in reverse, because somehow when they lifted off the ground and you reversed the shot convincingly, it looked like they were really slamming down hard.

Those kind of magical chance discoveries make any amount of frantic scrabbling around in a quarry in the wilds of mid-Wales worthwhile. When I look back at these sequences, they're all quite chaotic and – inevitably – a long way short of what we'd hoped for, with a fair amount of 'cut to monster going "Aaargh"' happening, but at least we managed to give the whole thing a certain sense of scale, if only by making a miniature suit of armour and putting a little kid squeezed inside.

It would be wrong to go on any longer without acknowledging the huge contribution of one of the friends I have learned much from – Julian Doyle. He'd been the production manager on *Holy Grail* and, knowing more about the practical side of film-making than either Terry J. or myself, was always finding ways to deal with the problems besetting us – whether this meant throwing toy animals into the air in his back garden (later to be matted into the scene at the castle when Arthur and his knights are pelted with a cow and various poultry) or squatting on the floor of his sitting room shooting 'The Book of the Film' by candlelight.

A veritable Julian of all trades, he worked on every Python film from *The Holy Grail* to *The Meaning of Life* and all of mine up until *The Fisher King*, his credits ranging through pre-production (his notes on my scripts were always particularly good in helping me to focus) to shooting and editing, with stints as writer, director and cameraman confirming him as one of the unsung heroes of my career's cinematic phase. As *Jabberwocky* got my post-Python bandwagon rolling, he was the one greasing the wheels.

We beat the Alien people to that 'skin stretching like vagina' thing by two whole years.

HOLLYWOOD

When JABBERW@CKY came out in the SILVER JUBILEE year of 1977, I got pilloried in the press because the reviews all said it wasn't as good as THE HOLY GRAIL.

Chapter

10

Always Look on
the Bright Side of Life

Draft poster for JABBERWOCKY –
never mind BOSCH and BREUGHEL, when is
GILLIAM the Questionable going to doff his
cap to ALICE IN WONDERLAND illustrator John Tenniel?

W

hen *Jabberwocky* **came out,** in the Silver Jubilee punk rock year of 1977, I got pilloried in much of the press because the reviews all said it wasn't as good as *The Holy Grail*. Things were especially parlous in New York, where I'd managed to make a bad situation worse by writing a note to the New York critics saying this wasn't in fact a Monty Python film but rather an homage to Breughel and Bosch. The fact that I should have mentioned two such great artists in connection with my (in their opinion) juvenile scatological crap obviously made them crazy, and all the reviews were about Gilliam the Questionable, rather than (Max Wall's character) Bruno the Questionable.

As painful as it was at the time, this mini-furore probably did serve some purpose in helping to define me as a separate – albeit somewhat embattled – entity outside the Monty Python group. It also established my superior art history credentials to those of the self-styled Big Apple critical elite, as – duh! – anyone who has the smallest familiarity with the aforementioned Pieter and Hieronymus knows that those two artists are about as juvenile and scatological as you can possibly get. And since half the images in the film were stolen from them, it seemed only fair to give them a bit of credit.

The funny thing about *Jabberwocky* was, whenever it went anywhere that people hadn't been primed to expect another *Holy Grail* or had never heard of *Monty Python*, it actually did very well. Even Python fans seemed to be taken aback by the level of filth, though. I remember one screening where this obsessive Python fan with a spotty face and green teeth (I'm not saying they all looked like that, it just so happened that this one did) came up and pronounced himself 'deeply offended by the sheer ugliness of it all'. I wonder who he saw in the morning as he brushed his teeth. Cary Grant?

In a way I was quite happy

with that reaction, as one of the most important things about Jabberwocky to me was that it should be anti-American film-making – not in an explicitly political way, but in terms of being the opposite of the Hollywood distorting mirror I'd grown up with, whereby all the pores were mysteriously gone from the skin and everyone's teeth shone like Doris Day and Rock Hudson's. You could say that in my determination to have everyone with crooked teeth and surrounded by great piles of ordure, I'd become more British than the British. I suppose when you make a conscious choice in terms of your national identity, you are bound to cleave to it more strongly than when it's just what you're born with.

The one thing I most wanted to do with *Jabberwocky* – and in this at least I think I succeeded – was to make it as tactile as possible. I also really liked the idea of two fairy tales in collision, so you have what's traditionally a happy ending, where Michael Palin gets to marry the princess and rule half the kingdom, but it's the wrong happy ending, because in this case he wanted to marry the fat girl next door who ate potatoes and treated him like shit. It was the sheer perversity of this which I loved, and I suppose again there's something quite un-American about that. I was Senator Joseph McCarthy's worst nightmare – a prom king with a grudge.

The adversarial character of my professional relationship with my ancestral homeland had been established way back in 1971, when I was working on *The Marty Feldman Comedy Machine* for ABC. That show was produced by

This is the plug-in-and-play title plate I did for Marty. He himself was difficult to photograph because his eyes pointed in different directions.

Larry Gelbart – the man who wrote for Sid Caesar, Jonathan Winters, and even Danny Kaye (my how the circles connect) and then gave the world the great TV series *M*A*S*H* – and, by the same curious British invasion logic that obliged Jimi Hendrix to make it big in London first before he could go to Monterey, the whole series was made in a big, ugly tower block on the North Circular. A couple of my fellow Pythons turned down writing gigs on it, because they didn't fancy going into the office from 9 a.m. to 5 p.m., five days a week, but I was happy to be commissioned to do the title sequence and half an hour of animation.

Perhaps inevitably, given that this show was being made for notoriously uptight American TV network ABC (who will figure again later in this tale), it was the occasion of my first proper run-in with the censors. I'd written this piece of animation, which I was quite pleased with, about the balance of fat within nature – the idea being that as one country puts on weight, another will inevitably be getting thinner. I broadened it out (as it were) so that when someone diets, that sets fat free to roam around looking for a home, and this turned out to be a great platform for visual gags, like the guy who's lingering, leaning against a lamp-post and a big blob of fat comes around the corner and scoots up his trouser leg, causing instant obesity, and making the malingerer topple over and roll down the street.

The row started with a famous Boucher nude that I'd cut out. ABC's in-house censor – who happened to be a bit on the extra-large side herself, but I'm sure that in no way affected her judgement – insisted that the lovely buttock-dividing crack of the model's arse (it was a rear view) would have to be covered. By this time, I was really making hay with Ronnie Barker's Victorian nudes, so I chose a frontally seated one, cut holes where the breasts should be, and protected the modesty of the lady's groin by cutting out a triangular-shaped hole, then submitted it to ABC and said, 'OK, if you don't want me to show the naughty bits, we can just not show them.' The response was a resounding 'No'. So it was ruled that I could neither show the naughty

bits nor even not show them! I remember joking with Barry Levinson, who was one of a number of film-directors-to-be working as writers on that show, that the only way we could get this stuff through would be if he 'took one for the team' and shagged the censor. He wasn't man enough to mount that Everest and so the fat animation did the only thing it could do and tossed itself off, which was probably all the censor did anyway.

Whenever I run up against that kind of bureaucracy – in whatever form it comes – I just seem to go berserk. My next response was to give ABC a minute-long sequence of animation where there was no movement whatsoever. It started with an empty landscape and this unseen guy's voice saying he's got this really great dog who does incredible tricks. He calls the dog into shot and asks the dog to roll over and play dead and then this very long off-screen argument ensues about whether the dog has moved or not (which it hadn't). In the end the guy thinks he sees some movement and this big hammer comes down and smashes the dog, as if to say, 'Alright, you want animation? I'll show you how it's done.'

It wasn't just the fact that someone had said 'No' to me that elicited this strong reaction. I wouldn't have objected if something I did had been rejected for not being sufficiently funny or well-realised. It was the manifest absurdity of saying that a classical painting could not be seen on TV that riled me. In this situation, I was being a traditionalist, not an iconoclast: 'What is this new framework you're imposing which means the public now can't see something they could have looked at in a gallery in Victorian times? Tell me what your rules are, because I don't understand them.'

I used yellow paper and red ink – 'Kerchunk, kerchunk, kerchunk' – stamp 'em up, cut 'em out and then layer them like old theatrical waves... I believe that's how they do it in China too.

The ABC censor had no objection to representations of Chinese communists — so long as their arse cheeks were fully covered. I made this rubber stamp because I needed a sea of loyal party members that Chairman MAO could swim through — I was ahead of ANTONY GORMLEY at that point.

That's what drives me so crazy

now about living in the age when the language of 'appropriateness' rules with an iron fist. Every time I hear that word 'inappropriate', something curdles inside of me, like when American schools removed thirty pages of Anne Frank's diaries because she had the temerity to mention her genitalia (apparently there were 'lips inside of lips' but she couldn't see because there was 'hair in the way').

All the right-wing parents were screaming the 'I'-word, but if you're going to teach kids about sex, you might as well use Anne Frank to do it. She's the perfect role model. On the one hand there's the undercurrent of jeopardy – 'Don't touch those bits, or the Nazis will get you.' On the other, her circumstances were different enough to those of the average good Christian American school-child to give you a bit of leeway – 'It's OK, she was Jewish, not like you.'

Over the years I took great delight in refining my response to the absurdities of censorship, with at least one *Monty Python* animation super-imposing Lord Longford's face over the genital area of Michelangelo's *David* to make the censor the thing that was being censored. It wasn't just the moving of near-

the-knuckle material a little further away from the knuckle to which I took profound moral exception, but any kind of outside interference in the material we'd worked so hard on. I suppose the BBC had given us delusions of self-determination by leaving us so much to our own devices when we were making the show. And in 1976, when we got wind of ABC (them again!) compressing six shows into two 60-minute 'specials', editing out 24 minutes of 'unsuitable' material to make room for adverts, the opportunity arose to put those delusions to the test.

ABC couldn't understand what we were complaining about when we sued them – weren't they offering us a much larger audience, so why should we care about our show being bowdlerised? But I was adamant about things like that, and I wasn't the only one offering to lead the resistance against Monty Python's more malleable tendency – Terry J. was just as insistent. In the end it was the eternally plausible Michael Palin and I who took the case to court. I hadn't yet shed my American citizenship, which was handy as there had to be a Yank on the affidavit for our case to be heard.

The case itself – satisfyingly abbreviated on Wikipedia as 'Gilliam v. American Broadcasting' – was definitely a big deal. There we were in the same courthouse where Nixon's former Attorney General John Mitchell had a year or so before become the first holder of that office ever to be given a prison sentence (for his role in trying to cover up the Watergate scandal). The room of judgement itself was the full Perry Mason deal – oak-panelled with 40-foot-high ceilings – and Mike and I definitely looked upon it as a performance space.

I can be pretty indignant once I get on my artistic high-horse, whereas Mike is much more naturally charming. He was the gentle persuader while I was the impassioned one, fighting for truth, justice and the American way. The judge was quite wry – after the trial was over, his clerk asked us to come back to his chambers and we found out he was a *Python* fan. The turning point in the case came when he said, 'Let's look at this,' so we sat down next to him in what would normally have been the jury box – we might as well have had popcorn – and we showed our version, and then ABC showed theirs.

It obviously made sense for it to be done that way – the original version first, and then the doctored one ABC were proposing to show after – but it showed what idiots the network people were that they didn't protest, because the contrast between the reactions in the court room totally played in our favour. Obviously everyone was laughing at the first screening, but by the time we got to the second, it was old material, so if anything, the destructive impact of the deletions was exaggerated.

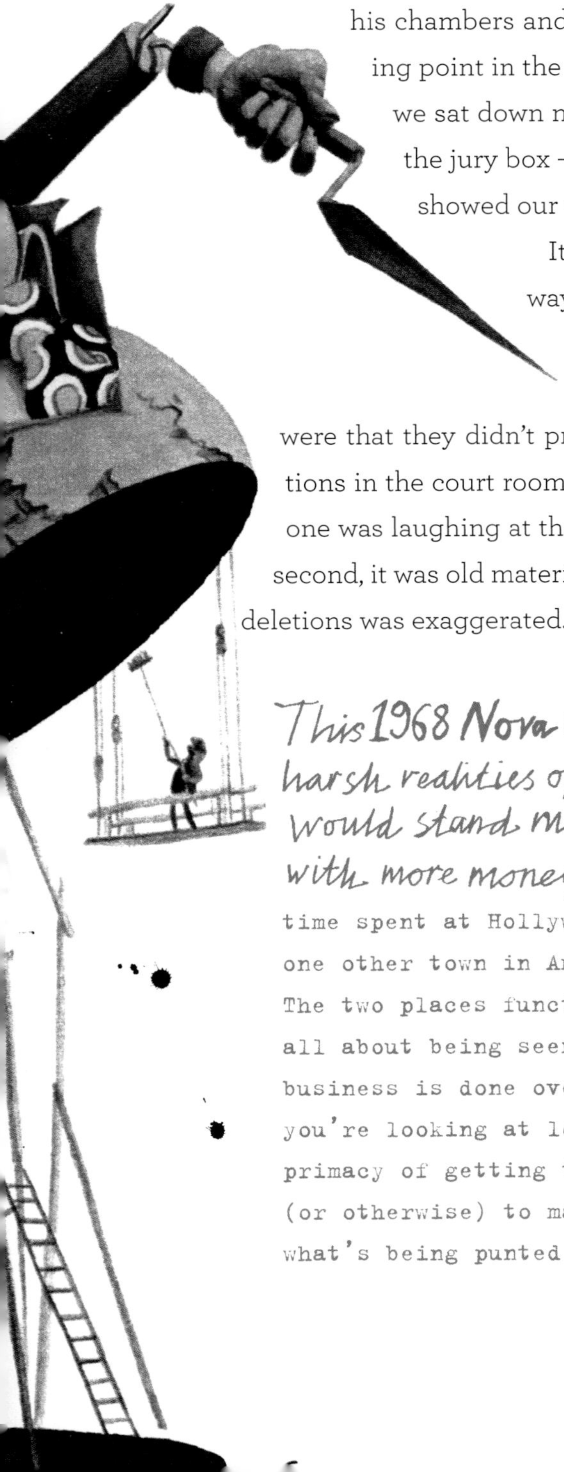

This 1968 Nova illustration showcased a clear eye for the harsh realities of money and power-broking which would stand me in good stead in my dealings with more moneymen. One thing I did learn from my time spent at Hollywood's sharp end is that there's only one other town in America like it, and that's Washington. The two places function in exactly the same way — they're all about being seen at the right places, and all the real business is done over breakfast. In Washington obviously you're looking at lobbyists rather than agents, but the primacy of getting the deal done over the likely benefits (or otherwise) to mankind seems to be the same whether what's being punted is an oil deal or a blockbuster sequel.

The problem was that it was too late in the process for us to have cried foul (the shows were scheduled to be shown in a couple of weeks, and you can't tamper with TV schedules in a capitalist society), so the initial judgement went against us, except in allowing us to put a disclaimer at the front of the show – which obviously we had a fair amount of fun with, to the extent that ABC then appealed the disclaimer (which they'd bowdlerised anyway), and then we appealed their appeal. In the course of a last appeal – and I don't know why this hadn't come up before – our original contract with the BBC came into play. There was a clause in that (which Terry Jones had insisted on – good work, Terry) stipulating that our material had to go out exactly as we made it, so it turned out that the BBC had no right to sell the shows on to ABC without that guarantee, and there was no option for the two broadcasting Goliaths other than to settle out of court with the six comedy Davids.

Not only did this result have important implications in terms of evening up the power balance between programme-makers and TV networks, it also secured our financial future. The BBC ended up handing over the rights to the shows everywhere in the world except the UK. This Python pension fund still pays the bills for all those years in between me making movies, when I can't get a job. It's allowed me the freedom to hold on between films until something that I actually want to do comes along, no doubt saving the world from a slew of inferior cinematic product in the process.

There is certainly satisfaction to be had from getting major broadcasting corporations to foot the bill for your artistic freedom, but we did have to fight for it, and the great thing was, it felt like the good guys were winning. I know the seventies are often seen as a period when many of the new freedoms and possibilities of the previous decade were closed down, but it didn't feel that way to us. Far from a period of retrenchment and stasis, this was a time when – for me at least – the underlying attitudes of the counter-culture were just as relevant as ever, and our business was finding new doors to push open wherever and whenever possible.

If there was anything we could do to fuck up the way the BBC normally did things, then fuck it, why not? I guess the political amphitheatre had been reduced in size from the broad front of the sixties' wider battles for social, racial and sexual equality, to a much more compact enclave within the broadcasting and film industries, but still, at least as far as I was concerned, it was the same struggle. And as if to show that we still had the stomach for a fight as the eighties hoved into view, Monty Python decided to build on the sure foundation of *The Holy Grail* by incurring the wrath of organised Christianity.

The seed that grew into *Life of Brian* was Eric

imagining a cheesy biblical epic called 'Jesus Christ – Lust for Glory'. This was a joke that made us all laugh, but it would never have become a film without the intercession of another contact Eric Idle made for us, appropriately enough a member of the band whose most outspoken member had once mischievously claimed they were in danger of becoming 'bigger than Jesus' (an idea which was not well received in America).

Eric and I had been out in LA promoting *The Holy Grail* when we first met George Harrison. It was at some kind of music business function or other (I wish the aptly named Idle would hurry up and write his autobiography, so I can find out which – I know it wasn't the Grammys). I remember the great session drummer Jim Keltner was there too, because he turned out to have gone to high school with Carol Cleveland. Eric and George quickly – and inevitably, given his penchant for embracing the great and the good (as he embraced me at the dawn of Python even when my connection to those two illustrious cadres was tenuous at best) – became friends, so once we'd all returned to England we would often be invited out to George's house at Friar Park.

He might have been 'The Quiet One' as far as The Beatles were concerned, but in the course of these visits, it soon became clear that he was the number one Python fan on the planet. He knew all the sketches backwards and forwards, and was kind enough to say on several occasions that he thought our impact on comedy was analogous to The Beatles' on music. His insistence that the spirit of the Fab Four had somehow passed on to us was obviously immensely flattering, but it also tied in quite neatly with his religious beliefs, not only because we started pretty much when they ended, but also because we shared several of the same points of origin – in the form of the Goons and Richard Lester – and 'everything is connected', as Hare Krishna devotees are often wont to say.

How George came to save *Brian* was that the whole thing

was ready to go – all the pre-production was done, and the crew were leaving for Tunisia on the Thursday – when EMI, who up until that point had been really keen to finance us, suddenly pulled the plug. All the flights were stopped – everything was on hold. What happened was that Bernie Delfont finally read the script – the pulling of the plug and the reading of the script were definitely connected. Just as so much of the rest of the world would once the film was finally released, he thought it was blasphemous, and decided to pass on the opportunity to provoke a special personalised pogrom.

We were still left with the small matter of a major overseas film production to finance. For a while we ran around asking everyone for money without having much luck, until Eric asked George if he was interested. George just said 'done' and that was it.

If only the rest of *Life of Brian*'s power-structure had been so happily free of complexity. Terry J. wanted the two of us to co-direct again, but I didn't want to do that any more, having been spoilt for such collaborative endeavours by the taste of absolute power (or the closest a film director can get to it – which isn't as close as you might think, because everything you do is totally dependent on other people anyway) I'd enjoyed on *Jabberwocky*. So we agreed a compromise that I would become the designer.

The **LIFE OF BRIAN** Gang (2) ~ On location in Tunisia, within easy reach of Franco Zeffirelli's old sets for **JESUS OF NAZARETH** (of which we made liberal use). I've managed to get somewhere near the middle of this one for a change, right down at the bottom, with Maggie holding our first child Amy three people to my left (or my right, as you're looking at it). I like the way Pythons are dotted randomly about with pretty much everyone else in their normal clothes except Cleese-y who seems to have found his biblical robes very much to his liking.

As was probably inevitable, I eventually changed from

designer to resigner, because if you expend a huge amount of energy designing something that costs money and someone doesn't shoot it in the way you know it should be shot, then you are (or at least I am) going to get frustrated. The aesthetic foundation of this frustration was the same as it had been on *The Holy Grail* – if you're doing a comedy that plays off a particular tradition (in this case the 'sword and sandal' epics I'd loved so well in my youth), then it has to be believable as an outgrowth of that tradition, which means it has to have a certain scope and quality to it.

On the handful of scenes I did actually end up directing – the arrival of the three wise men at the village being one – I worked really hard to give them those moments of epic scale. It's not that Terry's way of doing it was wrong, just that his default setting was to shoot everything more like TV, and as a result there were certain points – particularly the Pilate scene, where we'd built

this outrageous set with a rectilinear Roman room inside this three-storey Jewish hovel that you don't really get to see – where I felt important images were lost.

Looking back, I can see that as much as I might stamp my little artistic feet about the ways it could have been improved, *Life of Brian* not only got made but it also turned out brilliantly. In my more reasonable moments I will even concede that in the end we probably got quite a good balance between my grandiose ambitions and baroque angles, and Terry J.'s more nuts-and-bolts sensibility.

The **LIFE OF BRIAN** Gang (3) ~ with model of spaceship. We'd worked on **THE HOLY GRAIL** in Henry Moore's old studio but by that time Mike and I and Julian Doyle had taken on two former banana warehouses in Neal's Yard, Covent Garden, and set up a recording studio for Andre Jacqueman on the ground floor, and Peerless Camera Company (my FX company with Kent Houston) down in the basement. The studio room was 20 foot by 24, and we shot all of the space sequences upon which George Lucas would later compliment me in there. That room was also home to the sequence in *Time Bandits* when they're approaching Raglan Castle on their little coracle, which we did by rocking them back and forward on some inner tubes in front of black drapes.

Of all the Python films, it was *Life of Brian* that we had the most

fun on – it was certainly the one with the most improvised material. And when the film came out and caused so much trouble, I was in heaven. The fact that the Catholics, the Protestants and the Jews were all simultaneously marching in protest at the film's sacrilegious treatment of important religious themes was just the icing on the cake. It takes a lot to bring those guys together, and we had done it by the simple expedient of causing them all offence at the same time. There was a whole page in *Variety* about the protests, and each religion got a couple of columns to admit that the inappropriateness of what we had done was something they could all agree on. It was fucking great. Obviously Muslims didn't exist then, otherwise they would've been in on it too.

Here I am back on my own again – with the ruins of the spaceship in Tunisia, and then at home with the alien in South Hill Park, Hampstead.

It was wonderful to be accused of blasphemy, because it meant we knew we had irritated all the right people – everything Jesus had done for me had paid off. And because teaming up with George Harrison had served us so well, at the end of the process we formed HandMade Films together – which was basically Python and George, with Denis O'Brien managing both parties.

The complexities of HandMade's financial arrangements could be

(and, indeed, have been) the subject of a whole book on their own, so I'm not going to delve into them too deeply with regard to how *Time Bandits* came together. One of the fascinating things about film-making is that as a director,

ALWAYS LOOK ON THE BRIGHT SIDE OF LIFE

183

you're constantly having fifty or sixty conversations at once – and I don't mean just the ones you're having with yourself. The producers, the actors, the guy doing the lights, they all have their own different version of the film, and what's intriguing is that you become the conduit whereby all these different versions come crashing together and then ultimately develop into something else.

Sometimes they merge and move on, at others the confluence of these different conceptions is not so harmonious. But there's invariably a strange moment of surprise when you proceed from thinking you're all on the same course to realising how different what everyone wants is. There was a particularly vivid one of those incidents on *Time Bandits*, when I was talking to my old friend, the great percussionist/actor and adviser Ray Cooper (who at the time was head of production at HandMade) about how we were going to do the music, and I suddenly realised Denis O'Brien was expecting that George Harrison was going to contribute a bunch of songs – basically coming up with his version of 'Hi-ho, Hi-ho, It's Off To Work We Go', and turning the film into a live-action *Snow White and the Seven Dwarfs*.

When we were still developing TIME BANDITS, one of the reasons studios gave for turning it down was that nobody wanted to watch dwarves. Or so they said.
Thankfully that proved not to be the case. Forty years later HandMade Films was approached by Hollywood to license a new *Time Bandits*. It was pitched as a franchise of three films and they were offering huge amounts of $$$$. Their only stipulation was . . . NO dwarves!!! (A simple 'Fuck off!' from yours truly nixed another Hollywood producer's dream.)

Negotiating your way through these encroaching crowds of disparate and often conflicting perceptions is no less of a challenge than marshalling a theoretically inadequate number of extras into a plausible and satisfying crowd scene. In both cases there's a measure of trickery involved in delivering the illusion of a lot of people whose attention is all focused in one direction. When we were filming *Time Bandits* in Morocco, Sean Connery was up on the platform about to throw the Minotaur's severed head off into the crowd, and we only had maybe seventy-five people, all of whom I had to cram together in a little bit of space way down below in the courtyard. There was nobody in the whole vast area between them and the edge of the platform, but if you do it right, the perspective gives you the illusion.

I'd had to manage the same situation in *Jabberwocky*, when Michael Palin was standing in the long queue waiting to get into the town. In reality, all those people were standing maybe seven or eight feet apart, but I just lined them up very carefully with the camera at the right distance to make them overlap so it looked like a huge crowd. Some of these are an animator's tricks, some of them are a magician's, but they all boil down to what I consider to be one of the key skills in film-making – translating objects or people as drawn in my storyboards from two into three dimensions, and then understanding how they're going to behave once they get there.

A vital aspect of the shift from two dimensions into three is learning to deal with the difference between how you've imagined an actor is going to be and who they actually are. You've got to get the angles right here, too – dealing with leading men and women is no less of a skill than making a cupboard. Generally it's just a matter of letting them know you've listened to what they've said. At that point they feel like they've pissed on your territory so we all know who's boss, and from that point on they'll be co-operation personified.

With some people, it's just a question of making a single adjustment, as with Sean Connery's command: 'Don't film me getting on that horse.' This was on our first of fourteen days of shooting, which is obviously not the moment to alienate Sean Connery. Plus you realise he's not saying it to be a diva, he just

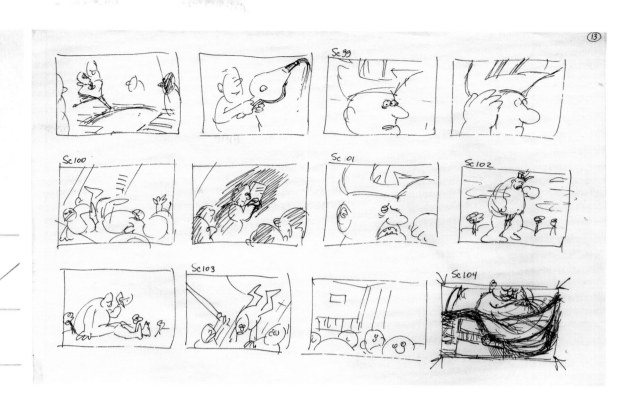

These are some of the rough sketches for
the 'giant with ship on his head' scenes in
TIME BANDITS. Obviously, there's a strong
Thief of Baghdad element about them.
That film is always there inside my **head**,
waiting to burst out at any moment
– it _scarred_ me. And here's the _finished_
version, in a collage for the poster.

knows he's getting on a bit and probably isn't going to look his best hauling himself up into the saddle, so you end up cutting to the kid and suddenly Sean is on the horse throwing him down the canteen and it all works fine. Real time is not what film-making is about – whatever keeps the pace moving is what you do, and if it keeps the star happy, so much the better. Necessity might be the mother of invention, but restriction is the mother of efficiency.

Of course, not every charismatic screen presence is as straightforward to deal with as Sean Connery. Casting Ralph Richardson in the role of God in *Time Bandits* did nothing to temper the grand old man's despotic tendencies. He was always playing games and testing people – before he'd even agreed to take the role, I had to go over to his place in Regent's Park on a Sunday morning, where he started doing impersonations of the music-hall entertainer Little Titch, which it was incumbent on me to recognise. Another time he suggested the Supreme Being should pull out a pair of dividers like a pair God used in a William Blake painting, but luckily I knew about the medieval manuscript that had inspired it. Bingo!

At each of these moments you're scoring points, and if you don't score enough he's going to be a nightmare. Ralph told me about a time when Jack Gold was directing him in something and he insisted that Jack – who was terrified of motorbikes – come for a ride with him, put him on the back of his bike and roared off around Regent's Park at an insane speed.

Nothing like that happened to me, but we did get into an absurd metaphysical debate about what God would wear. Ralph felt that God should be wearing a light linen suit, 'because he's so close to the sun', but I knew what he really meant was that he'd worn something quite similar in *Far from the Madding Crowd*, and wouldn't it be nice to wear it again? I said I felt God would be dressed more like a fusty headmaster, and one day – somewhat miraculously – Ralph turned up at the studio wearing exactly what I'd wanted. I knew he was testing me again, so the whole way through lunch he was waiting for me to talk about it, but I never did, until at the end he cracked and asked, 'What do you think of the outfit?' At that point, it was finally safe for me to say, 'It'll do.'

37A   Sc 55
Ref

A regal-looking SEAN CONNERY looks untroubled by
the Moroccan heat ~ relieved as he is not to be on horseback.

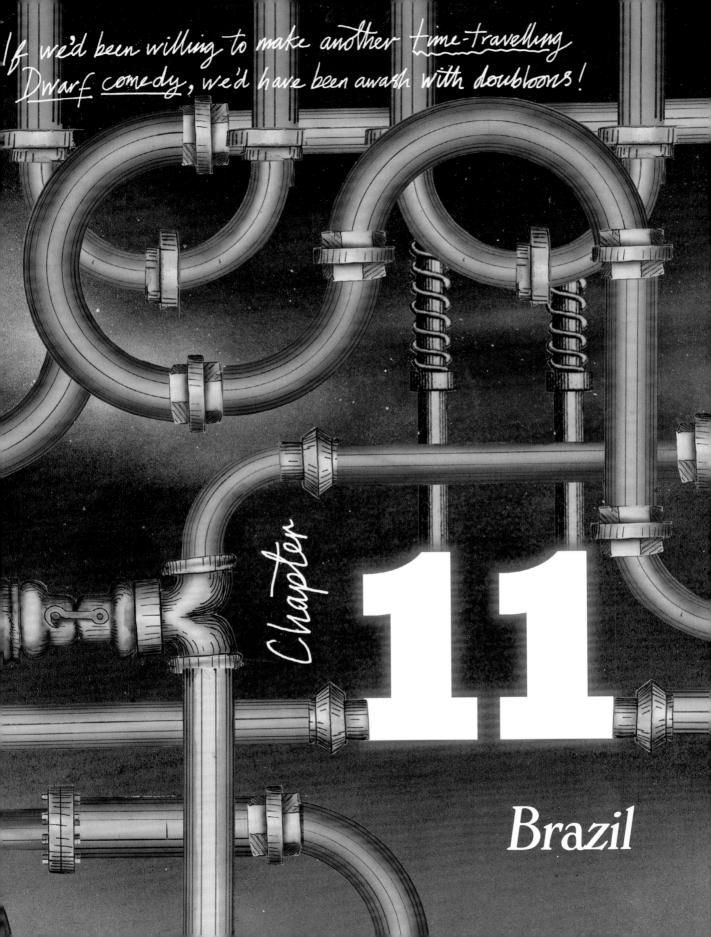

If we'd been willing to make another time-travelling Dwarf comedy, we'd have been awash with doubloons!

Chapter

11

Brazil

'This is what Hollywood does to talent' is clearly what's in my mind as far as this promotional meat-grinder is concerned. 'Get him, Mr Critical: how can he be so angry when he's done so well?' 'Because some people are born angry and they will find any excuse to hang on to their rage.'

The reason *Time Bandits* had happened

in the first place was because I was trying to sell the idea of *Brazil* to Denis O'Brien, but he had absolutely no interest in it. That was what triggered me to say, 'OK, if you don't want me to do something for grown-ups, I'll do a film for all the family.' It took no powers of persuasion at all on my part to get that one through, and when *Time Bandits* ended up being the most successful film I – or HandMade – ever did in America, that inevitably led to me being offered all sorts of other Hollywood projects that I didn't want to do.

Before I and my new producer Arnon Milchan could finally get *Brazil* off the ground (just a couple of feet off the ground, obviously, we didn't want to fly as high as the scale model of Jonathan Pryce would have to), there were two last big pieces to be fitted into the Monty Python jigsaw. There'd been a time somewhere around *The Life of Brian* when I'd started to become uncertain as to what my exact function in the group was, and the whole thing began to feel a bit frustrating. Obviously I knew I did the animations, but I wasn't sure how many more of those I had in me, and I'd enjoyed being a solo helmsman so much that I didn't really want to do timeshare at the wheel with Terry J. again.

I think all six of us were pulling in different directions by that point, and even though there were inevitably mixed feelings when the group finally disbanded, I'm glad we had the sense to quit while we were still good. It's always best to leave people wanting more – otherwise how can you justify getting back together for lucrative reunion shows in aid of Terry Jones' mortgage thirty years later? And *Live at the Hollywood Bowl* in 1980 and then *The Meaning of Life* in 1983 made for a pretty good send-off.

My wife Maggie made one of the great unheralded contributions to *Hollywood Bowl*. She'd been due to pop out our second child two weeks before, but somehow managed to keep her knees together till the shows were finished so I could get home to London in time for the birth. How best to commemorate this achievement? It seemed unfair to saddle the newborn with

If an idea is worth using, it's worth using twice.
This illustration for an article about health farms in the LONDONER in 1968 had found me making an exploratory foray down the same mincemeat-y mineshaft. I have included it to prove that I didn't steal the concept from Gerald Scarfe's cartoons for PINK FLOYD'S THE WALL.

the name 'Hollywood' outright, in honour of the circumstances of her birth, so we went with Holly Dubois instead, which ensured that even as an infant she would be unknowingly playing to a gallery of multilingual sophisticates – a precocious foundation which she would build on by making an acclaimed big-screen debut in *Brazil* at the tender age of four.

Airbrushed tombstone for THE MEANING OF LIFE title sequence – subtlety, thy name is not Gilliam.

For my last hurrah as a Monty Python animator, I decided to project the technical limitations that had served me so well on a truly metaphysical scale. This is God holding the world in his hands. Space is always hard, because if you're going to move through it you've got to have stars close to you, and yet you don't want them too big because otherwise they'll clutter up the emptiness. I believe Stanley Kubrick faced a similar problem in *2001: A Space Odyssey*, but I don't think he got around it by flicking white paint on to shiny black paper with a toothbrush.

This is not so much 'after Leonardo' as 'Poundland daVinci'...

The hungry train of human advancement is itself devoured by the filing cabinet of destiny – it's the circle of life, folks.

The creative dilemma I was wrestling with in the run-up to *The Meaning of Life* was defined not by the sophistication but the child-like crudity of the cut-out methodology I'd defined as my own over the past decade and a half. While the artwork I'd done for the various Monty Python books and album sleeves had got progressively more elaborate, it was a mark of the elemental simplicity of my animation technique that I took it to the top right from the beginning. *Beware of the Elephants*, which was only the second or third of those animations that I ever did, was as good as anything that came later. It was a bit like working on Photoshop – I never got past page three or four of that particular manual, either.

The truth was that even if some way of adding extra layers of
nuance had presented itself, I wouldn't have wanted to develop it. Partly because I lacked the patience, but largely because it felt like the brutal directness of what I'd done had been integral to its efficacy. It's the same with certain kinds of music that resist additional ornamentation – why would you want to get more complicated than Chuck Berry or the Sex Pistols? So once I'd got bored of working within the restrictions that stopped my mind wandering, there was no option but for me to do something else.

This was how *The Crimson Permanent Assurance* – my segment of *The Meaning of Life* – started out as an idea for an animation, but

Perfect people for a perfect world – one cloned family unit, fresh off the production line. **195**

then became a live-action short. Perhaps partly as a result of this formative shape-shifting, it also ended up being my first experience of going over-budget. I don't really know what the numbers were, but shortly after selflessly renouncing my directorial ambitions with regard to the film as a whole, I was deemed by the others to be totally out of control – drunk with power in charge of a limitless budget that no one had ever actually specified to me.

The basic story concerned a group of accountants who get angry with their new corporate masters of the universe and decide to become pirates on the high seas of international finance. If any amateur psychoanalysts out there wish to discern a subliminal echo of my own need to break out of my restricted role within Monty Python, I suppose it would be churlish of me to deny them this pleasure, but I don't remember that line of thought surfacing consciously at the time. And rather than being a product of anxieties about my own advancing years (I had by this point reached the grand old age of forty-two) the decision to use eighty-year-old actors reflected my determination to do for the elderly what *Time Bandits* had done for dwarves, i.e. dramatically expand their employment opportunities. I'm that guy who's all about helping the minorities … so long as they stay minorities of course – once they start becoming powerful, then it's a different matter.

The tone and feel of *The Crimson Permanent Assurance* were so different to the rest of the film that we had to remove it from its original slot in the middle of *The Meaning of Life* and run it as a separate mini-feature at the beginning, where it functioned like a sumptuous illustrated letter at the start of one of those medieval manuscripts I'm always banging on about, at the same time bearing witness to my increasingly marginal status within the group and growing willingness to fly the coop. Up on the big screens at the Cannes Film Festival, it looked fucking great – a real spectacle with genuine scale to it. Then when the actual film came on,

My 'Little Bo-Peep moment', welcoming Mike and Eric to heaven. I'm sure you'll agree, she's quite an enchanting girl.

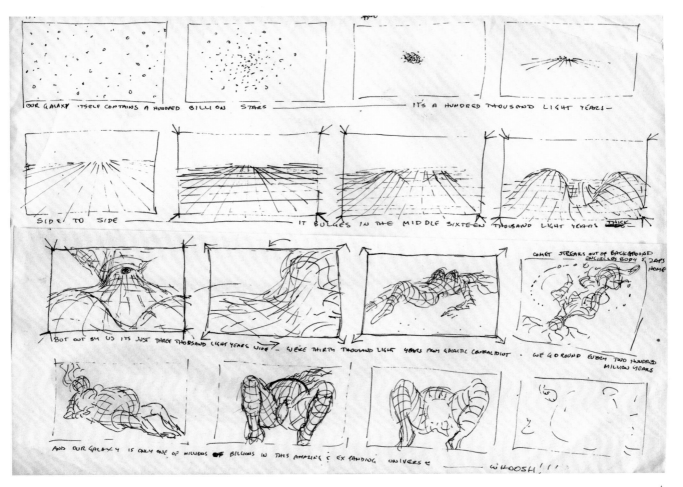

The storyboard panels contain the following handwritten captions:

OUR GALAXY ITSELF CONTAINS A HUNDRED BILLION STARS — IT'S A HUNDRED THOUSAND LIGHT YEARS —

SIDE TO SIDE — IT BULGES IN THE MIDDLE SIXTEEN THOUSAND LIGHT YEARS THICK

BUT OUT BY US ITS JUST THREE THOUSAND LIGHT YEARS WIDE — WE'RE THIRTY THOUSAND LIGHT YEARS FROM GALACTIC CENTRAL POINT — WE GO ROUND EVERY TWO HUNDRED MILLION YEARS

COMET STREAKS OUT OF BACKGROUND ENCIRCLES BODY & ZAPS HOME

AND OUR GALAXY IS ONLY ONE OF MILLIONS OF BILLIONS IN THIS AMAZING & EXPANDING UNIVERSE — WHOOSH!!!

This is my original drawing for the 'Big Bang' segment in Eric's "Galaxy Song", where the stars coalesce and become the space-time continuum, then you suddenly realise that it's a pair of breasts and she's been impregnated in space. As an indication of my readiness to move on, I got some proper animators to do this one for me.

it felt like you were watching TV, which given that this was how most people would ultimately end up seeing it, was probably for the best.

The happy memory of *Time Bandits'* big box-office numbers combined with the commercial and critical success of the last three Python films contrived to maximise my allure as a director and foster the general misconception of me as someone who knew what I was doing. But as hard as Arnon and I milked that moment, we were still struggling to get a full enough bucket to sustain *Brazil*.

If we'd been willing to do another time-travelling dwarf comedy, we'd have been awash with Hollywood doubloons, but having recklessly decided to exploit this moment of possibility to do the thing I'd wanted to do all along,

BRAZIL

getting the investment we needed was going to be much more of a challenge. I'd never been responsible for pitching a film before – other people had always been kind enough to do the money stuff for me – but this time Arnon and I were doing the rounds at Cannes.

He was running the show, and I was the guy who came in like
a trained monkey, leapt around and made a lot of chattering noises. You hope people are going to be swept along by your energy and enthusiasm, but more often what happens is the head honcho falls asleep. That's happened to me a couple of times, once with *Brazil* and again when J K Rowling wanted me to direct the first *Harry Potter* film (an assignment I was ultimately happy not to get, as by all the accounts I've heard from people who did end up doing them, the studio sat on you so heavily it became a bit of a nightmare). The younger junior executives are sitting there all bright-eyed and bushy-tailed, but the main guy is dozing – you're just noise to him.

We weren't getting much traction on Arnon's initial budget of £12 million, but then – in what turned out to be a counter-intuitive master-stroke – we put the price up, and the move from Oxford Street to Bond Street somehow did the trick for us. When I try to be devious, I generally fail, but sometimes when I'm out there as an innocent, it just happens. The thing that really sealed the deal was me turning down *Enemy Mine* – a big studio film that 20th Century Fox were desperate to get off the ground. *Time Bandits* had momentarily made me an A-list director, and now I was willing to say 'No' to a major studio project? The sado-masochistic logic of Hollywood decreed that the thing I'd turned them down for must now be something worth having.

As to the exact nature of the project for which we now had the go-ahead, the screenplay of *Brazil* had gone through a complex process of refinement at the hands of myself, my old buddy Charles McKeown, and one of the great English playwrights, Tom Stoppard – as a Czech born in Singapore, he understands the English language and its twists and turns far better than the locals. Foreigners are always going to look at things with a sharper eye, which is how Antonioni came over and did such a great job on 'Swinging London' with *Blow-Up*.

The practical process by which various drafts of the script evolved from the initial seed of me watching a beautiful sunset on a gloomy Welsh beach at Port Talbot is a story that has already been told in meticulous detail elsewhere. But the question of how *Brazil* related – and continues to relate – to its broader context, both personally and politically, is one in which I fondly imagine a fair amount of interest may remain.

In my capacity as one-sixth of an internationally renowned comedy troupe, I had often worried that I might actually be undermining people's abilities to change things. As any good commie from Lenin onwards would tell you, the secret of fomenting revolution is to let things get as bad as possible as quickly as possible, not to allow people to insulate themselves against the inequities of capitalism by having a good laugh at them. I believe the Roman satirist Juvenal knew this as the doctrine of bread and Flying Circuses.

It wasn't just the audience I was worried about – the emollient impact of all of this fun and laughter on my own counter-cultural instincts was no less a cause for concern. I think the underlying worry that comedy had given me a coward's way out was one factor behind my occasional firebrand-like utterances about my departure from America in the late summer of 1967.

Would I really have (as I've often said I might) joined a quasi-terrorist group like the Weathermen had I stayed? Probably not. It's like Mick Jagger saying he 'always wanted' to be a journalist. Does he really lose sleep at night over the decision to become a globally adored rock 'n' roll star rather than a Fleet Street hack? Somehow I doubt it, but the grass is always greener on the other side of the fence, however lush it might seem on yours to those looking over barbed-wire barriers of their own. I wanted to be a bomb-thrower and Mick wanted to pontificate about the state of the economy – if only we had followed our dreams!

When you grow up – as I did – reading Grimms' fairy tales and the Bible, there's no question that you see it as your duty to change the world for the better. And I think that's why, for all my frequent recourse to irony and/or sardonic sarcasm, my films have always been repositories of idealism – both in terms of the process of making them and of the subject matter of the films themselves. Cynicism can often be a way of covering up one's own inability to do great deeds. In a way I think that was what had so drawn me to the British sense of humour, because the Brits had almost patented that response – they'd failed at an empire, but then by learning to accept failure and make fun of it, they'd almost turned that into a positive thing.

One hangover from my missionary scholarship past has always been a sense of frustration that I haven't done more important things, whether in terms of my own creative work or going out to Africa to save a village from worms. Once I'd made the break from Monty Python, it was probably inevitable that this side of me was going to come more to the fore. And by the early eighties, the feeling I'd managed to string out throughout most of the previous decade that the radical agenda of the sixties was somehow being advanced via other means (every time I'd go back to New York with Python, black people seemed to walk a little taller, homosexuals moved with a more unrepentant sashay, and the city in general just seemed a friendlier place than it had been) could no longer really be sustained.

With Ronald Reagan and Margaret Thatcher

consolidating their initially shaky holds on power into an increasingly vice-like grip, it had become clear that the counter-cultural values that I'd taken as a consensus-in-waiting from the mid-1960s onwards were now in full-scale retreat. As far as those two great communicators were concerned, I could understand why all those public schoolboys in the British parliament loved to bend over and have Maggie's voice crack across their arses like a briar switch, but Ronald Reagan – the Disneyland president – was just ridiculous.

Here was someone who had never been anything more than a plausible front-man for any number of awful rich right-wing cabals. You never paid much attention to Ronnie Reagan – he was just kind of a joke. Then suddenly he was elected governor of California, and it seemed unthinkable that a B-movie actor could pull that off (there was certainly no way such a thing would ever happen again). When he spoke, he never really said anything, and yet somehow the lilting tones in which he said it reassured you that here was a guy who – despite all the incontrovertible evidence to the contrary – was actually on top of the situation.

Burt Reynolds told me a story once about being invited to the White House when Ronnie and Nancy were *in situ* (this works best if you can read it in a Reagan voice): 'Hey, Burt, you've gotta see in the dining room, there are all sorts of secret panels. Here, you just have to touch this and it opens up . . .' Of course, he can't find the secret button and is fumbling around all over the place until Nancy says (and this works best if you can read it in a Nancy voice): 'Oh, *Ronnie!*' and finds it immediately.

Then Ronnie takes Burt up to the Lincoln bedroom and says, 'I always feel so religious up here – really spiritual. I wonder, could you get down on your knees so we can pray together?' So there Burt is, praying on the floor of the Lincoln bedroom. When he leaves, Nancy and Ronnie are on the porch of the White House with their arms round each other saying, 'Whenever you're in town, Burt, just drop in – it'd be great to see you.' They're just these two slightly lonely old people who are only supposed to be running the country – it's not like there's really that much to do, is there? It would all be quite sweet if it wasn't for the awful geopolitical consequences of the kind of shit the people who actually were running the country were getting up to.

Preparatory collage for BRAZIL – upward motorway through high-rises.

This was where *Brazil* came in, and not only because the thing that always intrigued me about the villainous Mr Helpmann was that he's only the vice chairman, because to me there was nobody in charge. *Brazil*'s 1940s-inspired take on the future of 1980s Britain was located in exactly those places (like the spectacular Croydon power station) which had until recently been the engine-rooms of the empire, but were now – as Thatcher and Reagan's free-market fundamentalism hastened the end of the industrial era – in the process of a painful transition through partial dereliction to their ultimate destiny as luxury flats. All these stunning places we shot in, which were effectively remnants of the industrial era, have now either gone or been turned into cathedrals of Britain's lost imperial faith, like Tate Modern.

Those looking back on *Brazil* from a twenty-first-century perspective have sometimes been kind enough to see its depiction of a world where people do little but watch old films on tiny screens, eat off-puttingly extravagant cuisine and have ill-advised plastic surgery in the shadow of constant terrorist threats as in some way 'prophetic'. Keen as I am – with my messianic woodworking antecedents – to take on the mantle of prophet, I have to admit that all that stuff was already out there for those with eyes to see it in the mid-1980s. In those terms, I'd say *Brazil* was as much a documentary as it was a dystopia.

The IRA were bombing London on a regular basis, the

right-wing dictatorships Reagan was supporting in South America were reviving that great innovation of the seventeenth century – witch-trials – whereby if you were found guilty, you had to pay for your own incarceration, and in Germany university professors were being obliged to sign loyalty oaths in the belief that this would somehow cut off the supply of new recruits to the Red Army Faction. Against this turbulent backdrop, every time I went out to LA, I'd be sitting in hotel rooms and airports, and there would be pages and pages of plastic surgery ads in all the magazines. At that time, LA and Miami were the centres of this dubious practice, but now it's all around the world and someone who doesn't have surgery excites more comment than someone who does.

It's the same with the Ministry of Information, which I was obsessed with at the time, as an old-school Orwellian twist on the kind of totalitarian excesses that America was at best turning a blind eye to, and at worst actively initiating, in Latin America. Now it looks like a satirical dry run for the US Department

Another preparatory collage - 'Pipework through Bedroom'. One obvious influence on the ducts in BRAZIL was the famous external innards of the Georges Pompidou Centre in Paris, but inspiration also came from closer to home. I'd started to notice all these beautiful Regency buildings in London, where people were just smashing through all the ornate cornice work to put plumbing pipes on the outside. I remember thinking 'what is going on — does nobody have any aesthetics here any more?' I suppose they just wanted stuff, a sensation not unknown to users of the Internet, which somehow becomes more ubiquitous and invasive as it continues to bring us all these great things that we really want.

of Homeland Security or at the very least John Birt's BBC – probably the ultimate manifestation of that most destructive of Thatcherite tendencies whereby public institutions suddenly started to run themselves like number-crunching corporations rather than as public institutions for the people who actually paid for them.

The film's one tiny suspicion of prophetic content is delivered – like pretty

BRAZIL

much everything else in *Brazil* – by the ducts. I'd always been fascinated by pneumatic tubes in shops, wondering where do they lead and what is the person they deliver to up to. And I suppose now that people often refer to Internet service providers having digital content 'in their pipes', it can feel a bit like 'Central Services: we do the work, you do the pleasure', though of course one important difference is that in the film the ducts aren't just bringing you everything you want, they're also taking all the shit away. No one seems to have come up with a way of doing that via the Internet as yet.

In terms of elements of *Brazil* that were prompted by my own personal experience, the most obvious was probably the Acid Man. In the late seventies, my dad had been through a nightmarish experience when a patch of skin cancer was discovered on his ear and a highly recommended surgeon applied acid to it, then put a compress over the top and advised him to go and sit outside in the park for an hour or two while the acid worked its magic. By the time my dad came back into the surgery, the very edge of his ear was still there, but the whole lobe had been eaten away.

He was in terrible pain, but he seemed to have this amazing ability to cope with it. Dad was a quiet guy and very stoical – not always whingeing and moaning like me. There'd been another time when I was still a kid, when he'd been doing a chalk line on the ceiling, where you tap a big nail in and stretch the line that you're going to run your stud-work up to. He was up on the ladder tightening the line when the nail came loose, flew straight at him and went deep into his eye. He just pulled it out and drove forty miles home. I know those were different times when people in general made less fuss, but still, my dad made the Black Knight look like a faint-heart.

A few years later, he ended up having to have this operation where a tumour had grown behind his eye and they did a full-blown Python/Vanderbeek cartoon on him – lifted the top of his head off, went in there and took the tumour out, then stuck the top of his head back on again. It was after this that I became convinced that he was part lizard, because the optic nerve to that one eye had been severed – he was completely blind in it – yet when I asked him years later what that was like, he said, 'Oh, I still see a bit with it.' Devotee of the Enlightenment that I was (and am), I found this hard to accept, so Maggie and I did a test on him where we got him to cover his good eye while we hid a pea somewhere on the table, and of course he went straight to it. I suppose I've tried to emulate my dad's stubborn refusal to give up in the way that I've made movies – struggling on with an arm or a leg or both tied behind my back and my balls in a vice operated by the bond company.

As well as my dad's horrendous aural mishap, *Brazil*'s expansive narrative also found room for the newest Gilliam arrival. The only scene we had to reshoot because it wasn't quite working was the one where Jack Lint is at his office, spouting all these sinister details of the stuff he's been up to. I realised that what this scene needed to give it another angle was to have one of his children there (not twins, triplets – 'how time flies'), so drafted in my three-year-old daughter Holly. Having Michael Palin playing with this little girl while he's wearing a blood-stained smock and talking about torturing people turned out to be chillingly effective, and best of all – we didn't have to pay her!

Preparing to entrust my innocent daughter Holly to the tender care of the torturer, Michael Palin...

That's how you learn to make films, really – just by doing it. Giving an actor something else to focus on often helps with passages they're struggling with, because it takes their mind off the problem in hand. That's why in the party scene you can see Michael is eating all the time. Because he is such a brilliant performer, I was shocked by how nervous he was to be working along-side Jonathan Pryce, Peter Vaughan and Ian Richardson – people he regarded as 'proper actors' – never mind Robert De Niro. But that very twitchiness was part of what made Michael so great in the film, along with a vague sense of him coming from the same kind of background that George Orwell did, so had he been born fifty years earlier, he might easily have ended up as a colonial admin-istrator, writing about a Far East that was still under British control.

It's not fashionable now to imagine that the maintenance of empire could ever have been something people felt genuinely idealistic about, but no doubt for some in the generations before the whole thing fell apart, it was just the very important cause they were looking for – the Peace Corps of its day, even. My own very important cause, in terms of the shooting of *Brazil* at least, would be managing Robert De Niro.

Obviously I was very excited when Arnon Milchan – who had been his pro-ducer on both *Once Upon a Time in America* and *The King of Comedy* – told me that De Niro, who was a Python fan, wanted a part in *Brazil*. He came over and we spent a day talking, and Bobby was gracious enough to accept the smaller role of Archibald 'Harry' Tuttle, as I'd already given the part he originally want-ed to Michael Palin. From that point on, he started popping over to London quite a lot, and dealing with him became something of a full-time job.

He was so utterly thorough in his preparation that he had a friend who was a brain surgeon whose operations he was sitting in on (because I'd described Harry's precision as a repair-man as 'surgical'). Imagine coming out from being under anaesthetic after brain surgery and the first person you see is Robert De Niro! You're going to think you've crossed over to the other side . . . and then you're going to ask him for his autograph. By the time we were having to build mock-ups of every scene he was going to be doing, it was starting to drive every-one a bit crazy. Not least because the presence of someone who required so much attention began to have an impact on the other actors.

Kim Greist, a virtual newcomer who I had chosen to play the girl, in front of a long queue of better-known and possibly better-qualified candidates, started trying to behave in the same way – Robert De Niro was getting all that special attention, so why shouldn't she? In the end I had to tell her, 'Wait a min-ute, you don't actually deserve it, because you haven't done anything in your

career yet, whereas he has, which is why I will suck it up for him but not for you.'

On the first day of shooting, I was told that he'd been in his room in full costume at four o'clock in the morning. It was funny, because later on, when I needed to edit in some extra surgical-style repair footage using my own hands (because Bobby had been so nervous on the day that we'd only been able to film him using a couple of tools) I had to put his costume on, and I remember thinking, 'Jesus, it's so hot and cumbersome. This must be why he does all that preparation, because it frees him up when he's actually on camera. Thinking about everything else so intensely is his way of freeing himself up from over-thinking the lines – it's the self-administered equivalent of giving Michael Palin party food.'

I found that incredibly interesting. I've always tended to

see actors as something of a species apart. Having never studied acting myself, I don't really understand how their minds work, and I don't actually think it's my job to do that. In Monty Python we weren't trained so we just went out and did things – and I did them badly – but when you see the really great actors at work, you realise they've got all these little tricks that either help them do what they do or conspire to make our lives miserable – or most often, both.

At that point you just have to resign yourself to the fact that he is Robert De Niro or Sean Connery or Ralph Richardson or whoever he is, and we've somehow managed to get him in our film, so we've just got to make it possible for him to do whatever he does. Even if that means letting him have thirty-five takes. I just think people come in, and they kind of stake out their territory by putting their spoor down. Some of it's conscious and some of it's subconscious, but what the director has to do is to decide exactly how much of that behaviour you need to let them get away with.

And if you get that call right, they will reward you by coming up with something great – like Harry's thick glasses with the little lights on, which were totally De Niro's idea.

I think good actors will be willing to completely expose themselves so long as they're confident they are in safe hands and feeling protected – i.e. that their failures will not be used. My experience is that once they trust me they will go beyond their career 'health and safety' limits. They aren't called 'players' for nothing, and my job is to create a playground in which it's safe for them to risk falling flat on their faces.

It was all about creating an opportunity for him to show us that Marlon Brando could still touch his toes.

Chapter

12

Jump into the Fire

The most dangerous part of the film-making

process is the last stage of the edit. At that point, you obviously want what you've done to be successful – not so much because you're counting the money, you just want it to get out there and have people like it. The kicker is that by this time you're probably the worst judge of whether it's any good or not, because you've seen the film so many more times than anyone else is ever going to and are probably vacillating between thinking it's wonderful and an absolute piece of shit.

On the one hand, you're desperately holding on to what you've got, convinced that if you make one mistake at this stage, the whole thing will fall apart; on the other, you're desperately looking for the one change that is going to make all the difference. With *Brazil*, the latter impulse prevailed. The day the film premiered in Leicester Square, I went in and cut a large part of one scene out of the show print myself – it was the moment where Jonathan and Kim wake up together, just before he gets arrested. You convince yourself that this particular scene is going on too long and if you can just get rid of it, everything will work much better. It's a dumb trick to fall for, but I fell for it that time. Years later when the Criterion Collection released their restored version of the film I reassembled the severed scene.

Once *Brazil* was finished, Fox released it in Europe without

any problems, but Universal baulked in the States. I don't know how other people have the confidence they seem to exude in these situations, because I'm always terrified. But one thing I do have an instinct for is who the enemy is – I always

know when someone is trying to 'fix' things for the wrong reasons. In this case, the deluded fantasist Gilliam wanted the film to end with its feet on the ground, whereas the supposedly grown-up and responsible studio executives wanted to cut it so what had originally been written as a fantasy sequence would now be presented as reality.

Storyboard for BRAZIL's 'Sea of Eyes' fantasy sequence – one of several elaborate fantasy segments which had already been sliced (by me) from the script, long before Universal started trying to give us a fairy-tale ending.

The scenes that have to go first are often the ones that are nearest to the director's heart – it's almost as if you're in some Old Testament world where the first sacrifice has to be the thing you love the most. (It's like Bob Dylan says, 'God said to Abraham, "Kill me a son." . . . Abe said, "Where do you want this killin' done?"' Fuck, that's a great line.) The ones that go right at the end tend to be the ones which have cost loyal foot-soldiers the most – which is why it's some consolation now they can at least have some kind of afterlife as 'deleted scenes' on DVD or Blu-Ray.

I have no objection to sending the audience home whistling under the right circumstances, but the conclusion of a lapsed totalitarian dreamscape does not meet that criterion. Universal executives kept saying things like, 'The depressing stuff is really interesting, Terry, but that doesn't mean they can't escape from it . . . You saw *Blade Runner,* didn't you? *They got away.*' The problem was that in Ridley Scott's rose-tinted happy ending to Philip K Dick's original story – which had been released a couple of years before – the director had given the studio just what they wanted by letting them change the ending.

I can see the logic that lay behind that decision, especially for a commercially minded director like Ridley. You want the studio to get behind your film, and maybe even let you make another one – so when push comes to shove, you give way. What made me crazy was that later on, he got to do a 'director's cut' and put back in all the stuff that he'd collaborated on cutting out.

I don't know where my rebel streak comes from,

but for some reason it tends to move to the fore whenever purity or truth or any of these other ridiculously simplistic ideas get violated. I know what you're thinking: 'And this from the man who helped make adverts for whatever terrible films Universal could throw at him!' But don't you see? *That's how I know* . . . Because I was briefly caught up in that side of the business, I can smell that kind of bullshit a mile off. The problem for so many of the really good British directors who came out of advertising was that they'd been in that business for too long. Because I only did it for a year or so (and for at least half of that time I was in an active state of rebellion), I hadn't had time to internalise the doctrines.

The various battles I've had with studios and censors over the years have never been about resisting authority for its own sake, they've always (at least, from my end) been about protecting the work. With Python, for example, it was always very important to us that the programmes and books and records went out exactly the way we made them, and if anything I felt even more strongly about that once I was running my own cinematic show. I don't want to change my films after they're completed, because it's their flaws which make them historical records of what we were capable of doing at a particular time. When I sign my name to everyone else's work as the director, that's basically what I'm taking responsibility for: 'This is it, for better or worse, the best we could do.' So to go back and re-do that I think is a real cheat. (If this is the director's cut, why on earth did you put your name to it the first time?)

Once Universal started trying to fiddle around and re-cut the film, I kept getting calls from this editor they'd put on it who couldn't understand why I wasn't co-operating. He kept asking me, 'Don't you want to protect your film?' So I said, 'But you're disembowelling the thing . . . what am I supposed to protect – the bits of lifeless meat that are left? Fuck you!' The minute you start to go along with that shit, you end up like Spielberg taking the guns out of the policemen's hands in *ET* – in the original they had guns which they were about to shoot, and he airbrushed them out for the re-release. Maybe my appetite for the airbrush had been exhausted by using one to do cartoons with, but what the fuck was he doing? What was this – Stalin removing Trotsky from the Russian revolutionary photo-wall?

We weren't having that, even if it

meant the ice-pick in the night. We tried to hire a PR firm to help us get our point across, but Universal then embargoed the film so it couldn't be shown in America – even to a PR firm. At that point, it was guerrilla time. I took out a full-page ad in *Variety* asking Sid Sheinberg (who was the head of the studio) when he was going to release our film. That got a little buzz going, and then we offered to put any legitimate journalist who wanted to see the film on a bus to Mexico, where they could watch it legally.

It was around this time that the University of Southern California invited me to come and do a talk, so I brought the film with me, saying it was my audio-visual aid. But the operations manager of the school refused to show it, because that college is basically an extension of the studio system and they knew which side their bread was buttered. I was running back and forth on the phone to my lawyer who had Mr Middleman – (His real name! It might as well have been Mr Helpmann . . .) – from Universal on the other line. Then a student from a less hide-bound seat of learning (in this case Cal Arts, the college Walt Disney created, which trained all the animators who are now Pixar) said, 'We'll show it.'

At this point, Sid Sheinberg was caught in a cleft stick. I don't think he knew what to make of the original version of the film – he sensed there was something special about it, he just wanted a happy ending. They did actually bolt together their own happy-ending version, which ended up going out on syndicated TV (where it would be interrupted by adverts every five minutes). They called it the 'Love Conquers All' edit. This was doubly ironic, because Sid's wife – who'd played Mrs Roy Scheider in *Jaws,* so she knew a thing about sharks – loved *Brazil* just the way it was, so inside the house he was having to deal with her, while outside I was pursuing him through the national media, the poor guy.

By now a certain amount of noise was being created. In the intervening

HELP
The Ministry of Information
HELP YOU

Draft version of one of the on-set posters for BRAZIL.

years since we'd worked together in LA in the mid-1960s, my old friend Joel Siegel had progressed to being film critic on ABC's *Good Morning America*. He was very aware of what was going on and said maybe they could get us on the show. The key to that happening was persuading Robert De Niro to give an interview – which was something he very rarely did, because he was incredibly uncomfortable being interviewed, and it was truly wonderful of him to support us under those circumstances.

As it turned out, his social awkwardness worked in our favour. The host of the show was Maria Shriver – one of the Kennedy family who a short while later married Arnold Schwarzenegger and eventually became (at least, on a temporary basis) the first lady of California – and after a while she got so desperate trying to get anything out of De Niro that she turned to the less famous guy sitting next to him.

Once she'd asked if it was true that I had a problem with the studio, that was it, I was away. 'I don't have a problem with the studio,' I told the future Mrs Arnie, 'I've got a problem with one man. His name is Sid Sheinberg, and he looks like this . . . ' At that point, I whipped out the eight-by-ten glossy photo of Sid that I had presciently brought with me, ran up to the camera and showed it to millions of Americans.

Now it was all about keeping up the pressure. A couple of critics from the *LA Times* who had been at the USC event got behind us and started setting up clandestine screenings. Then someone looked up the rules for the LA Critics Awards and saw that there was nothing in them about films having to actually be released to be in competition, so they awarded us best film, best director and best screenplay, which was very sporting of them, especially as they had a reputation for being quite a conservative lot.

It's not often critics get the chance to do something positive, and having taken the opportunity with both hands, I have no doubt that the LA pen-pushing fraternity look back upon this as one of their proudest moments.

By this time, as may have already become obvious, I was really enjoying myself. I am generally someone who likes to be liked – there's no question about that – and the flipside of this generalised desire to get on with people is that when a conflict does arise, I am usually pretty good at reinventing my adversary as a horrible monster, which makes it easier for me to understand how a great guy like myself could have fallen out with them. I fondly imagine that the *Good Morning America* incident might also have proved to be a valuable resource for other directors – if they ever got caught up in a row with their studio, they could always say, 'At least I'm not Terry Gilliam.'

These are my rough notebook drawings for a theme-park attraction to be called 'The Body Ride', planned as one of the big draws at 'WonderWorld', an ambitious-to-the-point-of-sounding-fictional early eighties project to establish a UK Disneyland in the depressed former steel-town of Corby.

Few places in Britain had been more cruelly affected by the process of accelerated de-industrialisation that formed the backdrop to the writing of Brazil than this hard-pressed Northamptonshire New Town. How better to compensate its denizens than with an American-style theme park?

I was asked to design a ride and came up with this plan, inspired by the human digestive process- alimentary, my dear Watson.

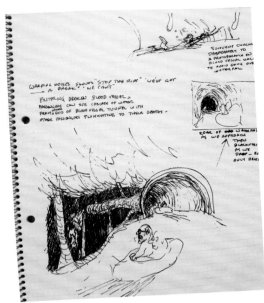

Sadly – although not surprisingly – WonderWorld never came to fruition.

Perhaps not so sadly, my sketch of the ride's final stage seems to be lost forever, so readers will have to guess through which orifice patrons would have made their exit.

One of the most thrilling things about the victory for free expression that *Brazil* did ultimately win (when poor old Sid threw in the towel and let us release it at just a few minutes shy of its original length) was how many different people had got behind us to make that happen – from the LA Critics, to the Cal Arts students organising screenings, to Robert De Niro breaking his vow of *omertà* to go on a chat show. I was disappointed, however, with Spielberg's apparent use of imagery from a scene in *Brazil.* At least to my learned friend in the ways of movie-making, George Ayoub, and my paranoid, bloodshot eyes, he had drawn rather too heavily for my liking on the scene of Sam's awakening for a scene in *Back to the Future*.

Obviously I'm the last person to be complaining about plagiarism, given the blatant debts I owe everyone from Breughel to Vanderbeek to Gustav Doré. I've always been fascinated by the sense that there is a *zeitgeist* out there, which everyone who is drawing or writing anything is feeding off, and that's how very different people will often seem to be having strangely similar ideas at the same time. In a broader sense, I think that's the way history works too – everyone wants to try and nail it down to this cause or that symptom, but I don't actually think it necessarily *can* be nailed down. An idea will be floating around for a while and then all of a sudden something shifts and we're all seeing things the same way – because it's the same energy everyone's plugged into.

In film-making terms, a lot of directors I've been friendly with – from John Landis to Martin Scorsese – have tended to shoot with a trailer full of reference videos (now it would probably be Netflix) so they can study various classic templates of the scene they've got in mind. But being one of those guys who sits in the National Gallery trying to get a perfect copy of the Rembrandt has never been what it's about for me. I'm much more interested in using what I think I remember of something as a template, rather than going back to check

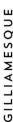

the actuality, because that way I know it's been through my alembic (the alembic being the distiller that alchemists use for turning base metal into gold, although in my case it does tend to work the opposite way round).

I've often spoken of the way the making of the film becomes the story of the film, but in this case, the *releasing* of the film became the story of the film. And the very existence of *Brazil* in its completed form came to represent exactly the kind of unlikely triumph over a malevolent monolithic adversary that the film's protagonists had hoped for. I think this was one reason why it came to resonate so strongly for those who had inhabited the real-life totalitarian landscapes to which the film was an imaginative response.

Palin and I were dragged off to Moscow and St Petersburg

for a couple of screenings in the midst of *glasnost* and *perestroika,* and the film seemed to be going down a treat. If anything the audiences felt our fantasy version of bureaucratic centralism worked a little better than theirs had. One of the highlights of that trip came when I was offered the chance to visit Eisenstein's apartment. Well, as the curator explained, it wasn't Sergei's actual apartment, but they'd laid it out as an exact replica and filled it with all his stuff. I was

already thinking about *Baron Munchausen* by this time, so when I saw a copy of one of the Munchausen books up on a high shelf, I reached up to have a look at it and clumsily knocked off a framed picture.

Early drawings of John Neville as Baron Munchausen. His physical resemblance to Jean Rochefort's later Don Quixote was not coincidental – first because both emerged from the illustrations of Gustave Doré, secondly because these long gaunt dreamers are opposing sides of the same coin, the difference between them being that Munchausen is a liar, but Quixote believes.

'*I'm tired and the world is tired of me,*' was Baron Munchausen's line.

And to be honest, I was feeling the same at this time. As often happened I found that it was actually my own children (by now Maggie and I had added Harry to the list) who ended up giving me a reason to carry on. I think the key to survival is trying to keep alive the 'inner child', whatever that is. We've all got that sense of wonder and the ability to be surprised but it's beaten out of people as they go through life. I've just been lucky to be able to find work that allows me to keep that little brat inside alive.

What should that picture be but an original drawing of Mickey Mouse signed by Walt Disney himself. I had already been considering the idea of doing *Munchausen* as a live-action Disney cartoon, and now the Soviet author of the only book I'd ever studied on the practicalities of cinema was conspiring from beyond the grave with arch venture capitalist Uncle Walt to give that ambitious plan the thumbs-up. How much more encouragement did I need?

The various existing versions of the Munchausen stories already seemed to be coalescing in those strange moments of synchronicity which always come into play in the formative stages of any film project. I had previously become very interested in *Baron Pràsil* – the Czech director Karel Zeman's 1961 version, which is a mixture of live action and animation, with real people walking through these amazing flat engraved sets. Then once when I was visiting George Harrison at Friar Park he showed me a film – the UFA version of the story, bizarrely produced by Joseph Goebbels.

That's how these things always come together. Something is floating around in the ether and then someone else comes at it from another angle and off you go. The money side of things was – inevitably – a little more tortuous. In fact, this was the first film of mine where the fiscal provenance went horribly skewiff. It started with Arnon having done a deal with Fox that I didn't know about and never saw a penny of. We only found out that they owned a chunk of the film once we were preparing to sign up with David Puttnam's number two at Columbia.

The other people I work with will often be telling me that my producer is a bit of an operator, and my reply to them is generally, 'Well, that may very well be true, but I'm only interested in one thing, and that's getting the film done – whether or not I get screwed in the process is an issue of secondary importance.' In this case, the discovery that both Arnon and 20th Century Fox would now own a chunk of the finished film obviously meant the end of my relationship with the man who has recently revealed himself to have been working as an Israeli intelligence agent throughout this period (Robert De Niro has said he knew, and I know even more). So in one sense, the people who warned me against Milchan were right, but at the same time, we got two films made together, and no amount of documentaries about his pivotal role in the Israeli nuclear weapons programme can change that.

Once Arnon was out of the picture, his German line producer Thomas Schühly stepped up to the plate. He'd previously worked on *The Name of the Rose*, and his first contribution was to keep firing accountants until they got the notional (perhaps fictional would be a better word) budget down to the amount of money we actually had, which was about £23.5 million. Our next challenge (no one could accuse us of starting small) was to try to get Marlon Brando to play the role of Vulcan.

I was out in LA staying at the Chateau Marmont hotel when his agent and friend Jay Kantor (who'd been a humble mail-room employee before the young Brando decided he liked the cut of his jib) informed us that Marlon would be paying us a visit. The call comes up from downstairs saying Marlon has arrived, so I tell them to send him up, wait the amount of time you'd allow for Brando to come up the stairs and open

This is one of my Munchausen sketch books, which I filled with fast and furious drawings of the same Roman architecture I'd photographed on my first trip to the Eternal City more than twenty years before. I loved doing these sketches, just sitting out in the street — on the day I did this one, I'd discovered that in the presepi — which are Roman nativity tableaux that come out around Christmas — the holy child is referred to as 'Il Bimbo Dio'.

the door to see him coming down the corridor in this great white linen suit and shades – *boom, boom, boom*. He'd put on a lot of weight. He comes in and we spend forty-five minutes or so having a very good time – relaxed and laughing, albeit in the awareness that there's a little game going on here. Having been trained to recognise this situation quite quickly by my experiences with Ralph Richardson – and others – I was intrigued to discover the exact nature of the game that was being played.

At this point I get a call from an anxious-sounding Thomas, saying that Marlon hasn't turned up. The way the Chateau Marmont is set out is that there's the main entrance higher up and the garage entrance down below, which is the way everyone normally comes in, but Marlon has had himself dropped off up at the front, and has thereby bypassed Thomas' welcoming committee. Unfortunately, the minute we relocate to Schühly's suite – where he's got a buffet set up and everything – Marlon suddenly becomes a very different creature. This isn't fun any more, it's business.

So I'm sitting next to this huge Mount Rushmore profile (Marlon's head is massive – even bigger than Richard Nixon's) and it seems to be carved out of marble with a brow that never ends. All the bullshit small-talk is kind of faltering, so I decide to stir things up a bit by saying, 'I've got to ask you about *A*

COLLEGIO ROMANO
ACCADEMA

VIA
OCLEGATA

Countess from Hong Kong,' which was a film Chaplin directed with Brando and Sophia Loren in. It's not a good movie and Brando is clearly not having a good time in it – turns out he just hated Chaplin, and being one of those guys who is very definitely either on or off, he gave a very uncomfortable performance.

The more I absorbed the place, the more I began to think of Munchausen as a baroque film – and how better to express my fascination for Rome than to make the film at the Cinecittà studios – the home of Italian cinema?

As soon as that film is mentioned, Marlon starts being very disdainful and dismissive about Sophia Loren – going on about how she was a terrible actress who'd made her career on her back. He launches into this story about a time when they were waiting for a shot, and he said, 'I bet you can't touch your toes.' He did it first, then as she bent down to do it, he grabbed her from behind and mimed as if he was fucking her doggie fashion. It's like a game within a game, though, because he's acting out this whole slightly grim story for us in turn, and I suddenly realise that the whole point of it was not about how it felt so good that he'd humiliated Sophia Loren in front of the whole crew, it was all about creating an opportunity for him to show us that Marlon Brando could still touch his toes.

Rome's allure has been so strong for me over the years that it's been suggested that I might be a closet Catholic … and there could be something in that, if it were only possible to get rid of the priests and just have the architecture.

RED ORANGE BRICKS
YELLOW BRICK COLUMNS
LAVENDER CREST ABOVE DOOR

PIAZZA DELLA PIGNA

As he shifted his huge bulk to pull off this improbable physical coup, you could almost see Marlon thinking, 'You think I'm a fat old fuck, but I can still touch my toes.' At this point, I started to think we had some chance of persuading him to be in our film – what fascinated me was the realisation that Marlon Brando actually cared what we thought of him. After he left, Thomas told me that we'd all been invited to Jay Kantor's birthday party later on, but that even though Brando had been alright with me, he'd been making life difficult for everyone else.

By this time I thought I'd sussed out how to deal with Marlon, so I got his number in the literal as well as the metaphorical sense and called him up. When the phone stopped ringing, it just clicked, so I didn't know if it was an answering machine or Brando was there, but on balance it felt like the latter, so I left him a long message saying how I'd enjoyed meeting him very much but I didn't know why he was giving our producer Thomas such a hard time – 'He's a huge fan, but you're shitting all over him. Why would you do this when you don't need to?'

Later that night, we went to Kantor's party, and when Brando saw me across the room, his curious gaze just fixed on me in a 'What's this guy's game?' sort of way. I never got to find out how far my pro-active strategy would have taken us, because I said to Thomas that the only way to get him was to call his bluff with the whole getting-a-squaw-to-come-out-and-pick-up-his-Academy-Award thing and tell him we'd pay him $2 million, but only if we could give the money directly to the American Indians. I think we would've got him that way, because his own moral scheme would have left him no option but to accept. Unfortunately, Thomas didn't have the balls to do it, and insisted on a more conventional approach, which didn't work.

It all worked out for the best in the end, though, because we got Oliver Reed instead, and he was an absolute joy. I loved working with Ollie. A lot of people were a bit nervous about him, but he only went crazy once. It was during the scene where he throws the Baron and all the others into a whirlpool, and I don't quite know what was going wrong, but suddenly he just decided to go for the assistant director – he didn't actually punch him, but the physicality was definitely there as a back-up to the verbal assault.

I was lucky enough to be on the other side of the maelstrom at the time (in both senses) so by the time I got there, it was just a question of trying to calm down this terrifyingly Vulcan-like figure. Almost the next minute it seemed like Ollie felt embarrassed by what had happened – maybe he'd just got himself in the place he needed to be in, and all it took was the trigger of someone doing the wrong thing to make him explode more or less in character.

Either way, the next scene we shot he asked me if he could 'try something'. Of course I said yes, and then he just batted his eyelids like a love-sick cow as Uma Thurman's Venus spoke, which was both hilarious and sublime – sometimes you almost feel like those things are happening as an act of atonement. I never really know what to say in situations where an actor has got upset on a personal level, so I just try to get in there and look understanding – as if I'm doing something to make it better when really I don't have a clue. I think how a lot of the best actors tend to work is almost by a series of controlled explosions, and in those situations it is sadly inevitable – as any one-armed mining engineer will tell you – that the odd unscheduled blast will occasionally sneak in.

Much as Columbia wanted to cut costs, making
BARON MUNCHAUSEN in black and white just
wasn't an option.

Chapter **13**

Old Man

often say, 'If you haven't read the story, you don't know you're in it', but the sad truth is that knowing you're in a story doesn't necessarily change the ending. In fact, that kind of self-awareness can become a problem in itself – you start to realise the pre-set patterns are waiting for you like dog shit on the pavement, and it's just a question of which one you're going to tread in.

Because the producer Thomas Schühly's heroes were Dino De Laurentiis, Alexander the Great and Napoleon, he was very excited about working on such a grand project and insisted on calling BARON MUNCHAUSEN 'the new CLEOPATRA.' But I kept telling him to shut up because the Italian crew all got new cars and houses from the last one, and if we kept telling them that we had all this money, it was inevitable that they would take everything we had and more.

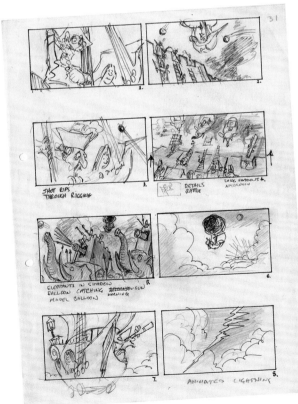

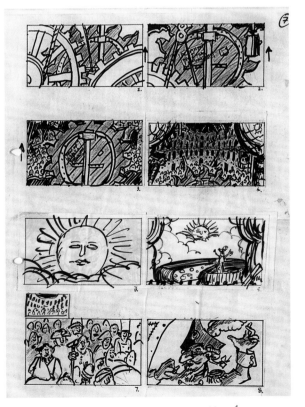

My most ornate storyboards for my most ornate film... Who could possibly have guessed that this was going to be expensive?

If I can immodestly presume to construct an analogy on the capacious foundation of the *oeuvre* of Orson Welles, let's say *Brazil* was my *Citizen Kane* – the time we took on the studios and won – then *Munchausen* was my *Magnificent Ambersons*: payback time from the men in suits. *Brazil* had come out and done OK. It made decent money – not loads, but enough – and was widely recognised as an achievement of some kind. But this guy who'd made it was clearly trouble and his come-uppance was long overdue, so once things started to go wrong on *Munchausen*, I knew I'd clicked out of *Kane* and into *Ambersons* mode. That sense of falling into another story is like a flying dream without the actual flight.

On *Munchausen,* where the original budget was roughly £23 million,

we were probably pushing £30 million by the time things had really gone tits up. The insurers Lloyds of London had come in to produce the film for a while (from which point things actually progressed quite smoothly, because they brought in a sensible woman, Joyce Herlihy, who'd been the production supervisor on *Jabberwocky,* and she made intelligent decisions without just blaming me for everything) until they reached the limit of their liability, and then it reverted back to the bond company, Film Finances.

The role of the bond company is one of the most significant – and least discussed – aspects of movie-making. For a suitably handsome percentage, the bond company guarantees that if you go over budget, the film will still get finished, and (at least in theory) it'll be them that coughs up the money. They operate along basically similar business principles to the bail bondsman in a Western, except there are no actual bullets in the shoot-outs. There is an element of waiting for people to go for their guns though, because a bond company will often sign off on a blatantly fictitious budget, confident that the producers will chip in the extra cash to avoid the stigma of calling them in.

What did they mean the director was 'out of control'? Everyone of these elephants was integral to the storyline ...

OLD MAN

227

By the time *Munchausen* got to the post-production stage, the studio had been subject to regime change and were happy to see the projects of David Puttnam's old guard doing badly so the new boys would shine by comparison. At this point the bond company will generally start dumping all their other bad debts on you, under the old Hollywood adage of 'If it's down already, you might as well bury it.' The way the accounting of major financial institutions is set up often tends to militate against fiscal common sense and in favour of profligacy. I remember talking to one of the people from Lloyds about the racehorse Shergar, who had been stolen a couple of years before, but they were 'convinced' was still alive. They'd paid out millions on the basis that he wasn't, so we asked, 'Why don't you just get a private detective and stump up a few thousand to track him down?' And the guy said, 'It's not worth it, the money's already been written off.' If you blow the whistle that a mistake has been made, you'll probably end up in even bigger trouble, so it's probably best to just sit back and let the millions keep on flowing (which in this case, was probably good news for us ... up to a point).

Even Baron Munchausen's four Academy Award nominations could not dispel the bad financial ju-ju, which had been intensified first by a web of intrigue between the bond company and the studio, and then by the studio's decision to limit the film's American release to a fraction (and a small one at that) of the usual number of prints. My new-found pariah status in Hollywood was not entirely without an upside, though. As a consequence of the

difficulties I subsequently had getting projects off the ground, I've definitely made fewer films than I would've liked. However, given an easy ride, I probably would have knocked out some real stinkers, but I was saved from myself by my own notoriety, so maybe there is some kind of guardian angel at work in my career after all – it's just that he or she is a pretty fucked-up, ironic character.

The cast has a group premonition about the pathetic release the studio would give the film.

Bitter resignation to the malevolence of destiny aside, there was at least one sense in which the toxic aftermath of *Munchausen* really did prove to be a blessing in disguise. There's nothing quite like an enforced renunciation of the ego for paving a new avenue of creative fulfilment. Such was my determination to control as many aspects of the film-making process as possible that I'd always sworn I was only ever going to make films from my own scripts – it all had to be me, I was going to do everything. But of course then reality kicks in and decrees otherwise, and you realise that there's actually nothing better than coming across something someone else has done which you just think is wonderful.

There I was, flicking distractedly through the latest version of *The Addams Family* script and thinking, 'This isn't really doing it for me,' when in the same package from my agent, Jack Rapke, along came *The Fisher King*. It was already past midnight when I started reading it. I was just about to go to bed, but I thought, 'I'll take a peek anyway,' and right from the first page I was thinking, 'Fuck, this is good.' I just understood it – the dialogue was great, I could identify with the characters and even the fact that it wasn't full of special effects was working for me – 'OK, you've done the big one, now let's come down to something more practical . . .'

The painful truth was that the main reason Richard LaGravenese's

script had been sent to me in the first place was because they wanted Robin Williams to be in the film. Robin had been in *Munchausen* and was my buddy, and therefore I was the bait – that's all, just a little worm stuck on the end of a hook.

This is the kind of moment when it becomes very clear what your power is – if you have any left – but I think one useful attribute I can legitimately claim is the ability to recognise reality. Of course, that's the secret weapon no one in Hollywood expects me to have. They all think I'm a dreamer and a fantasist, and OK, in a way I am, but I can also recognise reality – there it is, sitting over there. That doesn't mean I want to join it for lunch, but if I have to, then I will . . .

A man at war with the fates – pondering the potential benefits of a spell in the cinematic wilderness.

The director seduces a doubtful Robin with an ancient ritual dance.

Being a honey trap for Robin Williams might not

be much, but it's better than nothing. So long as I can snag the big names, then I can still do my job – I think that was what I learned there, and it was a lesson I was happy to take on board. Do I want to be Steven Spielberg – to have all that money and be able to do exactly what I want? In one way I do, but the problem is I want to be able to tell the stories I think need telling. To be fair, Spielberg's *Amistad* did change the black man's future enough for them to have walk-on parts in *Lincoln* and be grateful. I accept that. But it does not fall to all of us to make that kind of grand contribution to humanity.

The rest of us less saintly and philanthropic directors must gather our crumbs of validation wherever we can find them. And *The Fisher King* – perhaps as the universe's reward for my willingness to set aside my customary monomania in taking it on in the first place – would offer my bruised ego as much balm as any other film in my brickbat-bestrewn cinematic pantheon.

Because it was Richard's first script and he'd written it on spec, I asked if I could see the earlier versions. Just as I'd expected, they were even better than the one the studio wanted me to make . . . i.e. the pressure to compromise had already been brought to bear. But that wasn't going to happen now I was in charge. Not only did I go back to the previous drafts of various key scenes, I also worked as hard as I could to stop myself putting my fingerprints all over the film. So often in that situation the director will come in and piss all over the script just to claim it as his own, but I was determined not to do that out of respect for Richard's writing, and the most satisfying aspect of this rare act of self-abnegation was that the one time I gave in to pressure to incorporate one of my ideas, it actually worked out really well.

The original scene was just a homeless woman singing in Grand Central Station and Jeff Bridges' character stopped whatever he was doing and was captivated. I looked out over the Grand Central Station concourse and thought, 'All these people in the rush hour are moving faster and faster, trapped in their own worlds – wouldn't it be wonderful if they looked at the person they were passing and fell in love and started

dancing?' When I shared this silly romantic notion with everyone, they were very receptive, but I didn't want to do it because I was determined this should be Richard's film and not mine. But he liked the idea too, so in the end we did do it, and it was great, and now every New Year's Eve people come to Grand Central Station to waltz with an orchestra playing.

One of the things that isn't my job as a director is to teach acting. Actors have all these phrases they've learned to use to describe what they do – let's call it the thespian lexicon – which I have never got round to learning and don't feel I should. So when I'm directing I don't ever try to do their lines, but rather just communicate a certain energy – which sometimes communicates itself a little too effectively, to the extent that the actors can end up just doing a version of me, which sometimes works and sometimes doesn't (perhaps this is what happens to my old *Help! fumetti* veteran Woody Allen as well).

(Very) rough sketch for Grand Central Station waltz sequence.

No doubt the strength of my identification with the central characters is a factor in this too. Jeff Bridges in *The Fisher King* was probably the best example. It was only when the film was finished and people started asking me, 'Don't you see what he's doing?' that I realised. He'd picked up all sorts of my movements and mannerisms – I don't know whether just naturally, by osmosis, or as a

Gilliam and Bridges co-star in Battle of the Mullets.

OLD MAN

231

The Red Knight brings us a long overdue splash of colour...

form of deliberate defence mechanism. (I was so in his face and he couldn't escape me, so he thought he might as well reflect me back.) Either way, Jeff caught me out a couple of times on set by saying, 'Sorry, I'm not quite sure what you mean,' and asking me to do the line, which of course I couldn't, because the kind of energy I bring to the set is like Harvey Kurtzman's autistic son. I've got so many thoughts in my head that it's like the river of my language has run dry, and the fact that I can't quite get the words out makes me crazy.

It always intrigues me to find out what people's reactions to my films are once they're finished, but I'm wary of setting too much store by them – first, because my ego is probably well enough developed already without feeding it extra protein shakes; second, because if you take the praise seriously, you're going to have to give the criticism the same weight. But some of the responses to *The Fisher King* did give me great satisfaction. I remember David Crosby telling me that he had been in a car crash that resulted in the death of his wife, a tragedy for which he felt very responsible, and that he'd lived with the guilt of it for many years. But he found watching *The Fisher King* a very cathartic experience, to the extent that he actually felt the burden lifting from his shoulders.

One woman told me she'd come out of a screening at a New York cinema and walked twenty-five blocks in the wrong direction before she realised what she was doing. And there was a Universal PR girl who said she'd gone home after seeing *Brazil*, got in the shower and wept uncontrollably (of course, it is possible that those tears stemmed from the realisation that she was going to have to help me with the publicity). I love it when the films really get to people – for some reason I find a lot of Christians coming forward to tell me how much they've been affected by them – because then you know you've managed to take someone to the point where they are lost in your world.

When I did this illustration for a piece on Paul Newman in *The Sunday Times* in 1968, I didn't imagine that we would become friends, but after *THE FISHER KING* there was a project he wanted to talk to me about, and we got on really well.

Paul had this dirty grey Volvo estate that he used to drive around Vermont in, but he'd put this massive engine in it, and he loved pulling up next to some guy in a fancy car who'd be thinking, 'Look at that old fart,' then Paul would rev up like he was on the grid at the grand prix and go roaring off round these blind corners. He took me out in his boat once, and that got the blood flowing in just the same way. He seemed to have some arrangement with the coastguard which meant he didn't have to abide by the speed limit in the bay, so you'd be flying over the waves — Boom! Boom! — hanging on for dear life.

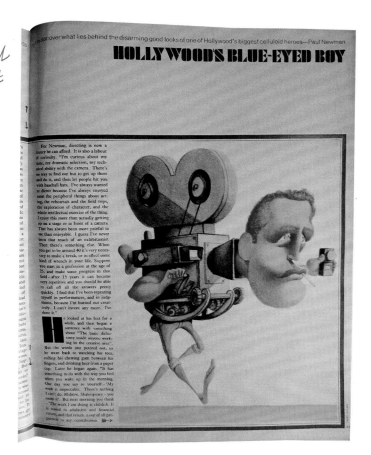

HOLLYWOOD'S BLUE-EYED BOY

One of the things I most enjoyed about the sequence of three American films which *The Fisher King* initiated was that I'd been living in England for so long by that point that I felt like I was coming back to the land of my birth almost as a foreigner, which always tends to be the widest-eyed and most observant perspective to have. The same process of uncontrolled de-industrialisation that had been so helpful in supplying locations for *Brazil* had been in operation in the US too. So by the time I got to Philadelphia to make *12 Monkeys*, there were these three beautiful decommissioned power stations waiting for us.

I love it when you can just sneak in and use a building that is already there instead of designing the space yourself, which would cost money and probably produce something much less interesting. I suppose in a way this approach is the live-action location equivalent of cut-out animation, but I also prefer the idea of adapting real places rather than starting from scratch, because when I watch a film that has effectively been designed by a single mind, I never get the same kind of scruffy, human thrill out of it.

One of the main misunderstandings of my films comes from the kind of trailer-speak where the man with deep voice says, 'We are going into the mind

OLD MAN

of Terry Gilliam...' Fuck! That's the last place Terry Gilliam wants to be. In fact, that's the reason he makes films – so he doesn't have to be in there. This is also why I find it so mystifying when people bracket me and Tim Burton together – because we're so completely different in our approaches to what might broadly be called 'fantasy'. The point of the worlds he makes is that they're complete: the trees all look one way and the grass looks another. It's beautiful – wonderful stuff. But what I do is all about the messy, weird, unexpected things that only come out of the way reality works. Whether it's an argument with a producer, or money or time running out, these are the pressures that restrain your greed for all possibilities and enable you to focus on what can actually be achieved.

With *12 Monkeys,* I again felt a real sense of responsibility with

regard to David and Jan Peoples' script, just because I liked it so much. David had scripted *Blade Runner*, and he also did *The Unforgiven* – which was originally written for Dustin Hoffman at the time of *Little Big Man,* but then it didn't happen until Clint Eastwood picked up the option. So it was almost fifteen

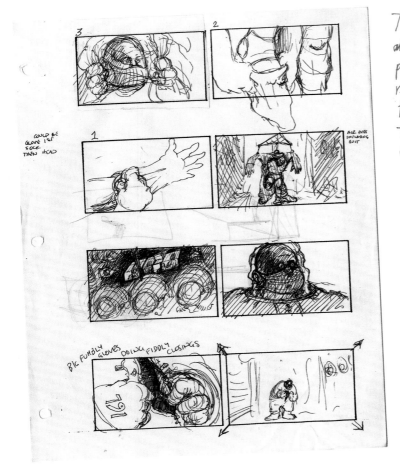

The first time I met Bruce Willis we talked about the scene in DIE HARD where he was picking glass out of his feet. I told him how refreshing and interesting I thought it was to see the man who was supposed to be the big, tough guy showing that kind of vulnerability, and he told me, 'Well, that was my idea.'

So when we were preparing to do 12 Monkeys I said, 'I don't want Bruce the superstar, I just want Bruce the actor — you've got to come with nothing, nobody, zip . . .' Of course, he responded to that in his own way — by bringing a pantechnicon with a gym in it to the set — but in terms of his actual performance, he certainly delivered. And if he had any reservations about being hoisted into a suit which looked a bit like a condom, he never shared them with me.

COULD BE GLOVE 1ST SOCK THEN HEAD

AIR INTO INFLADING SUIT

BIG FUMBLY GLOVES DOING FIDDLY CLOSINGS

791

A _12 MONKEYS_ grafitti stencil used to deface the world's walls as part of the film's guerilla marketing campaign.

years later when David got a call from Clint asking, 'Do you want to see your movie?' He went to a screening and there it was – not just brilliant, but word perfect as he wrote it. It's good if one of those best-case scenarios can come to pass for a screenwriter every now and again, because the hope keeps the rest of them hungry.

We did have one big fight over whether Bruce Willis should beat up or kill a second guy, but other than that, I like to hope the experience of working with me wasn't too disillusioning for them. (We may have set the bar a bit high for Richard LaGravanese, though – as _The Fisher King_ was his first film, he left us thinking the writer being welcomed onto the set every day and treated with respect was normal.) My memory was fading even then, and I've never had the time to sit down and write a diary every night (not being cunning enough to realise – as Michael Palin did – that this was where the real money was all along), so given that something interesting usually seemed to happen in the course of the making of my films, we thought we might as well get it on record. Apart from anything else, this would give us evidence to refer back to in the event of any subsequent legal disputes. Hence *The Hamster Factor*, the feature-length documentary which was made on *12 Monkeys*' Philadelphia set.

Fighting off strong local competition in the race to

become Boswells to my Johnson were two graduate film students from Temple University named Louis Pepe and Keith Fulton. We gave them a digital camera, and I agreed to wear a mic every day and wander around swearing at everyone while forgetting it was on, and they came back to us with what I still think is an excellent and unusually honest documentary about the making of a film.

The great thing about *The Hamster Factor* from my point of view is that it captures a key moment in the film-making process, which as far as I know had never previously had its moment in the spotlight. And that's the National Research Group screenings. To me, from a creative point of view, that sequence is as scary as anything that happens in Pepe and Fulton's next documentary, *Lost in La Mancha*. After the NRG screening of *12 Monkeys*, you see my editor Mick Audsley and I enthusing about how well it's gone while they're handing out the response cards, and then I'm in the foyer being very polite to the producer Chuck Roven's wife Dawn Steel (who'd been the Columbia executive responsible for shuffling *Munchausen* onto the back-burner after David Puttnam became a non-person, but luckily I am not one to hold grudges).

Next day – *Boom!* Reality bites – we get the results from the screening back and they're killing us. David and Jan who wrote the script are there as we look through them, and it's like a wake. This is the point at which there's enormous pressure on you to

I always do a cartoon for the cast and crew after a shoot. The sigh of relief encoded in the 12 Monkeys *one is almost audible.*

WE DID IT!
....BEFORE IT DID US!!!

rip out your film's guts on the Aztec altar of commercial compromise – the studio executives are like the high priests, handing you the ceremonial dagger. The great thing about *12 Monkeys* was that we ignored everything they told us, and the film miraculously managed to still be successful. This was either a rousing vindication of the uncompromising spirit of true artists or clear evidence that pig-headed stupidity can actually win through, or most likely a bit of both.

Two posters I did for cinematic events not organised by the National Research Group. (Below) A collage tribute to Hokusai's *The Great Wave off Kanagawa* for my poster for the 1991 London Film Festival.

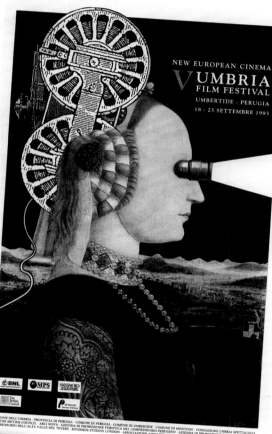

(Above) This time it's Piero Della Francesca's portrait of the Duchess of Urbino that is getting the treatment – the occasion being the film festival, which I am now the president of, near the house in Umbria that I bought in 1990 as a souvenir of BARON MUNCHAUSEN.

Ever since the *Holy Grail* sound-effects debacle, I've been a great believer in screening my films for people from the earliest possible moment, not only to check people are laughing in the right places, but also because it's the best way of seeing where you need little cuts, or extra lines to stop things sagging. The important thing is to solicit the audience's opinions in an appropriate way afterwards. If they're your friends, they'll probably be very polite and you'll have to take them to the pub and get them pissed before they'll tell you what they really feel. The contrasting problem with the random groups of strangers the National Research Group bus-in from the shopping malls of America to represent what the public wants is that they're not experiencing the film as they normally would, but rather as someone who has been told their opinion is important (i.e. a critic). That's why the response sheets for *Airplane!* came back so negative – because no one wanted to admit to laughing at something so coarse.

This is the moment in the process where you need people
in the fox-hole who are ready to fight the last battle with you (although paradoxically I also find the presence of the odd panicking faint-heart can be useful too – it strengthens my resolve by giving me something to react against). All of this noise is hurtling at you, everybody's got an opinion, and in a way editing all those opinions is as much of a challenge as editing the film was in the first place. When someone's raising a particular issue, are they really talking about what they think they're talking about, or is it actually an egg we laid fifteen minutes ago which is now coming home to roost in fully realised chicken form?

The one thing I changed as a consequence of that horrendous *12 Monkeys* screening was the scene where Bruce Willis has kidnapped Madeleine Stowe and they're in the woods together, and we let the music push the emotion too quickly. Effectively the film was saying, 'There's romance in the air,' but the audience wasn't buying it, which was totally fair enough. Bruce was quite keen for us to emphasise the love-story angle, so that might have shaped the premature musical drift.

When you're trying to trick the studios into letting you make European art films on Hollywood money, having stars of his and Brad Pitt's magnitude on-side is a vital part of the equation. But once you're actually cutting the film, you're not thinking about Bruce or Brad so much, you're really just asking yourself, 'Is this working?'

The actors are a long way away when you're in the editing room, which can make things interesting when they see the finished cut. Robin Williams was really pissed off when we showed him *The Fisher King*, because there's one very emotional scene outside Amanda Plummer's flat where he's taking her home for the first time and talking about having a hard-on the size of Florida. Robin worked his arse off on that scene and was really unhappy with me that he wasn't in shot as he poured out his heart. The camera just stays on Amanda's face as this tear begins to well up in her eye and then drops. 'Robin, I don't need to see what you're doing,' I reassured him, 'because we're seeing the result of what you're doing, and that's *so much more powerful.*'

I'm not sure if he entirely bought that, but it's often those

kinds of bruising encounters which give a film its finest moments. There's a funny argument between me and the producer Chuck Roven in *The Hamster Factor* about a scene which I really didn't want to do. It comes right at the end of the film, where he wanted me to show that the boy had been changed by the experience of what he saw in the airport, but I was going to finish on the plane when the lady scientist from the future says 'Hi' to David Morse, who has just released the virus that will wipe out most of humanity.

By that time, I was in 'Fuck you, I'm the director' mode, so I was doing everything I could to make it impossible. We were already on the edge of being over budget, so instead of problem-solving like I normally would, I set out to make the whole thing as difficult and expensive as possible, hoping that Chuck would just throw in the towel. I told him, 'Alright, if you insist on doing this, we're going to have to have a crane on top of another crane.' It was just out of spite that I did that, but in the end this ludicrously extravagant shot which I only set up to piss the producer off worked beautifully and gives the film a much more emotional and well-rounded ending. It's just connecting the circle a little bit more, so you see the boy watching the plane flying overhead which is actually (spoiler alert) the salvation of the future, although of course he doesn't know that.

This wasn't a shot I planned, but the producer kept pushing me – which I like – and then something good which wouldn't have happened otherwise came out of the friction between us. To me that's a much more interesting way of understanding how films are made than the hoary old myth (admittedly more prevalent among directors than anyone else) of the director as some kind of isolated heroic genius imposing his vision on the world. They're always throwing the 'auteur' thing at me (which so many people so desperately want

What I like about this picture is that Bruce Willis and Brad Pitt have been made up to look rough whereas I've got an actual black eye, having had my head kicked in front and back by a horse while out riding at the weekend. I like to do something as different to directing a movie as possible in any leisure time that may occasionally arise on a film shoot, just to clear my mind. By a strange coincidence, my assistant on *12 Monkeys* was a former amateur jockey who'd had to spend almost a year in hospital being metallised after the horse she was riding missed a turn and ran straight into a building.

It's interesting looking at stills of Bruce: his essential Bruce-ness often doesn't come through, because he's saving it for the movie camera. Brad on the other hand makes no such distinction. He was fantastic on that film, even though it came just at the point in his career where he was becoming a huge star, so he would have been entitled to be distracted by all the attention he was getting. One of the things I'm always trying to do with my films is take really handsome guys and make them less good-looking on the big screen so I feel better. The women on the other hand — and Madeleine Stowe in *12 Monkeys* was the perfect example — tend to be the ones on the set who get me through all the traumas of the production and generally make life bearable.

to believe in, because who doesn't want to be God?), but my joke is that I'm not an auteur, I'm a 'filteur' – the thing on the end of the cigarette that lets certain toxins through, but not others.

The whole thing starts with me – even though at the beginning the majority of the ideas might be mine, when I gather together the rest of the team their ideas are invariably surprising, which starts a creative leap-frogging game amongst us; it's my job to sort through and hopefully pick out the good ideas. My decisions won't always be correct, but at least the fact that it's me making them should give the result of me doing a series of things I didn't originally intend a certain discernible personality. Although, that said, I do think our romantic impulse to individualise the term 'artist' causes a lot of the problems – Rubens had a bunch of assistants, Hockney probably has someone to do the grass, and you don't think Damien Hirst pulls the wings off those butterflies all on his own, do you? What the artist does is bring the whole thing together and then take responsibility for the success or failure of the whole endeavour by signing his or her name to it.

All of which threatens to bring us back to the absurdity of the 'director's cut' again . . . If you even look at that phrase taken out of context you can see how ridiculous it is – after all, who else's would it be? Before I go into another dyspeptic rant, this is probably an appropriate moment to acknowledge how different the grizzled, slightly world-weary version of me who appears in *The Hamster Factor* seems to the ultra-confident young (well, early forties) buck, fearlessly trading *bon mot*s with Tom Stoppard in the more generic 'making of' short that accompanied *Brazil*, just a decade or so before. The reason for that is simple. I *was* a completely different person. When I look back at the *Brazil* me, he was still going strong – unstoppably even, at least in his own mind – whereas that's not so much the case from the nineties onwards. Where did that other guy go? You could say it was Munchausen's syndrome that did it for him . . . except that it wasn't the syndrome, it was real.

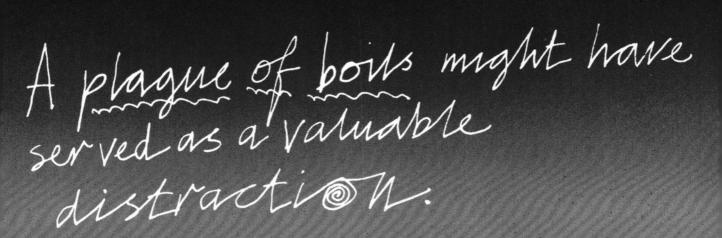

A plague of boils might have served as a valuable distraction.

Chapter

14

Desolation Row

m

y initial meeting with Hunter S. Thompson was in the same place I'd first rubbed shoulders with Marlon Brando – the Chateau Marmont hotel in Los Angeles. This time it was me and Johnny Depp and Benicio Del Toro who were the welcoming party. Various people – including my (and Hunter's) good friend Ralph Steadman – had been on at me for ages to make a film of his book *Fear and Loathing in Las Vegas,* but previously I'd always said, 'No'. What made the difference this time was Johnny and Benicio already being cast – I'd met Johnny briefly at Cannes the year before, thought he was incredible and really wanted to work with him.

Hunter was busy playing Hunter Thompson, which was basically what he'd been doing for the past thirty years. The thing about him was, even when the whole act was starting to get wearisome, he still retained the capacity to flip the whole situation on its head and come out with something quite brilliant. I remember Ralph had just done his 'Gonzo' art book, and Hunter's response was, 'Hitler took the high road, Ralph, and you took the low road . . . ', which I thought was very funny. And while I can't say we forged an instant bond, at least the ice was broken more effectively than it had been with the film's previous director, Alex Cox.

Alex had gone up to Hunter's place in Colorado, got himself physically thrown out and effectively lost the job, which was why Tony Grisoni and I now had to write a new script. I thought this was a total no-brainer – 'Just do the fucking book.' For me, *Fear and Loathing* said everything I felt about the end of the American dream, and there was a nice twist from a personal point of view in that it seemed to pick up the story of my former homeland from pretty much the emotional point at which I'd left it behind. The script was done in eight days (OK, with rewrites, ten days), and although we'd reckoned without the purists who would be mortally offended because we'd left out a comma or an exclamation mark, Hunter himself didn't seem to have a problem with our efforts.

Visiting him at his home in Aspen was a trifle nerve-wracking at first. Sitting in his canvas chair in his kitchen, Hunter was like a hurricane waiting just off-shore. Luckily there was no loss of life and limb during my visit. In fact, he was great, and watching him surrounded by acolytes and waiting for the world to come to him – he always seemed to be being filmed for some documentary or other – you could see that all this noise which came from his fearsome reputation was in fact a rather poignant strategy for distracting himself – and everybody else – from how long it was since he had actually done anything great. (I guess him running for sheriff had been the end of it, but I suppose he wasn't the kind of guy who could just sit back quietly and let the world move on.)

That said, the day he came down on the set to film his cameo on *The Matrix* flashback, I wanted to kill him. We had Harry Dean Stanton up in the judge's tower at great expense and Hunter was throwing bread rolls at me and basically doing everything he could to draw attention to himself – just trying to make everyone say 'Stop it, Hunter', to prove what a maverick he was. Then, when the time actually did come for the Hunter show to start, he refused to sit where we'd put him because, 'As a journalist, I'd always have to be on the edge of things.'

So we're all tip-toeing around him trying to get him in position – then Laila Nabulsi, his Palestinian ex-girlfriend who was one of the producers of the film, suggested we pick out the best-looking extra and seat her at the table he's meant to be at. Of course, he's over there like a shot, but then on the first take when Johnny walked past he's too busy talking to her to notice him. Only on the second take was some small reaction registered, and then by the third he'd gone again. At that point, we just rolled our eyes and said, 'OK, for fuck's sake get him out of here.' This is why I never normally work with material by living authors.

Johnny would be late on set every morning, because he

had to stay up all night talking to Hunter on the phone. He'd actually lived in his basement in Aspen for a while – just absorbing Hunter, stealing any kind of talisman he could touch or feel. He wore his shirts in the film, at the start of the shoot he even took his car – the Red Shark – and drove down to Vegas in it. Johnny really loved Hunter, and of course the feeling was mutual. There's nothing better than being portrayed by someone who looks better than you do. In the end, Johnny's performance was absolutely spot on. Some people complained that he was too much of a 'caricature', but they'd obviously never met Hunter.

The only real problem I had on the set – Hunter excepted – was that obviously Benicio Del Toro was every bit as much of a method actor as Johnny, and sometimes that would entail a certain amount of getting lost and fumbling around, and demanding a kind of attention which I didn't necessarily have the time to give. So in the course of the shooting I probably found myself

The Shark stops for gas, which it did often — that car's petrol consumption was outrageous.

drifting ever more onto Johnny's side, because that was easier, but looking back at the film now, I can see that Benicio was extraordinary. Ralph Steadman said he wasn't sure if he could really be Gonzo because he didn't quite have the humour and the lightness of touch, but what Benicio did have was the intensity – a kind of dangerous, animal quality, which worked brilliantly as a foil to Johnny.

After she saw the film, Ruby Wax said she hated me because I'm the man who made Johnny Depp look 'unfuckable'. I told her I was just trying to level the playing field for the rest of us.

There's a scene in the North Star Café where Ellen Barkin (an amazing actress, who had been kind enough to forgive me for misguidedly dropping her from *Brazil* at the very last minute in favour of Kim Greist) was playing the waitress. Benicio wanted so much to put the pie in her face, but I just said 'No, you can't', because if he had done, all of that strength of feeling would have been lost in the gesture. One of the things Johnny told me about Hunter was that he eats everything in his path – he will leave nothing unconsumed. So at the end of that scene when Benicio's gone and Johnny looks at Ellen, and you can see he's feeling embarrassed

At last Benicio gets the director's attention.

and guilty, he gets up with the plate of food in his hand as though he's going to leave, but then turns round and puts it back on the table, almost as an offering.

We just invented that moment – it wasn't in the book – but we were both so embedded in the characters that we felt in the right frame of mind to extemporise. The lizard tail and the underwater room were hatched in a similarly playful spirit – we just did them because we could. It was great fun working with someone like Johnny, who at his best is as fast as the Pythons. The news seemed to get out that the whole film was going well, because all these people like Cameron Diaz and Harry Dean Stanton and Lyle Lovett were agreeing to appear in cameo roles just because they wanted to be part of it.

Johnny had put so much into his performance that showing him the finished film for the first time was quite traumatic. There were just a few of us watching it at the De Lane Lea screening room in Soho, but when the lights came up, Depp was nowhere to be seen. He'd snuck out during the credits and was in the bathroom throwing up. I think watching yourself on the screen can be quite

Living carpets and reptilian transformations – who wouldn't want to be part of this?

horrifying for an actor, because if you're as conscientious as he was at that stage then all you're seeing is your failures and the things you don't think you quite got right.

Getting Hunter to see the film was like trying to lure a coyote into a phone booth. We were all terrified of him seeing the film and not liking it. It turned out he was even more terrified, and while we kept setting up screenings for him, he kept finding ways to duck them. In the end, we managed to corral him into a friend's home screening room up in Aspen, and luckily – albeit I suppose inevitably, given his penchant for never going anywhere without a camera crew of some kind in tow – someone was there to film the moment when the lights came up and he was just lying on the floor, howling with laughter.

We were pretty happy with that. Obviously then he had to come and fuck up the New York premiere by showing off and throwing one of those gigantic cartons of popcorn all over the place. Forget everyone else who has worked on the film, it's Hunter's night. My new right-hand man and cinematographer Nicola Pecorini and I were so pissed off that we left and went down to a local bar. Hunter was a weird one – I admired him enormously, but he was better appreciated at a distance.

That film got one of the best reviews of my career – from a fifteen-year-old kid who said, 'It's not hypocritical.' You can't hope for better than that. In commercial terms, we thought we'd been very clever counter-programming next to *Godzilla*. Unfortunately, that giant irradiated dinosaur trampled all over us. On its initial release *Fear and Loathing* only made about $10 million in America and was thereby deemed to be 'a disaster', although as far as I was concerned

Laila Nabulsi's mum got me an Egyptian galabeya - which really does protect you from the desert heat. It's not just about looking cool, kids, it's also about staying cool.

Obviously the communists aren't the main threat any more - now it's the Islamists. But if the not-so-glorious day ever comes, I can always show them this picture from my Florence of Arabia phase in the Nevada desert...

this was lazy use of language. That word needed redefining in cinematic terms, and I was the man to do it.

But before the time would finally come for me to be impaled on my own Quixotic windmill, a trio of non-celluloid calamities lay in wait – afflicting first me, and then the world. I will address these events in ascending order of geopolitical significance. The most footling was that I found myself subject to personal excoriation by that perennial middle-ranker among critical non-authorities, the *Evening Standard*'s Alexander Walker, for the crime of securing partial (and it was no more than 10 per cent of the overall budget) UK lottery funding for our European co-production of *Don Quixote*.

Johnny Depp in THE MAN WHO KILLED DON QUIXOTE – what could possibly be more British than this?

By the time Walker accused me of being the not-so-thin end of a sinister wedge of 'Americans coming to Europe to grab funding', I had been a law-abiding UK taxpayer for thirty-three years – more than half of my life. I'd come over here, taken your women, been a part of the most notoriously English of comedy groups – what more did I have to do to prove my Anglophile legitimacy? It was like the whole thing with HandMade Films, which we'd initially wanted to call 'British HandMade Films', but you had to apply somewhere special – possibly to the Queen's Keeper of Patriotic Adjectives – to use that designation, and for some reason they turned us down. (George Harrison and Monty Python together? Who else did we need on board to make us British enough – Sir Laurence Olivier? Johnny Rotten?)

Even setting aside the fact that a high proportion of the 'British' films for which Alex tub-thumped so patriotically were actually financed by American studios (which would therefore take the lion's share of the revenue in the happy eventuality of there being any profits), surely any meaningful notion of what a British film might actually mean would be substantially based on the contributions of such 'foreigners' as Joseph Losey, Dick Lester and Stanley Kubrick anyway? And, perhaps, Hollywood should be thanking Hitler for many of its greatest filmmakers, Billy Wilder, Otto Preminger, Fred Zinnemann and Fritz Lang, who defined America from the 1940s to the '60s.

As so often when an outrageous journalistic slur is perpetrated, there was a personal grudge behind this one. When *Time Bandits* had come out, Alex had given us a very equivocal review, which was later generously overlooked by the person who asked him to do the blurb on the back of the video (which of course he was very happy to do, as there was a pay cheque involved). But I found out and asked if it might be possible to get someone who actually liked the film to help us promote it. This got back to Alex, who was such an old bitch that from then on he did everything he possibly could to make life difficult for us. Luckily natural justice intervened, in that Alex's greatest excitement in life was the Filipino dictator-ess Imelda Marcos lending him an island which he had a film festival on . . . until the brave people of the Philippines rose up and overthrew her. And lo! Alexander Walker's island was snatched from his grasp.

A far sadder and graver illustration of humankind's perfidious capacities was supplied by the vicious knife attack on my good friend George Harrison at his home near Henley on the night of 30 December 1999. As if the twentieth century hadn't managed to pack in enough foul deeds, it saved one more for its penultimate night, when the ex-Beatle, philanthropist and film financer was stabbed more than thirty times by a mentally ill ex-heroin addict with a kitchen knife.

George was someone who never really did anything but good, and was incredibly generous about supporting people whose work he approved of. He loved hanging out with his mates and playing music, and spent the rest of his time lovingly restoring the thirty-six acres of gardens at Friar Park – the magnificent Gothic revival mansion which he'd put up as collateral to enable us to make *Life of Brian*. And he didn't just pay other people to do it for him and turn up every now and again to order them around like most rock stars would – he physically did it himself, basically turning himself into a manual labourer.

Before he bought the place, it'd been a convent school – Serge Gainsbourg's wife Jane Birkin had gone there. But by the time George arrived, all the artificial lakes had been filled up with rubbish and the alabaster fireplaces had been whitewashed. Restoring Friar Park became his life's work. He'd be out there working every fucking day, and I didn't blame him because it was an amazing place. All the lakes connected up and you could get in a boat and row down into these man-made caverns. It also had Europe's largest

My end-of-shoot drawing for the crew.

alpine garden with a great Matterhorn in the middle of it with more caverns inside. Basically, it was an Edwardian Disneyland.

In a way it was appropriate that the building helped finance

The Life of Brian, because Frank Crisp, the Victorian lawyer and microscopist who'd been responsible for its lavish fittings, had himself been ardently anti-clerical. He'd designed the stonework to feature monks eating babies and even the brass light-switches were a monk's head, so you tweaked the nose when you turned them on or off. Old Frank must have been turning in his grave when the place became a convent school (and I don't know if the nuns made special covers for the light switches) but I suppose the fact that one of its old girls was Jane Birkin of 'Je t'aime' infamy must have given him some posthumous comfort.

Obviously George himself was a very spiritual person, but he never lost his wonderfully bitchy and sardonic Scouse sense of humour. Within twenty-four hours of receiving those horrible injuries, he'd given a quote to the hospital spokesman to the effect that the attacker 'certainly wasn't auditioning for the Travelling Wilburys'. And when I remember him pottering around Friar Park, it's actually Voltaire's *Candide* – a true Enlightenment talisman – that he reminds me of. George Harrison getting nearly killed by a maniac who was looking for Paul McCartney but turned up at the wrong house certainly confirmed the anti-Leibnizian suspicion that all is not for the best in the best of all possible worlds. And no one ever took Voltaire's advice to '*cultiver notre jardin*' more literally than George did.

The legacy of the Enlightenment was getting a pretty rough time of it at the beginning of the twenty-first century. Tourists . . . terrorists . . . so closely related thanks to my bad enunciation. And by my holiday planning as well.

Ten years before, I'd missed a great chance to holiday in Egypt because I was shooting *The Fisher King* . . . the first Gulf War was rolling into action but I was stuck making a movie. 'What is he talking about?', you are probably wondering. 'The war wasn't in Egypt, and he's not a war correspondent.'

Right on both counts. But I was desperate to go. The place was deserted. Thanks to the high standards of American education, many Americans seemed to think that Iraq was next door to Egypt and therefore possibly directly in the sights of their not-so-smart bombs. And just a few hours away the pyramids were waiting for me, without a tourist in sight. Heaven! But I was working. Damn!

Years passed, until one day a busload of Dutch tourists taking in the ancient sites of Egypt was brutally ambushed and blown up by a gang of Muslim fundamentalists. With no film commitments, this was my chance. I grabbed my seventeen-year-old daughter Amy, and we rushed off to Cairo and points south. Security was high, the fundamentalists were busy celebrating, and the Nile was empty of tourists. Bliss. Utter bliss. The people were lovely, contrite, and delighted to see they hadn't been abandoned. The bartering rates were generous . . . 200 camels for my daughter . . . a once-in-a-lifetime bargain! Impossible to say 'No'. But, fortunately, blood turned out to be thicker than my burning desire for livestock.

Sadly, we didn't have too long to wait until my next happy holiday. I had planned to be in Marrakech, Morocco, at the beginning of October 2001. But the horror of 11 September changed all of that. Paranoia was rampant. All Arabs and Arab countries were suspect. All Muslims were the enemy.

I had been to Morocco many times. We had shot part of *Time Bandits* there. But I found, despite all of my experiences in North Africa, I was having doubts. I was nervous. Everyone I knew was cancelling their travel plans. Fear of flying was universal. But it was my second daughter Holly's birthday.

And did I want her growing up with the kind of mindless fear that was raging all around us? No. The only way to deal with this was to leap into the darkness. Confront it head on. A slight change of destination took us to Fez, one of the most wondrous cities in the world. Tickets in hand, we hopped onto a Royal Air Morocco flight and into the semi-unknown.

Just as Egypt had been during the first Gulf War, Morocco was empty of foreigners. The people of Fez welcomed us with open arms and empty shops. A city of apologies. Their sad, heartfelt, mantra was 'Islam is Peace'. We completely agreed. We dined in strangers' homes. We made new friends while prejudice and paranoia engulfed the West. In America, Homeland Security was conceived and beginning to metastatise. The future of fear was growing in the belly of George Dubya and Dick Cheney's double-backed beast. The question was – and is – how many more of these wonderful holidays will my children have to take before the madness abates?

The Windmills of My Mind – the latter stages of Orson Welles' career were blighted by his failure to complete an ambitious cinematic adaptation of Don Quixote, but there was no way I was ever going to let that happen to me...

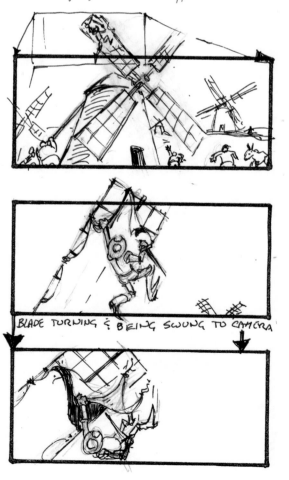

BLADE TURNING & BEING SWUNG TO CAMERA

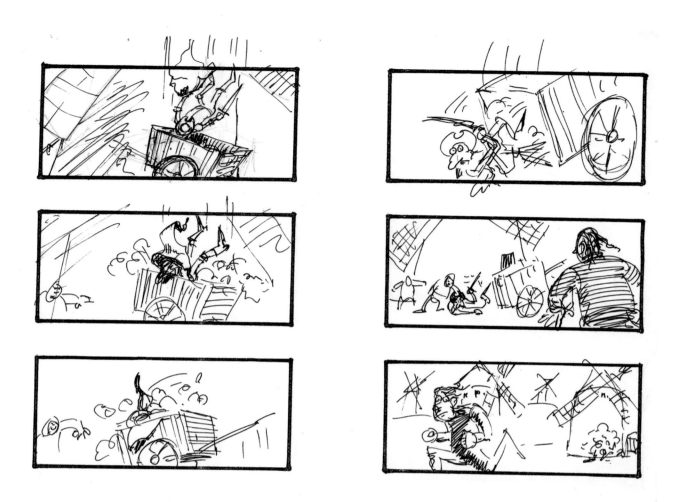

The events of 9/11 would present several of the world's most irrational despots – Osama Bin Laden, George Bush – with an insoluble 'How do you follow that?' dilemma. Luckily for me, I had already got my retaliation in first. With the calamitous late-2000 abandonment of *The Man Who Killed Don Quixote,* I had achieved the ultimate refinement of my cinematic methodology. Never mind all those years of 'The process of the film becomes the subject of the film' – that shit was old news. Why not take it one step further, to the point where *the film itself did not even get made*?

With *Don Quixote,* my identification with the hero's failure to

attain his romantic dream was so total that the film itself became the balloon in the *papier-mâché* head. It turned out that the actual product was *Lost in La Mancha* – the documentary about the film not getting made. When I was much younger and fascinated by architecture, I had once designed an extension to our house in Panorama City which never got built. In this case, however, we built the extension before the house. (I've still not lost hope of completing the main building, but that's how things tend to go with unattainable romantic ideals, isn't it? If we do ever get to make it, people will probably only be disappointed that it's not lived up to their ideal by being all about Don having fights with windmills anyway.)

In the 'comedy film' (as it was once described to me by a woman at a film festival, who was appalled to subsequently discover that these mortifying events had actually taken place and were not an elaborate cinematic hoax) *Lost in La Mancha,* I played the part of Terry Gilliam – a role I'd been preparing for more or less effectively throughout my (then) sixty-or-so years on this earth. It was –

Tragedy makes the best comedy, always. Not that it was funny at the time. LOST IN LA MANCHA captured some of the hazards we encountered – filming in an air force fly-zone, the lead actor struck down with ill-health, biblical floods on set.... What they didn't capture on camera were the buzzards. They were flying overhead, just waiting for us to die. As Jean Rochefort and I seem to have just noticed here.

On the set of DON QVIXOTE in a momentary interlude of actual filming.

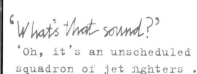

'What's that sound?'
'Oh, it's an unscheduled squadron of jet fighters . . .'

quite literally – the performance of a lifetime, as I broke the hearts of audiences everywhere who suffered with me for all the artists in this pathetic, sad world.

The funny thing was that when the going really got tough, the documentarians – Louis Pepe and Keith Fulton, our *Hamster Factor* A-team – had actually wanted to piss off home. 'Just keep fucking shooting, you jerks!' I had to shout at them from the depths of my encroaching despair. 'You might not have a film about the making of a movie, but at least you'll have a film about the unmaking of one, and that might actually be much more interesting.'

At the moment in the documentary where the tempest hits and everything's washing away in the floods, there's one shot where you can see the camera is looking out through the windscreen of a car. That's because Louis and Keith were in there hiding, because they only had one camera and they didn't want to get it wet. All the really interesting shots of the water spilling across the set came from the stuntman's own hand-held camera – trained as he was to run towards the danger, he was out there filming like mad.

Not an impromptu Hokey-Cokey, but teaching Johnny to walk with stones in his shoes ...

The film might not exist – at least, not at the time of writing – but it really comes alive in the stills.

I know this is a bit of a hobby horse of mine, but I really do think the Western world has given up something very important by losing touch with the Bible. Whether or not you actually believe in God doesn't matter – it's like the Greek myths . . . if you've not read them, you won't understand what the world is actually like. What counts is ingesting this huge system of iconography and mythology at an impressionable age, which then gives you a template: 'Oh, I see, the world's falling into that pattern now.'

On the set of *Quixote*, for example, I could become Job – a plague of boils might even have served as a valuable distraction when the news came through that my leading man Jean Rochefort's extreme physical agony was going to make it impossible for him to sit on his horse – and an understanding of what it means to be tested is very useful when you find yourself in trying circumstances. For all its much-vaunted scientific rationality, I don't know if the modern world appreciates that fact as well as it should. I'm as much to blame for this as anyone. Although whenever I've heard one of my children complaining that something 'isn't fair', I've always tried to ask them, 'What has "fair" got to do with it? What has happened to make you think you live in a just world? I blame the parents . . . it must be our fault for bringing you up too fairly and hiding you from reality.'

DON QUIXOTE – *graveyard of dreams… and belief (in film-making, if not the higher power).*

I must've been asked about the extent of my religious faith when I first went to Occidental College, because it was a Presbyterian scholarship, but I don't think we ever had the talk about whether Jesus is of the same material as God, which may have been for the best, as these issues have killed a lot of people over the years. I was certainly never questioned about the Trinity. The idea of the oneness that can be three is a mystery I've never managed to quite get my head around (it always makes me think of the Three Musketeers, and then I get confused about D'Artagnan – the extra one, the lad from the country who joined up) . . . I suppose that's why it's a mystery.

I've got all sorts of weird f*@ck!ng sh*t
floating around up there in my head....

Chapter

15

All Things Must Pass

he **Bible** also lays a sure foundation in terms of how best to approach literary or cinematic source material (as opposed to HP Sauce material – for safe dining, always use a condiment). You have this text which many people view as something sacred and immutable, yet which is actually the product of lots of different people's work and a huge number of different drafts, if only in terms of angry old men with beards excising all references to female disciples (this, incidentally, is roughly how *Life of Brian* script meetings went, and poor old Mary Magdalene was historically up against even worse odds than the Pythons' woman for all seasonings, former *Mad* magazine Miss Teen Queen, Carol Cleveland).

In the twilight realm of artistic attribution, questions of authenticity tend to be a lot more complex than they might initially appear. For instance, people who tell you *Don Quixote* is dry as dust (and within this broad category I would definitely include the Spanish, who are taught the book at school and therefore grow up hating it) tend not to have read the Tobias Smollett translation. I haven't read it either, but the important thing is, I know it exists.

The idea of simple replication has never really interested me. This is why I much prefer to refer to my probably inaccurate idea of something than the actuality of the thing itself. The relationships of both *Brazil* to George Orwell's *1984* and *12 Monkeys* to Chris Marker's *La Jetée* (which we persuaded the Writers Guild of America to let us say our film was 'inspired by' rather than 'based upon') were deliberately developed along these lines, with me taking care not to read or watch the originals until after my films were finished. This way I can be confident I haven't ripped anybody off, because what I've done is actually based on a pre-emptive foretaste, a recollection from the future – the memory I will have of these things once I've finally got around to reading or watching them.

If I choose to base what I'm doing at any given moment on the way I think I will remember having felt in ten years' time, who's to stop me? And if I keep saying these kinds of things for long enough, maybe one day there will turn out to be some truth in them. The only outcome I would lose sleep over is that I might be accused of being 'post-tentious' – pre-tentious is bad enough, but post-tentious would be a sickener.

Over time, I have definitely found that the closer you get to what you think is the essential core of something, the blurrier and more confusing your vision tends to become. For instance, when I set out to make *The Brothers Grimm*,

They were headless and slightly larger than life-size, and when you looked into their neckholes you saw a monitor playing film of events in the history of the square, and a camera took a picture of your face which was then projected onto the entire wall of a modern office building alongside the visages of Potsdamer Platz's earlier denizens.

I was very keen to strip away the extra layers of bogus gentility and ornamentation which I assumed the Grimms' repertoire had acquired since it was first published. And then I found out that the whole success of the stories was entirely down to the brothers' opportunistic bowdlerisation. Oh yes, this is good.

First, they sent all their mates out collecting folk tales, then they wrote them down and tidied them up a bit for publication. But the first edition of the huge book that resulted didn't sell too well – finding only an academic audience – so the Grimms began to make subtle alterations to suit the sensibilities of a middle-class reading public. For example, in 'Rapunzel' the way the witch originally realised something was wrong was by discovering her tower-bound captive was pregnant. It wasn't just her hair she'd let down – the prince had fucked her! This particular rough edge was thoroughly smoothed over in time for the bestseller, and it wasn't the only one.

The two films I ended up making in the years 2003–5 – my rarely screened Canadian child-in-jeopardy adventure *Tideland* being the other one – were both in their own different ways designed to make the point that it's

Heath Ledger was one of those people who had so much energy he couldn't help but pass it on to the people around him – look at the speed my hands are moving, it's like I've got wings!

OK for kids (and adults for that matter) to be shocked and scared by fairy tales. Because life itself – as my experiences making *The Brothers Grimm* with the Weinstein brothers would confirm – actually is scary, and fairy tales are one of the strategies humankind has developed to prepare us for that.

Making one of these films was a revitalising experience of unfettered creative freedom, the other was basically quite miserable, although working with Matt Damon and Heath Ledger was a delight. *The Brothers Grimm* began to live up to the latter part of its name from the moment Chuck Roven and I were pitching it to MGM Studios.

Chuck and I put on a real show for the executive in question, and he just sat there watching us with his dead eyes then said, 'Why do you want to make a film about animals eating children?' It wasn't a great start, but somehow we got the go-ahead anyway, only for MGM to pull out once we had all flown to Prague to do the 'tech scout', which is when you've done all your casting and

found your locations and you're driving the various heads of department – props guys, lighting people, grips – around to show them where you're going to be filming. With no George Harrison around to save us any more, the vultures inevitably gathered at the roadside, scenting the cinematic carrion now splayed out on the road.

Although I'd sworn I would never work with the Weinsteins, the need for new backers had become sufficiently urgent for me to set those scruples aside. Around this time, I flew out to LA hoping to bump into Martin Scorsese at the Vanity Fair Oscars party, as one does. Marty had just finished making *Gangs of New York* with the Weinsteins. He said, 'It's a horrible experience, but if it's the only way for you to make the film, you've got to do it,' and he was right. There's a point you reach with a project where the momentum is such that you don't really have any option but to jump in with both feet, irrespective of whether what you're jumping into is a shallow puddle or the San Andreas trench.

Because Matt would normally be the quieter guy, where Heath would be the one who everyone falls in love with when he walks in the room, I thought it would be fun to get them to play each other's roles.

At last, here is my son Harry who, because he spouted the immortal words 'The Brothers Grimm!', was featured in the cinema trailer.

Given that *The Brothers Grimm* was my first film since the collapse of *Don Quixote*, I was feeling pretty beaten down at this stage, and I didn't really feel I could afford to look the Weinsteins' gift horse in the mouth, even though it was already standing on my foot. First, the Weinsteins wanted Heath Ledger out, but I insisted we weren't going to do the film without him. Then we reworked the script a bit, although I'm not sure if we improved it. By the time we'd had to sacrifice Samantha Morton – who would have been amazing – in favour of their choice of Lena Headey, and they'd sacked my friend and cinematographer Nicola Pecorini (who was the one who had alerted me to how good Heath was in the first place), I basically felt like I was no longer responsible for what was happening. It was like I was back in the army, and 'Not my problem, mate' is a pretty bad attitude for a director to have on a film set.

Tideland couldn't have been a happier contrast (even if the downside of working free of interference did turn out to be that hardly anyone got to see the film I was so proud of). And not only as a chance to get back in touch with my inner child, who I'd always suspected was a little girl ... (I said something along those lines at the press conference and a lot of people were shocked, because they didn't understand how I could be serious about my work and still joke about it. But from my point of view, doing that is the only way to survive the loss of control which is such an integral part of the publicity and review process – the post-partum depression phase of film-making, when you find out that you have been judged – otherwise it would drive me mad. Even if you describe a film as 'the fourth part in a trilogy' and everyone just ignores the gag and takes you at face value, at least you know you've had an impact on the conversation.)

This was the moment in TIDELAND when we lost the sympathy of half the audience.

Jeff Bridges' rock star is about to shoot up and the little girl has cooked up the heroin for him and filled the needle. She knows exactly what's going to happen . . . . We had an ex-junkie who was on methadone to advise us, and we knew we'd got it right when he said, 'Oh fuck! That looks good.'

The idea of children always being these innocent, vulnerable little creatures is just bullshit.

Children are made to bounce when you drop them. They're designed to survive. That's the dilemma as a parent – you're so fearful that anything might happen to your kid, but once you follow that through you're already saying they can't look after themselves.

I'm not one of those people who thinks having children around keeps you young. The moment mine were born, I felt old and vulnerable and frightened that something bad would happen to them. I'd never really worried about things before, but suddenly all I wanted to do was be sure I would die before they did. I didn't care when that was, so I suppose fatherhood had at least one positive side-effect in terms of making my own mortality (which I'd always been aware of, in fact I've thought about it every day since I was a kid) more palatable – 'I better move fast if I want to beat the kids to the punch . . .'

When the circus comes to town you've got to get the elephants out, you've got to make noise.

The week before *Tideland* opened

I'd been doing interviews on radio and television in New York, but my daughter Amy pointed out there were no posters anywhere, no ads: 'It's coming out on Friday and there's nothing anywhere. We've got to do something.'

So I got the *Tideland* poster and I mounted it on a piece of dirty old cardboard and scrawled 'STUDIO-LESS FILMMAKER. FAMILY TO SUPPORT. WILL DIRECT FOR FOOD'. Then we headed to the studio where they record *The Daily Show*. There's always a big queue outside.

The distribution company had no money for decent ads, but they were driving me around in a big black limo! We arrive and park unseen around the corner. Amy goes to the front end of the queue with a video camera and starts filming as I come up from the back end with my sign, shaking a plastic cup with a few coins in it and crying, 'God bless you, I'm an independent filmmaker but I'm dependent on your goodwill, sir.' People turn away, refusing to look at this deadbeat. The security guys try to get me off the sidewalk and I resist – 'Sir, it's a public space, I have a right . . .' Little by little people began to recognise me and by the end we had gathered a big crowd of fans, including the writers for the Jon Stewart show.

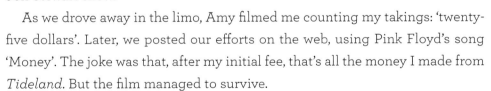

As we drove away in the limo, Amy filmed me counting my takings: 'twenty-five dollars'. Later, we posted our efforts on the web, using Pink Floyd's song 'Money'. The joke was that, after my initial fee, that's all the money I made from *Tideland*. But the film managed to survive.

When I decided to renounce my American citizenship (in 2006), I felt duty bound – if only as a sop to my imaginary late-sixties bomb-throwing Mick-Jagger-as-a-humble-stringer alternative self – to present it as a political gesture. In fact, the single biggest factor in my decision was the discovery that were I to die as a US citizen, America's external revenue service profiteering division would assess the value of all my worldly goods for capital gains tax.

The house Maggie and I live in – which we've inhabited for thirty years – is probably (through no fault of our own, and entirely thanks to the insanity of the North London property market) now worth about twenty times the amount it was bought for. So if I breathe my last as a fellow citizen of Terry Jones and Michael Palin, my wife won't have to pay any capital gains tax on it because it's our primary residence. Whereas had I continued formally to throw in my lot with the land of Mark Twain and *South Park*, she'd be left with no option but to sell our family home to pay the death duties.

I'd had no qualms about paying taxes in two countries for forty years. I never minded contributing to the upkeep of roads and schools (never mind the American army, which had so generously given me an honourable discharge) in a country I no longer lived in – it gave me a warm fuzzy feeling when I did occasionally pop back to use the facilities. But while we were shooting *Tideland* and the 2004 presidential election returned George W for another bite at the White House cherry, that did feel like the political icing on a cake of financial self-interest as far as I was concerned. I couldn't believe the American people would be so foolish and self-destructive, but once they had been, it became much harder to justify throwing my grieving widow out onto the streets on their behalf.

The actual process of becoming un-American

was quite funny. First, I had to go down to the embassy and formally say, 'I want to give up my US citizenship.' Obviously I was trying to divest myself of something which long lines of people all around the world would give their right arms for, so it had to be done properly. It turned out the phrase 'give up' wasn't the 'correct' one. The word I would have to use was 'renounce', which actually sounded far more powerful and violent and angry than I had originally intended.

It was a bit like in *Brazil* – 'I'll have a rare steak.' 'Say the number, please! You have to say the number!' I had to fill out lots of forms and have a session with the diplomatic counsel, then go away for a month to consider in depth the insanity of what I was doing, before coming back to affirm that no, I still really, honestly didn't want to be a US citizen any more. It was actually quite touching the way the people at the embassy kept trying to persuade me to reconsider, as if America's worst fear was to be parted from its artistes, especially if they were one-sixth Python.

The OPERA

Being asked to direct a production of Hector Berlioz's *The Damnation of Faust* by the English National Opera in 2011 was exciting and terrifying at the same time. I lost so much sleep over doing this, but it was a good school to go to as far as opera was concerned, and being in your seventies is no reason not to be acquiring new skills, or to stop being a go-Goethe.

I've always really liked German culture, which has tended to get dragged down in the eyes of the world by what happened after the Austrian corporal took charge. The idea was to use the story of Faust as a filter for the whole bloody aftermath of German romanticism, so the production could range from beautiful mountains to a Hungarian march, which took us into the First World War, to an Amen chorus as a backdrop to the rise of the Nazis – basically it was Goethe's *Cabaret* with a dance sequence for Kristallnacht which even *The Producers* might have thought twice about.

The concept of 'the Faustian bargain' is one that everyone, not just film and opera directors, does well to keep in mind. In our production this cube which he carried on his back was Faust's way of regulating and regimenting the world in the goose-steps of the Enlightenment. I should also acknowledge Tristram Kenton as copyright holder of these two photos, as it is important to give credit where credit is due.

TION

Having somehow pulled off *Faust*, I foolishly thought I knew how to do opera. Then I spent almost two years thinking how to make *Benvenuto Cellini*. Like *Faust* it was an opera seldom staged. Even Berlioz had three failed attempts at it.

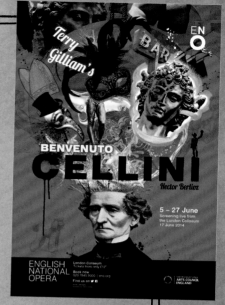

I've long been fascinated by Cellini's autobiography, the only one by a Renaissance artist. He was a brilliant sculptor and goldsmith, but he was also a murderer, a liar, an arrogant bastard: 'You've been given this gift, this talent and you're destined to do something extraordinary. But everything conspires against it happening and you lose faith.' Berlioz was that kind of character; Cellini was like that too. Can't think why I identified with him so much.

Luckily, Leah Hausman, from whom I learned so much on *Faust*, was my co-director, but my old 'Alice in Wonderland hubristic nightmare' returned: a hundred performers on-stage, singers, stilt walkers, jugglers, sword fights, giant carnival puppets, and lack of rehearsal time. It was identical to the madness Cellini went through as he attempted the impossibility of casting his famous statue of Perseus. He and I had become the same person!

Right up till the last minute, I knew we were not going to pull it off. But somehow the show opened. To five-star reviews, sold-out houses – and only eight performances. Opera makes no sense!

The thing about both

The thing about both *The Hamster Factor* and *Lost in La Mancha* that I'm most proud of, looking back, is that as uncomfortably close as those two documentaries are to the clogged and straining heart of the film-making process, you don't leave them with any sense of that process having been de-mystified. In fact, if anything, by the end of them the actual creative moment is still more mysterious.

I don't mean that in a *The Agony and the Ecstasy* kind of way, where Michelangelo – who was not gay by the way (at least, not the way he's played by anti-gun-control zealot Charlton Heston) – gets his inspiration from laying back and looking up at the clouds: 'Oh, it's an elephant up there, or perhaps a pretty boy, maybe I'll do that one instead . . . but *I'm not gay.*' To me, the real mystery kicks in when I'm so focused on trying to drag as much of life or memory or whatever into one particular moment – whether the boundaries of that moment are defined by the camera's viewfinder or the edges of the piece of paper I'm drawing on – that nothing else matters. The rest of the world disappears and anything, or anyone, that tries to get in the way has to be destroyed.

I think that being able to concentrate all my attention on a single goal is maybe my one real talent (along with my amazing ability never to learn to do things properly, so everything is always done at a basic elemental level with no grasp of theory whatsoever – that's another skill which can't be taught). The intense clarity of those periods of total engagement is so wonderful that when they end you – or at least, I – feel completely blurry and out of focus. At that point I tend to go into an intense depression that lasts maybe six months, and I've got to let it run its full course because otherwise it never quite goes away. I can only come back up once I've actually touched the bottom.

As debilitating – and frequent – as these depressive interludes are, I've never been tempted to try to stave them off with psycho-analysis. I realise this probably sounds very superstitious, but I've never read Freud for the same reason – because I wouldn't want

Wandering alone in the forest of cinematic despond . . . Or on the set of THE BROTHERS GRIMM . . . or both.

to mess with what gives me the good stuff. I know I've got all sorts of weird fucking shit floating around up there in my head, but I don't want to analyse it – I want to put it to work. And I think there's a further aspect of my protestant diligence ethic which also militates against any form of therapy. Given that I'm lucky enough to earn my living through creative work – already a profoundly self-centred occupation – in that context, buying myself an imaginary friend to talk through my problems with would seem to be taking self-indulgence to a ridiculous level.

Temperamentally, I've always been inclined to admire the no-nonsense self-reliance of craftsmen more than the self-indulgent whimsicality of artists. Obviously a lot of that does go back to my father, and I presume my lifelong fascination with the character of the wood-carver's son Pinocchio (this wooden thing who desperately wants to be a person, but we're only interested in him because he is made of wood) comes from the same source. At my most self-pitying moments in the midst of one wide-screen disaster or another, I have been known to visualise myself as a kind of Pinocchio messiah who takes on the sins of the world, and then gets nailed to himself.

'Freud Analysed' illustration, published in *The Mirror* magazine 11 October 1969, the same week MONTY PYTHON'S FLYING CIRCUS made its TV debut. And no, Sigmund, I don't want to hear your theory as to why I might not be having flying dreams any more.

The ultimate 'Dear Jean' letter – a Get Well Soon card to Monsieur Rochefort.

Losing one leading man

in the middle of filming – as we did when Jean Rochefort's double herniated disc killed *Quixote* – was very bad luck. Losing two was starting to look like carelessness. I wish I could say that somehow wrestling *The Imaginarium of Dr Parnassus* onto the screen after Heath Ledger died in the middle of the shoot was the heroic last stand of a director who refused to bow down to the dictates of a malevolent destiny. But it wasn't really like that.

Everyone was utterly stunned when the news of Heath's death came through – it was beyond horrible. It was impossible, unbelievable, unbearable. Not only had we lost a wise and joyous friend, a part of our family, but an extraordinary talent who, I have no doubt, would have been the greatest of his generation. I just said, 'I don't give a fuck about the film. I give up. It's finished. I'm old and tired and worn out and I want to go home.' Luckily, I surround myself with people who don't listen to anything I say. My daughter Amy – who was one of the film's producers – Nicola Pecorini and my friend Ray Cooper kept telling me, 'You can't do that, you've got to finish it for Heath.' Whatever arguments they used took a full week and a half – or maybe even two – to rouse me from my slough of despond. Even then, I didn't personally have the strength and resilience to find a way forward, they just pushed me to the point where I had no other choice, so it became the line of least resistance.

With Lily Cole and Christopher Plummer on the set of DR PARNASSVS – only two of the three people in this photo are in costume.

My thought process started off like this: 'OK, you've got to get someone to replace Heath, but there's no one person who is good enough, and even if there was, I don't want to work with him even if he was available – which he won't be at this short notice – and we don't have time to re-do the whole film.' Then I realised, 'He goes through the magic mirror three times, so maybe we could get three different actors to play him.' I was partly thinking of Luis Buñuel's *That Obscure Object of Desire*, where two different actresses play the same character, but mainly about how if the part was divided into three, Heath's three replacements would only need to turn up for a few days.

Early drawing of DR PARNASSUS's stage
The spooky resemblance to similar draughtsman-like groundwork for abandoned summer-camp production of *Alice in Wonderland* almost half a century before may or may not have been an omen.

I'm very determined and will, foolishly, go head-to-head with any brick wall. But lately there are more times when I just give up and become totally and depressively fatalistic. That's when people like my daughters Amy and Holly become vital. Viz: Parnassus. It was Amy who just wouldn't let me let the film die.

It's amazing how often the most satisfying and effective solutions to seemingly insurmountable film-making problems turn out to be completely counter-intuitive. If you need someone to play a giant, it's always best to ask a fat short-arse. And if you're agonisingly short of one A-list male lead, why not just get three to replace him?

I was determined that it was only going to be people who really knew and loved Heath, so my first call was to Johnny Depp, who said he would do anything to help. His promise stopped the frantic retreat of the money people, who knew the film would never be finished, and bought us time to get Jude Law and Colin Farrell to join the ride to the rescue. Not only was it extraordinary for those three to step in at such short notice, they gave their fees to Heath's daughter. Heath's spirit seemed to be infusing all of us. In fact, when we finished *Dr Parnassus* I thought it was one of the best things I'd ever done.

I remember watching it all the way through and thinking, 'This is so good – I can't make a better film than that.' As it turned out, not as many people as I'd hoped agreed with me, and Sony Classics, the American distribution company, didn't help by barely promoting the film despite the stellar cast (unlike the Italians, who did a bang-up job, making almost twice the money in Italy that we did in the US). At times like that, you do find yourself wondering 'What's going on here? Have I been wrong, and they've been right all along?' But then you – or at least, I – just think, 'Fuck 'em.'

I hate people that think what purports to be reality is truth; one of the reasons theatres keep turning up in my films is partly a warning. I'm saying, 'It's not necessarily real but it may be more truthful.'

What's happening in cinema today is that Stan Lee has become God. You'd think I'd be in favour with this all-powerful movie deity, given that I got his daughter a job on *Jabberwocky*. I'd met Stan through Harvey Kurtzman while working at *Help!* – he was a lovely guy, although I have no clear memory of him other than that he looked exactly like Stan Lee – and he asked if I could find her something. I ended up getting her a potentially quite testing gig as Max Wall's PA. So maybe he's never forgiven me for that.

Either way, as the computer-game element in films comes more to the fore, less and less is allowed to be left to the imagination. I remember my son Harry being really into those Tony Hawk skateboard games when he was growing up. He felt like he'd really experienced what it was like to use a skateboard, but when he actually got a real one, he was surprised to find that reality kept getting in the way and gravity was a much stricter (not to say more painful) teacher than Tony.

I'm no better. Nothing is more fun than *Grand Theft Auto*, and you certainly wouldn't want a lift home from me after I've been playing it. (Maybe computer games are just nature's way of saying there are too many people. Somebody's got to institute the cull, because Thomas Malthus' unholy trinity of wars, plagues and famines aren't quite doing the job any more.) But it's the same with any half-decent movie that has high-speed action sequences, and as a director I can't really argue that films don't seriously affect people, because why would I bother making them otherwise?

Of course, having a lot of gunplay in a movie or a computer game doesn't automatically turn people into serial killers, in the same way comic books didn't automatically change kids into communists (although arguably they did have that effect on me) back in the 1950s, when Harvey Kurtzman was being excoriated as a pernicious influence on America's youth. But I do still love that quote Al Jaffee gave a few years back, when he said, '*Mad* was designed to corrupt the minds of children, and from what I'm gathering from the minds of people all over, we succeeded.'

One of the many funny things about comic books is that the Catholic Church invented them. I discovered this in Rome when I saw the way they used to have the texts the priest would read from unfurling over the lectern – almost like a scroll – with a series of ornate illustrations across the bottom, upside down on

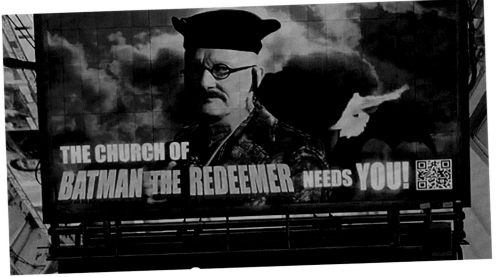

Now that Marvel comics dominate the film industry, comic books are king, so if you've got to believe in something, why not BATMAN THE REEDEMER?

the page, but the right way up for the illiterate church-goers (which was most of them), who could then follow the action in pictorial form while the man in the dress chuntered on in Latin.

This pioneering use of frame-by-frame storytelling was not just the origin of the graphic novel, it also – imagery being all the more important when you're illiterate – foreshadowed the current relationship between Hollywood and the American public. It's amazing the kind of prophetic nuggets you can come up with sometimes if you go digging around in the distant past. That's why whatever kind of story I'm dealing with, I've often found that the best way to connect the past, the present and the future is just to mix the three of them up.

Tom Stoppard and I had been talking a few years earlier about how we could make a BRAZIL about NOW. Neither of us knew how to do it. The world has become increasingly amorphous, unfocused. In ZERO THEOREM I played with the idea of solitude as the focus: a man disconnected from the connected world. "Alone but never lonely."

More interesting stories are being told than in the cinema. Personally I prefer the big cinema screen, but have you seen the size of the TVs you can buy today? I sit very close.

In *The Zero Theorem*

we had a billboard proclaiming 'The Future Has Come And Gone – Where Were You?' but the joke was on us. Many of the futuristic ideas we incorporated in the film were *passé* by the time we finished. We had made a period film! It's as if the future is coming to us faster than we are heading to it.

I think it was the author William Gibson who suggested that global stocks of cognitive dissonance are currently so high they threaten to make the traditional idea of science fiction redundant. And once you reach my age, you tend to find that the individual days become really long, but the years get shorter, which only distorts your temporal perspective still further.

Looking back, it seems my life has been a series of continually looping circles, almost Eastern in their spinning. One thing connects with another, and the same things keep re-happening. I don't even want to understand it, I just know it's a fact.

The 2014 Python live reunion

gave me a similar feeling. Suddenly we're back as a group, working together day after day, performing the old sketches. The intervening thirty years had disappeared completely. It was like 'What the fuck has happened? I'm back playing a buffoon. I thought I was supposed to be a "serious film director". *Have you not seen my reviews?!*'

Nevertheless, it was fun to be outrageous again and the audience response was astonishing. Back when I was directing *Faust* there had also been standing ovations. Ray Cooper said, 'Isn't that a wonderful feeling?' And I said, 'Yeah, it's terrific. I just don't want to become addicted to it.' I don't want to need it.

But, the truth is I am keen to please people, as many as possible. I want them to love what I do, but that desperate 'I' is kept chained, gagged, and locked in a lead-lined box under my bed. It's why we live 6,000 miles away from Hollywood. I fear that if I spent time there I would succumb. *'Yes, sir, I would love to sell out … If only you'd give me a chance!'*, but that other 'I', that Gilliam and his 'reputation', have put paid to that.

You see, *that* Gilliam doesn't want the responsibility of having to please all the people all the time. He just wants to be able to make the things that thrill him.

He's delighted when a film or a show does well critically and financially, but he doesn't want that to be the measure of success. It's the object, it's the thing he made, that counts, not the applause. The applause fades away, he will be gone, but the things he made will remain.

Of course, no amount of playing with narrative time-frames or split personalities will shake you free from the essential human chronology of life and death. I've got it in my will to be put in a cardboard coffin, though Maggie's insisting on wrapping it in a blue ribbon, and then buried on our hill in Italy, with an oak sapling planted in my chest. The old plan – because Highgate Cemetery is at the bottom of our garden in London – was that I'd be cremated

RESURRECTION PYTHON: News of our deaths had been exaggerated.

Here we see the serious and retiring auteur at work, immune to the attention-seeking tendencies of the other Pythons.

I wanted to call the live show "One foot in the grave". We settled on "One down, five to go".

and then they'd throw the ashes over the wall. Either way, it's important to be prepared. I've never been one of those people who's ill at ease with the prospect of their own mortality – death is the only thing in your life that's actually guaranteed to happen, so you might as well be ready for it.

Four years ago, on one of the very rare occasions that I have ever tried to do anything useful in the garden – almost as if to ensure that my wife would never ask me again – I went to change a blade on the lawnmower and it slipped and cut through an artery and several tendons. My hand was a mess, and my daughter Holly had to drive me to the Whittington hospital, which is just down the hill from our house.

Unfortunately, it was the weekend of the Highgate Pond Square festival, and the streets were gridlocked. So there I am with this tourniquet twisted round my arm – which I'm holding out of the window of Holly's Mini, trying to keep the blood which is spurting out off the upholstery – she's honking the horn and I'm shouting, 'Get the fuck out of the way!' but still no one's moving. The fact that I'm wearing Bermuda shorts and flip-flops only intensifies our resemblance to one of Ralph Steadman's illustrations for *Fear and Loathing*.

Finally we make it to the Whittington hospital and the lady on the desk just carries on talking on the phone even as my life-blood is draining away on the floor. I guess this kind of shit is normal to her. As they're wrapping my arm up in bandages to try and staunch the flow, I'm looking up at the ceiling and

An early 1990s Valentine to Maggie (she gets one every year, that's how dewy-eyed I am) with Amy, Holly and a caped Harry in attendance to testify to the enduring romance of family life.

all these wires are hanging down off it. A very nice Iranian doctor comes in and says, 'I don't think we should operate in here, it's too dirty.' So they bind me up as best they can, give me this little chit and put me in one of the minicabs which is waiting outside because that is cheaper than using an ambulance. The cab driver is telling me all his tales as if this is just a normal cab ride. Eventually he gets me to UCH down on the Euston Road, and after I've been sent back out the front door and round the side a couple of times, because I came in the wrong entrance, I finally get the treatment I need.

Of course all the people who looked after me were fucking great, but you couldn't actually invent the stupidity of the delivery system – ducts would have been a step forward. At one point I started to tell the doctor, 'You've got to be careful, I make my living with this hand.' But Maggie said, 'Shut up, you're making him nervous.'

2007's Valentine Jihadist viewed the lovers' festival from a somewhat more TERMINAL perspective.

I LOVE MAGGIE – FROM THE VALENTINE JIHADIST 2007

That was the first and (so far) only time I've had a general anaesthetic. Inevitably the guys who were giving it to me were Python fans, and they were joking about the gruesome scene that might await me when I woke up, but as it turned out it was the most perfect experience – totally cinematic, but not so much a dream sequence, more a jump cut. There you are being wheeled down the corridors on the gurney, the doors of the operating theatre open in front of you, then the next thing you see is a close-up of a big face saying, 'How do you feel?'

For forty-five minutes of my life in-between, there was nothing – it was as blank as the tape at the start or end of a reel – and that's what I assume death is like. I'll tell you something. From my experience, it's not so bad.

Preparatory collage for
as yet unmade screenplay
THE DEFECTIVE DETECTIVE

—this arboreal tableau corresponds to many people's view of the afterlife

(ie there's a bar in it).

And so... it's Goodbye from the <u>Gilliams</u>.

AMY   HARRY   MAGGIE   TG   HOLLY

OK... I know it's a bit cuddly but we all deserve
something for staying awake this long.

THE END

(Yes, finally.)

END CREDITS

The lie at the heart of an autobiography is the billing. As quasi-autobiographer I'm given top billing, but the truth is that T. Gilliam's Life is a product of all the people along the way that did the hard work: pushing it, stumbling over it, picking it up and carrying it, and too often just getting in the way of it. Some are big parts worthy of equal billing, some vital supporting roles, others are bustling extras providing a sense of scale and colour. Whatever role they played they gave my life the laughter, drama, and meaning that made it worth living. Nevertheless, I'm still the only one who gets his name in the title.

David Aaron, Steve Abbot, Jim Acheson, Dan Ackroyd, Douglas Adams, Margaret Adams, Pani Ahmadi-Moore, Simon Albrey, Nick Alder, Alan Aldridge, Molly Allen, Paul Allen, Woody Allen, Chuck Alverson, Wes Anderson, Tex Antonucci, Dave Appleby, Ron Arad, Arcade Fire, David Arquette, Peter & Wendy Asher, Julian Assange, Rutie Atsmon, Daniele Auber, Mick Audsley, Paul Auster, Richard Avedon, Tex Avery, George Ayoub, Jille Aziz, Oana Babes, Edward Baer, Giampaolo Bagala, Bill Bailey, Richard Bain, Kenny Baker, Joan Bakewell, Banksy, Andra Barbuica, Humphrey Barclay, Ota Bares, Ronnie Barker, Ellen Barkin, Patrick Barlow, Francesca Barra, Clare Barrett, Terry Baylor, Jim Beach, Lou Beach, John Beard, Emanuelle Béart, Hildegard Bechtler, Terry Bedford, Jeffrey Beecroft, Chris Beetles, Steve Begg, Tor Belfrage, Steve Bell, Larry Bell, Monica Bellucci, Hercules Bellville, Tarak Ben Ammar, Peter Bennett-Jones, Jonathan Benson, Aaron Bergeron, Stephen & Clara Berkoff, Hector Berlioz, Gianni & Marisa Berna, Bernini, John Berry, Chuck Berry, Derek & Pam Berryman, Bernardo Bertolucci, Paul Bettany, Chrissie Beveridge, Sanjeev Bhaskar, Peter Biziou, Preston Blair, William Blake, Julian Bleach, Martin Body, Raluca Bogda, James Bonas, Helena Bonham Carter, Connie Booth, Walerian Borowczyk, Borromini, Hieronymous Bosch, Rosa Bosch, Rob Bottin, Mel Bourne, Susan Boyle, Marlon Brando, Finn Brandt, Goran Bregovic, Kathleen Brennan, Jeff Bridges, Steve Bridgewater, Jim Broadbent, Barbara Broccoli, John Brockman, Richard Broke, Tim Brooke-Taylor, David Brown, Linda Bruce, Peter Brueghel,

Brunelleschi, Rob Brydon, Paul Buckmaster, Luis Buñuel, Milly Burns, Tim Burton, Gary Busey, Kate Bush, Gaia Bussolati, Sid Caesar, Massimo Cantini Parrini, Peter Capaldi, Cristiana Capotondi, Jofre Caraben, Claudia Cardinale, Elaine Carew, Paul Carr, Lewis Carroll, Jenne Casarotto, Patrick Cassavetti, Loyd Catlett, Brian Catling, Pete Cavaciuti, Benvenuto Cellini, Miguel de Cervantes Saavedra, Kirstin Chalmers, Lon Chaney, Charlie Chaplin, Graham Chapman, Val Charlton, Harry Chester, Luca Chiarva, Tamara Choi, Roger Christian, Gwendoline Christie, Ian Christie, Julie Christie, Bob Clampett, Nicky Clapp, Eric Clapton, Lee Cleary, John & Jenny Cleese, Carol Cleveland, Jonathan & Pauline Clyde, Joel & Ethan Coen, Paul Coker, Stephen Colbert, Lily Cole, Sean Connery, Nicholas Connolly, Billy & Pamela Connolly, Paule Constable, Richard Conway, Steve Coogan, Peter Cook, Wendy Cook, Ray Cooper, Francis Ford Coppola, Harry H. Corbett, Valentina Cortese, Clotilde Courau, Lucinda Cowell, Harriet Craven, Grover Crisp, David Cronenberg, Mackenzie Crook, Dave Crossley, Robert Crumb, Joanne Crump, Penelope Cruz, Barry Cryer, Alfonso Cuaron, Mitch Cullin, Adrian Curelea, Tim Curry, Uma Da Cunha, Roger Daltry, Matt Damon, Mychael & Jeff Danna, Louis Danvers, Lucy Darwin, Daumier, Marcus Davey, Dennis Davidson, Ray Davies, Mario Davignon, Jack Davis, David Day, Massimo De Luca, Robert De Niro, Chiara De Palo, Derek Deadman, Douglas Dean, Roger Dean, Bob Dearberg, Benicio Del Toro, Don DeLillo, Piero Della Francesca, Christi Dembrowski, Winston Dennis, Johnny Depp, Myrtle Devenish, Ron Devillier, Danny DeVito, Cameron Diaz, Philip K. Dick, Walt Disney, Malcolm Dixon, Paul Docherty, Stanley Donen, Martin Doone, Gustav Doré, Fyodor Dostoevsky, Michael Douglas, Ditch Doy, Yam Doyev, Bob Doyle, Margarita Doyle, Julian Doyle, Mike Drazen, Druillet, Christie Dubrinski, Damian Dudkiewicz, Kath Duggan, Francois Duhamel, Joe Dunton, Albert Dupontel, Joe Durden-Smith, Albrecht Dürer, Shelley Duvall, Guy Dyas, Bob Dylan, Jake & Fiona Eberts, Pierre Edelman, Edith McGuigan, Mike Edmonds, Ade Edmondson, Beth Edwards, Daniel Edwards, Mark Egerton, Sergei Eisenstein, Willy Elder, Derek Elwood, Oana Ene, Harry Enfield, Sergio Ercolessi, Max Ernst, José Luis Escolar, Kenny Everett, Penny Eyles, Bob Ezrin, Kate Fahey, Paloma Faith, Jimmy Fallon, Robert Farr, Colin Farrell, Michael Fassbender, Gail Fear, Marty Feldman, Federico Fellini, George Fenton, Claire Ferguson, Jodelle Ferland, Valerie Ferland, Dante Ferretti, Howard Feuer, Ralph Fiennes, Mike Figgis, Chuck Finch, Tony & Lesley Fish, Carrie Fisher, Serena Fiumi, Brendan Fletcher, Jürgen Flimm, Michael Forbes, Graham Ford, Roy Forge Smith, Forkbeard Fantasy, Milos Forman, Lisbeth Fouse, Stephen Frears, Stan Freberg, Dawn French, Don French, François Frey, Rupert Friend, Uri Fruchtmann, Stephen Fry, Keith Fulton, Neil Gaiman, Paul Gambaccini, Pablo Ganguli, Andy Garcia, Ed Gardner, David Garfath, Andrew Garfield, Norman Garwood, Matt Gauci, Gill Gayle, Frank Gehry, Larry

Gelbart, Bob & Jeanne Geldolf, Steve Geller, Gina Gershon, Amy Gilliam, Beatrice Gilliam, Harry Gilliam, Holly Gilliam, James 'Gill' Gilliam, Scott & Susan Gilliam, Sherry Gilliam, All the Gilliams, Jean Giraud, Alan Glazer, Rodney Glenn, Bob Godfrey, Christophe Goffette, Jeff Goldner, John Goldstone, Bobcat Goldthwait, Valeria Golino, Caroline Goodall, John Goodwin, Edward Gorey, Hilton Goring, Frank Gorshin, Assheton Gorton, René Goscinny, Marcel Gotlib, Goya, Robert Graham, Keith Grant, Boris Grebenshchikov, Green Ginger, Kim Greist, Gerry Grennell, Terri-Jayne Griffin, Isobel Griffiths, Keith Griffiths, Tony Grisoni, Harold Gronenthal, Robert Grossman, Lee Grumett, Adrian Guerra, Sabrina Guinness, Christian Guinn, Craig Haagenson, John Hackney, Samuel Hadida, Victor Hadida, Nancy Haigh, Jim Hampton, Tim Hampton, Tomás Hanák, Robert Hansen, Alma Har'el, Bill Harmon, Ben Harper, Max Harper, Saga Harper, Ned & Megan Harper, Peter & Pamela Harper, Dhani Harrison, George & Olivia Harrison, Charles Hart, Moss Hart, Leah Hausman, Michael Havas, Václav Havel, Nicholas Hawksmoor, Harold Hayes, Alex Hayesmore, Polly Hayward, Lena Headey, Lucas Hedges, Joseph Heller, Duitch Helmer, Katherine Helmond, Andy Henery, Lenny Henry, Judy Henske, Jim Henson, Katy Hepburn, Joyce Herlihy, Norma Heyman, Jim & Gay Hickey, Debra Hill, Ellen Hillers, Hank Hinton, Peter Hoare, William Hogarth, Hokusai, Roger Holden, Buck Holland, Bob Hollow, Peter Hollywood, Ian & Sophie Holm, Nathan Holmes, Rachel Holroyd, Nicholas Horne, Alex Horowitz, Bob Hoskins, Emil Hostina, Tomoyasu Hotei, Kent Houston, John Howard Davies, John Howe, Hugh Hudson, Jeremy Hume, Barry Humphries, Tom Hunter, John Hurt, Anjelica Huston, Charmaine Husum, Eric & Tanya Idle, John & Sue Ignatius, Neil & Yvonne Innes, Ted Irwin, Eddie Izzard, Tracey Jacobs, Sharre Jacoby, Andre Jacqueman, Al Jaffee, Mick Jagger, Henry Jaglom, Anne James, Clive James, Fred Jannin, Ricky Jay, Michael Jeter, Penn Jillette, Elton John, Nick Jolly, Bill Jones, Chuck Jones, Sally Jones, Simon Jones, Terry & Anna Jones, Scott Joplin, Neil Jordan, Phill Jupitus, Jon Kamen, Michael Kamen, Shekhar Kapur, Henrik Karlberg, Kat Krazy, Lindsay Katina, Charlie Kaufman, Dena Kaye, Ian Kelly, Jim Keltner, Mel Kenyon, Mark Kermode, Cookie Kershaw, Beatrice Kessi, Jeremy King, Lindy King, Denis Kitchen, Max Klinger, Charles Knode, Harry Knowles, Ernie Kovacs, Jirí Králík, Paul Krassner, Kai Krause, Beatrice Kruger, Stanley Kubrick, Toyohara Kunichika, Utagawa Kunisada, Utagawa Kuniyoshi, Akira Kurosawa, Gary Kurtz, Adele Kurtzman, Elizabeth Kurtzman, Harvey Kurtzman, Meredith Kurtzman, Pete Kurtzman, Emir Kusturica, Jean Labadie, Richard & Ann LaGravenese, Rowan Laidlaw, Irene Lamb, John Landis, Fritz Lang, Chris Langham, Erica Langmuir, Peter Langs, June Lanterman, John Latimer, Jude Law, John Le Mesurier, Jane Leany, Evgeny Lebedev, Heath Ledger, Stan Lee, Tom Lehrer, David Leland, John Lennon, Annie Lennox, Felix Lepadatu, Lerner & Loewe, Richard Lester,

Kathy Lette, Barry Levinson, Gary Levinson, Art Lewis, Nancy Lewis, Sandy & Sarah Lieberson, Katrina Lindsay, Ric Lipson, Laurie Lipton, Tomas Liska, Csaba Lökös, Richard Loncraine, Peter Lord, Richard Lotts, Lyle Lovett, Victor Lownes, George Lucas, Mario Luraschi, Hamish MacInnes, Alexander Mackendrick, Louise & Ray Mackintosh, Ian MacNaughton, Don Macpherson, Gergely Madaras, Elio Maiello, Roberto Malerba, Dario Marianelli, Antonio Mariotti, Chris Marker, Pippa Markham, Aaron Marsden, Gabriella Martinelli, Groucho Marx, Anastasia Masaro, Nick & Nettie Mason, John Massey, Jack Mathews, Henri Matisse, Simon McBurney, Paul McCartney, Winsor McCay, Luke McCoubrey, Bob McDill, George McDill, Alex McDowell, Dave McGiffert, Dave McKean, Raymond McKelvey, Charles McKeown, Steve McLaughlin, Larry McMurtry, Janet McTeer, Jay Meagher, Georges Méliès, George Melly, Chris Meloni, Mel Metcalfe, Natascha Metherell, Arnon Milchan, Ian Miles, Linda Miles, Kenny Miller, William Miller, Ray Millichope, Spike Milligan, Fred Milstein, Helen Mirren, Eleanor Mondale, Sarah Monzani, Keith Moon, Alan Moore, Dudley Moore, Mike Moran, Bobby Moresco, David Morgan, David Morse, Art Mortimer, Samantha Morton, Tamzen Moulding, Peter Mountain, Marco Mueller, Frank Muir, Peter Mullan, Peter Mumford, Cillian Murphy, Bill Murray, Gordon & Stella Murray, Paula Murrihy, Laila Nabulsi, Michael & Carolyn Naish, Joe Napolitano, Vince Narduzzo, Constantine Nasr, Boris Nawratil, Liam Neeson, Ted Nemeth, Franco Nero, John Neville, Patrick Newall, Mike Newell, Paul Newman, Harry Nilsson, Yuki Noguchi, David Nord, Torquil Norman, Maxime Nourissat, Michael Nyman, Denis O'Brien, Derek O'Connor, Denise O'Dell, Lynda Obst, Bill Oddie, Alan Odle, Keith Olberman, Max & Jackie Oliver, Tim Ollive, Julia Ormand, Gabriele Oricchio, Steve Otano, Frank Oz, Al Pacino, Rachel Palin, Tom Palin, Will Palin, Michael & Helen Palin, Nicholas Pallesen, Petr Palous, Basil Pao, Vanessa Paradis, Nick Park, Alan Parker, Trey Parker, Van Dyke Parks, Beatrix Pasztor, Bill Paterson, Phil Patterson, Omar Paxson, Nicola Pecorini, Barbara Pelligrini, David & Janet Peoples, Louis Pepe, Gabriella Pescucci, Hazel Pethig, Lloyd Phillips, Tom Phillips, Joaquin Phoenix, Piranesi, Brad Pitt, Jim Plannette, Ian & Marianne Pleeth, Christopher Plummer, Amanda Plummer, Bill Plympton, Carlo Poggioli, Roman Polanski, Patricia Poienaru, Sarah Polley, Slava & Yelena Polunin, Adrian Popa, Adrian Popescu, Nic Powell, Sandy Powell, Michael Powell, Roger & Erica Pratt, Monique Prudhomme, Jonathan Pryce, Richard Pryor, John Ptak, Chris Purves, Jack Purvis, David Puttnam, Ingo Putze, Stephen & Timothy Quay, Don Quixote, Steve Rabineau, Arthur Rackham, Michael & Emma Radford, Tommy Raeburn, Joseph Raisi-Varzaneh, Ken Ralston, Rankin, Jack Rapke, Dave Rappaport, Paul Rassam, Odilon Redon, Oliver Reed, Rémi Renoux, Matthew Reynolds, Lucille Rhodes, Christina Ricci, Christine Rice, Keith Richards, Ian Richardson, Ralph Richardson, Deborah

Ricketts, Alan Rickman, Bradley Roast, Glenys Roberts, Geoffrey Robertson, W. Heath Robinson, Jean Rochefort, Roy Rodhouse, Marcus & Hattie Rooke, Sebastian Rose, Tiny Ross, Rosto, Tim Roth, Arnold Roth, Giuseppe Rotunno, Chuck Roven, Mercedes Ruehl, Pat Rushin, Willie Rushton, Ken Russell, Nola Safro, Soupy Sales, Vinicius Salles, Crispian Sallis, Mark Samuelson, Jennifer Saunders, Adrien Sauvage, Pietro Scalia, Gerald Scarfe, Maria Schell, Fred Schepisi, Debbie Schindler, Volker Schlöndorff, Julian Schnabel, Annabel Schofield, John Schofield, Thelma Schoonmaker, Thomas Schühly, Schuiten, Marty Scorsese, Baltimore Scott, Ridley Scott, Roger Scott, Ronald Searle, Peter Sellers, Daniele Sepe, Irv Sepkowitz, Andy Serkis, Penny Service, Dr Seuss, Kiran Shah, Senna Shanti, Ivan Sharrock, Harry Shearer, Michael Sheen, Sid Sheinberg, Theresa Shell, Gilbert Shelton, Stacey Sher, Jodi Shields, Dave Shostac, Linda Siefert, Joel Siegel, George Siena, Mike Silcock, Joel Silver, Margery Simkin, Ros Simon, Pete Sinclair, Shel Siverstein, Angelo Smimmo, Randy Smith, David Soar, Michele Soavi, Steven Soderbergh, Mike Solinger, Sergio Solli, Bart Soroczynski, Bill Spahic, Nicky Spence, Lizzie Spender, Dave Sproxton, Morgan Spurlock, Michael Spyres, Harry Dean Stanton, Ringo Starr, Alison Steadman, Ralph Steadman, Maggie Steed, Jasna Stefanovic, Gloria Steinem, Karen Stetler, Eve Stewart, Bob Stilwell, Sting, Matt Stone, Tom Stoppard, Peter Stormare, Samantha Storr, Madeleine Stowe, Phil Stubbs, Trudie Styler, Ken Sullet, Graham Sutton, John Swinnerton, Tilda Swinton, Dorka Tamás, Quentin Tarantino, Shahla Tarrant, Bertrand Tavernier, Yvette Taylor, Derek Taylor, Alison Telfer, François Testory, David Thewlis, Mélanie Thierry, Jeremy Thomas, Neville Thompson, Hunter S. Thompson, Uma Thurman, David Ticotin, Jennifer Tilly, Micky Titchmarsh, David Tomblin, Eric Tomlinson, Leigh Took, Pete Townsend, Verne Troyer, Mark Twain, Jan Unger, Tomi Ungerer, Jaco Van Dormael, Nyla Van Ingen, Gertrude Vance, All the Vances, Stan Vanderbeek, Peter Vaughan, Simona Vescovi, Pascal Vicidomini, Caroline Vie, Bill Vince, Jean-Pierre Vincent, Monica Vitti, Max von Sydow, Dick Vosburgh, Bruce Wagner, Tom Waits, Lesley Walker, Max Wall, David Foster Wallace, Carol Waller, Sarah Walley, Kevin Walsh, Christoph Waltz, David Warner, Craig Warnock, Dave Warren, Peter Watson, Ruby Wax, Simon Wegrzyn, Paula Weinstein, Julie Weiss, Orson Welles, Colin & Sherry West, Natasha Westlake, Bill Weston, Maggie Weston, Tom & Dorothy Weston, Ben Whishaw, Delphine White, Michael White, Willard White, Karen Wikstrand, Billy Wilder, Marsha Williams, Richard Williams, Robin Williams, Bruce Willis, Corinne Winters, Jonathan Winters, Ronnie Wood, Wally Wood, Joanne Woodward, Wendy Worth, Frank Lloyd Wright, Jerry Yester, Taiso Yoshitoshi, Yelena Zagrevskaya, Dick Zanuck, Frank & Gail Zappa, Karel Zeman, Robert Zemeckis, Edoardo Zuchetti . . . **and finally, the most philosophically influential of them all, Mel Brooks and his 2000 Year Old Man.**

Index

References to images and captions are in **bold**.

INDEX